JONATHAN CAPE
PAPERBACK
JCP 87

NATIONALIZATION
IN BRITISH INDUSTRY

LEONARD TIVEY

*Senior Lecturer in Public Administration
at the University of Birmingham*

Nationalization
in British Industry

REVISED EDITION

JONATHAN CAPE
THIRTY BEDFORD SQUARE LONDON

FIRST PUBLISHED 1966
REPRINTED 1972 (TWICE)
THIS REVISED EDITION 1973
© 1966, 1973 BY L. J. TIVEY

JONATHAN CAPE LTD
30 BEDFORD SQUARE, LONDON WCI

ISBN 0 224 00835 8

Printed and bound in Great Britain by
Richard Clay (The Chaucer Press) Ltd, Bungay, Suffolk

Contents

Preface

THE NATURE and scope of this book are explained in Chapter 1. It is intended to serve as an introduction to the study of nationalization, and no more; all the problems that it raises can be more fully pursued elsewhere. But for the student and general reader there may be some virtue in brevity: from a short book the interrelations of various topics may emerge more clearly, and so it may be easier to see the subject as a whole. It should be stressed, however, that no attempt has been made to discuss the problems of the power industries, or of transport, as such; for this purpose the reader should turn to studies in industrial economics.

I would like to thank friends who have commented on various parts of the book, including Messrs E. L. Pritchard, A. L. Minkes, D. Rimmer, J. M. Samuels, S. C. Littlechild, G. F. McRobie, Dr N. S. Ross and Mrs S. Trench. Their advice has always been stimulating and helpful, and often acceptable. The faults that remain are my own.

L.J.T., February 1966

THE REVISED EDITION

There have been numerous alterations to this edition. Most are minor adjustments; a few are rather longer additions. The main intention of both is to bring the book up to date, but in some cases – particularly in Chapters 6 and 7 – there has been some modification of viewpoint. I would like to thank the Information Division of the Treasury for help with the table in Chapter I; Miss Gill Lucas for helpful research assistance; and Miss Marjorie Davies, secretary to the Department of Political Science, for excellent typing. Nevertheless, I am still responsible for all the faults herein.

University of Birmingham   L.J.T., July 1972

1   The Scope of Nationalization

THIS IS a book on a political subject. Politics is concerned essentially with divergence and disagreement, and this is therefore an account of controversies and the outcome of controversies. Politics is also concerned with the way disagreements are resolved, and hence the book also discusses the arrangements for the administration of institutions and the settlement of policies. Finally, since politics is often about a conflict between ends rather than means, the purposes which the institutions try to serve are discussed.

The institutions to be considered are the British nationalized industries. The political fact of their nationalized status is the main focus of interest for this book. It is this status that the industries have in common, and it is this that makes them worth discussing together.

They are, nevertheless, industrial organizations. They buy, produce and sell as economic units, and it is impossible to conceive them apart from their economic nature. Much of the material must be presented, therefore, in economic terms. The object is not to solve, or even to express views on, the economic problems as such, but to consider them as part of the policy-making process. For economists, the aim is to show how the nature of institutions shapes the issues with which they grapple – to show the extent to which these issues can be attributed to, or are affected by, the nationalized status of the industries. It is deceptively easy for economists to examine industrial problems as if they were in a vacuum; but in fact, the control, organization and purposes of nationalization are central facts that cannot be realistically ignored.

The general plan of the book may be briefly indicated. The next chapter describes the development of ideas about nationalization, both in the sense of public ownership and of its embodiment in the public corporation. The third chapter describes the circumstances in which nationalization first took place, the parliamentary process of legislation and the basic structure of public corporations as they have emerged. The fourth chapter sets out briefly something about nationalization in practice and the industrial record of the corporations. These three chapters are largely historical and factual, though for the sake of brevity some general judgments have been used to summarize complex situations.

The rest of the book is concerned with the examination of problems and controversies. In Chapter 5 these are problems of internal organization; in Chapter 6 they are problems of external relations: with the Government, with Parliament and with the public. Chapters 7 and 8 consider fundamental issues. In one the objectives to be aimed at in industries already nationalized are considered; in the other there is a return to the theme of Chapter 2, the case for nationalization and public ownership as such. In these later chapters the intention has been to set out the problems and arguments fairly, but this has not prevented assessments being made and conclusions drawn on many matters.

The scope of the book is conveniently limited by institutional boundaries: it covers the public corporations running nationalized industries in coal, electricity, gas, inland transport, air transport, steel and the Post Office. It should scarcely be necessary to stress the economic importance of these bodies. The table opposite sets out the public corporations, as the pattern had evolved by 1971, and shows their assets and the numbers employed by them. These figures give some idea of the relative importance of the various bodies and of their place in the country's economic system. The situation in other countries is briefly described at the end of Chapter 3.

Changes in recent years which have affected the list include the addition of the British Steel Corporation and the Post Office. London Transport is now supervised by the Greater London Council instead of the Ministry of Transport, and is regarded as municipalized rather than nationalized; however, it should be emphasized that it remains a statutory public corporation. In a similar way the Passenger Transport Executives in conurbations are independent public corporations supervised by local authorities. Other changes in the structure of publicly owned transport are described in Chapter 3. The list excludes some bodies which are

NATIONALIZATION IN 1971

	Average net assets (£ million)	Number of employees (thousands)	As percentage of working population of Great Britain
National Coal Board	667	356	1·4
Electricity Council and Boards	4,958	188	0·8
North Scotland Hydro-Electric Board	269	4	–
South Scotland Electricity Board	455	14	–
Gas Council and Boards	1,760	116	0·5
British Steel Corporation	1,235	252	1·0
Post Office	2,681	415	1·7
British Overseas Airways Corporation	251	24	0·1
British European Airways	166	25	0·1
British Airports Authority	73	4	–
British Railways Board	863	273	1·1
British Transport Docks Board	127	11	–
British Waterways Board	8	3	–
National Freight Corporation	108	63	0·3
National Bus Company	97	84	0·3
Scottish Transport Group	25	18	–
TOTAL Nationalized industries	13,743	1,850	7·5
Working population, Great Britain		24,827	100·0

close to the nationalized industries – the Bank of England, the United Kingdom Atomic Energy Authority, the British Broadcasting Corporation and the Independent Broadcasting Authority – since they are not industries in the normal sense, and have special methods of finance. Not in the list, and little discussed in the book, are companies in which the Government holds shares.

It is now common practice to describe Britain's economy as 'mixed'; that is, it is partly private enterprise and partly in public ownership. Associated with this notion are the concepts of 'public sector' and 'private sector' of the economy. These terms should be used with very great care. They originate in the national income accounting used for evaluating and guiding general economic policy, and their application in political and administrative discussion can be highly misleading. In the present context it should be remembered that the 'public sector' includes many institutions besides nationalized industries, most of them bearing very little similarity to the public corporations discussed in this book. In particular it includes Government departments and local authorities, both of which operate public and social services of considerable economic weight. The structure and purposes of the other parts of the 'public sector' are often very different from those of industrial organizations, and the idea of a 'public sector' as an harmonious administrative unity is a myth.

The private sector includes both private-enterprise firms and individual people. All business activity takes place in a civil order shaped over time by governments, and its success depends in part on the success of the Government's economic policies. In addition, the Government actively promotes for private industry, in one way or another, research, productivity, marketing, training and technical education and exports; it operates a protective tariff and in special cases provides finance. In short, the expression 'mixed economy' implies not only that some industry is privately owned and some publicly, but also that the economic efforts of government, firms and individuals are closely interwoven and do not operate independently.

The public sector is generally reckoned to comprise about 25 per cent of the economy, measured in terms of production, and to employ about a quarter of the country's working population. The nationalized industries themselves produce about ten or eleven per cent of Britain's wealth annually, and they employ seven or eight per cent of the labour force. Their position as basic industries or services, however, makes them crucial to the rest of the economy.

This book, then, is about the 'nationalized industries' as listed. This is nearly the same as the 'public-enterprise sector' or the 'public sector of industry', but not quite since it excludes municipal enterprise and some other bodies. It does *not* anywhere near approximate to the 'public sector of the economy'.

2 The Origins of Nationalization

'NATIONALIZATION, then, is not an end, but a means to an end,' wrote R. H. Tawney in 1921, 'and when the question of ownership has been settled the question of administration remains for solution.'[1]

Both questions are discussed in this book; and in seeking the sources of nationalization in Britain, we shall find it convenient to distinguish two developments, approximating to these questions. The first was political – there was in the first half of the twentieth century a growing belief in the need for a measure of public ownership of productive forces. The second was administrative – there was in the same period a great increase in the number of institutions of a 'semi-independent' type, neither part of the ordinary governmental structure nor yet totally separate from it. The conjunction of these developments in the programme of the Labour Party in mid-century brought about the main nationalized industries in their present form.

In this chapter the two developments will be examined in turn.

BELIEF IN PUBLIC OWNERSHIP

It is prudent to be clear about 'ownership' itself before considering its private and public forms. The concept of ownership is not a simple one. It implies a relationship in which men exercise certain rights over goods, or 'property'. The rights must be recognized by law, for ownership is inherently a legal concept.

Among the rights usually involved are the right to dispose of the goods – by gift, by sale or exchange, by bequest; the right to use and the right to deny use to others; and the right to enjoy the fruits of the property. These rights are not immutable – they may be varied by differences in the law, by different systems of tenure or by social custom. Nevertheless, with the growth of modern industry, the existence of this group of rights ensured that the owners of industrial property – urban land, factories, mines – became the employers of labour and the managers of the various enterprises. This is capitalism – a system in which ultimate control lies with the persons who have a legal title to the capital.

Not all property belongs to individuals. Groups of people can enjoy ownership rights collectively, and in practice most modern industry is now in the hands of business firms – companies or corporations. Moreover, there is the distinction between private and public ownership. Some property is owned by the community as a whole and controlled by the Government of the nation. This book deals with those *industries* that are owned in this way in Britain, and not with other Government property.

Modern ideas of public ownership began to take shape in the nineteenth century. Many socialist ideas, including that of common ownership, have a much longer history. Indeed, in Plato's *Republic* the ruling classes hold all their possessions in common. There was a tradition of socialist ideas in Europe in the Middle Ages, and in Sir Thomas More's *Utopia* of 1516 the ideal society takes the form of a co-operative commonwealth.

But these and other antecedents are of doubtful relevance. The industrial revolution brought with it a revolution in thinking about society, and the ideas that are most significant for twentieth-century nationalization arose as criticisms of the new industrial civilization. (The word 'socialism' first appeared in 1827 in a magazine of the co-operative movement.) Socialism is now generally taken to be a rival system to capitalism for the organization of economic affairs. Politically it has meant more than the substitution of common ownership for private ownership. It has been associated with the general emancipation of the working class, and it has emphasized the need for greater equality in economic and social matters. The socialist movement has always been divided, moreover, into many schools of thought; some, like Marxism, claiming to be scientific, and others stressing Christian or other moral values. But all socialists have insisted on the evils of capitalist ownership and have endeavoured to find better arrangements. The crucial point about modern socialism, as distinct from earlier schemes for common ownership and communal living, is that it concentrates its attention on 'the means of production', not personal possessions. Industry in the nineteenth century became an affair of large organizations, and it is the public ownership of industrial enterprises of this type that nineteenth- and twentieth-century socialists have advocated.

This is no place to relate the wider history of socialism in Britain.[2] After the death of Robert Owen and the decay of his ideas for co-operation and model communities, socialism achieved little prominence in mid-Victorian England. It was on the international scene that Marx and Engels were giving a new profundity to socialist ideas. Common ownership of the means of production was a cardinal aim of the Marxist programme, and it thus became a leading element in left-wing thought everywhere. But Marxism never secured the dominance in England that it did in Europe. The Fabian Society and other groups advocated non-capitalist ownership on practical and moral grounds, and preferred a pragmatic political strategy. The eventual accomplishment of some public ownership in Britain cannot be understood merely as the rise and triumph of a single doctrine. Not merely were its socialist advocates a varied and often dissonant army, but its progress was aided by many non-socialist forces. Thus it is possible for some socialists to be critical of common ownership in the forms it has taken, and where it does not reflect the other values that they seek to promote.

The economic trends which led to public ownership were twofold. On the one hand there was technological development which bred industrial change; and many of the new industries and services needed to be organized as monopolies for full efficiency. On the other hand depression brought special difficulties to particular industries. It was argued that these needed reconstruction by national ownership.

Many of the arguments for public ownership, however, were not economic in character at all. In the nineteenth century, protests against the evils of industrialism were also protests against capitalism. John Ruskin and William Morris were critics of the moral and artistic state of civilization – they found industrial Britain ugly and philistine. When Ruskin entitled an essay 'A Joy for Ever, and its Price in the Market', he was satirizing the application of economic criteria to the deeper satisfactions of human life; and his criticism of uncontrolled free enterprise was that it over-valued economic success, not that it failed to achieve it. Again, the criticism of R. H. Tawney in the twentieth century was moral and religious: a capitalist society was an acquisitive society – one in which material gain was honoured before service and co-operation. Finally there were criticisms from a specifically political standpoint. H. J. Laski, for example, argued that the wealth accruing to private industrialists gave them unfair political advantages, and that neither individual liberties nor democratic proceedures would be respected by capitalist owners of industry if their position were attacked.

The defence of capitalism depended largely on the theory of free competition, as developed by economists. This varied its degree of dogmatism and sophistication, but fundamentally it always asserted that economic welfare was best promoted by individuals seeking their own betterment, for in society they could only do this by providing goods and services for their fellows. Given competition, privately owned firms would have both the motives and the pressures to make themselves efficient. Politically and morally, capitalism was seen as essentially liberal – it did not impose restrictions on individual efforts, it rewarded talent and enterprise, and it limited the power and influence of the Government. In the long run, it was claimed, all human freedoms were involved in freedom of economic activity, for on this freedom rested the ability of men to live independently of the control of Government.

Five factors

It is possible to distinguish five main factors which led to the mid-twentieth-century political situation which shaped industrial nationalization in Britain. The first four are described in a very rough chronological order of origin – thus the co-operative movement began in the mid-nineteenth century, the Labour Party started in 1900, the movement for workers' control flourished around the First World War and the need for planning emerged between the wars. Finally, there were non-socialist influences at work. But the influence of all still persists.

(1) *The rise and limitations of consumers' co-operation.* If business undertakings are not controlled by the owners of the capital, other groups may take charge. In the British retail co-operative movement, which began with the Rochdale pioneers in 1844, control is ultimately in the hands of the consumer members. Though these consumers may have small capital holdings, their rights over the management of the societies derive entirely from the fact of membership. Any person may join, and each member is entitled to one vote, which cannot be multiplied either by investment or by purchases. The retail societies are thus, in principle at any rate, controlled by members who are essentially consumers; these societies control, in turn, bodies like the Co-operative Wholesale Society which engage in manufacturing and distributing. The workers in the movement are employees, subordinate to the management in the usual way.

This movement, which had sales of £50 million by 1900 and over £1,150 million in 1971, was a clear, large-scale breakaway from capitalist organization. Its success can be considered a convincing demonstration of the viability of other such forms of enterprise. But with the coming of the twentieth century the limitations of this approach became apparent. It was based on retailing: consumer control over manufacturing was remote and confined to lines to be traded in the shops. Producer co-operatives do exist in Britain, but they are small-scale and not of significance on the national scene. The system has made no impact on the basic industries or on the risky, expanding manufacturing business. Many great industries sell little to the individual consumer but trade mainly with other firms. Reformers have never ceased to hope for further applications of the co-operative principle, but in the twentieth century it has never seemed likely to suit the problem industries. Moreover, in recent years the co-operative movement has met with severe difficulties of its own, both because of a decline in active participation by members and because of weakening commercial performance. In the 1960s these problems began to be tackled by reorganization, amalgamations and managerial efficiency. But in the event the movement did not provide convincingly the promise of effective management, and other means of non-capitalist organization were therefore thought necessary.

(2) *The Labour Party and its programme.* In 1900 a group of trade unions and socialist societies came together to found the Labour Party, which aimed at securing distinctive representation of the workers in Parliament. In itself this implied the desirability of democratic political action and the imposition on industry of change by legislation. At first there was no agreed doctrine of what those changes were to be. Many leading trade unionists supported the Liberal Party and were openly non-socialist. Others regarded socialists without hostility, but as rather impractical idealists. Resolutions favourable to nationalization were first passed by the Trades Union Congress in the 1880s and 1890s. In 1894 a motion for the nationalization 'of the means of production, distribution and exchange' was successful, but in 1895 this demand was modified to mean nationalization only of land, minerals and railways. At the time of the foundation of the Labour Party, the trade-union element could not be regarded as committed to widespread nationalization. Nevertheless many unions were in a radical mood, dissatisfied with the results of working with the Liberals and very conscious that political action was necessary to protect their own position and to help the workers generally. In the period before the First World War, various nationalization motions were carried by the T.U.C. and some nationalization Bills introduced in the House of Commons, for purposes of demonstration, by the minority of Labour Members of Parliament; but these actions were overshadowed, in the Labour movement as well as outside it, by more urgent industrial and political issues.

The real beginning of the Labour Party's concern with public ownership came at the end of the First World War, and it roughly coincided with the Party's replacement of the Liberals as the main rival to the Conservatives. The experiences of war had forced trade unionists, like others, into a more radical frame of mind; and they had been impressed by the effectiveness of Government control of industry during the war, which seemed to show that business competition was not necessarily the most efficient method of conducting affairs. Trades Union Congresses during the war demanded increasingly wider measures of nationalization.

The Labour Party was put on a new footing in 1918, with a new constitution. Clause Four of this document stated the objective of the Party:

> To secure for the producers by hand or brain the full fruits of their industry, and the most equitable distribution thereof that may be possible, upon the basis of the common ownership of the means of production, and the best obtainable system of popular administration and control of each industry and service.

The Labour Party's election programme in December 1918 was called *Labour and the New Social Order*, and included wide proposals for social and fiscal reform. Moreover, it contained specific and far-ranging proposals for public ownership: land was to be taken into common ownership gradually; coal, railways and electricity were to be nationalized; industrial and life insurance were to be taken over; municipalities were to control the drink trade and be encouraged to take up new enterprises such as the retailing of coal and milk. Monopoly industries were also to be nationalized when convenient.

Henceforward the Labour Party was clearly a socialist party aiming at large measures of public ownership in industry. The growing strength of the Party and the militancy of the large trade unions – who were by this time also demanding nationalization – meant that public ownership became for the first time the key issue in British domestic politics – a position it retained for forty years.

The Labour Party made chequered progress between the wars, forming Governments in 1924 and 1929 but never securing a large majority in the House of Commons. It was never, therefore, in a position to implement the nationalization plans which it put forward repeatedly at elections. In the 1930s there was much dissension between the left wing, led by Sir Stafford Cripps, and the rest of the Party. But ideas about priorities for nationalization crystallized, and a workable programme was indicated in Dr Hugh Dalton's book, *Practical Socialism for Britain*, in 1935. This advocated among other things the public ownership of transport, coalmining, power, steel, armaments and gradually of the land.

The depression and industrial strife of the inter-war years, of course, confirmed socialists in their dissatisfaction with capitalist ownership, and reinforced their determination to carry through drastic changes. By the outbreak of the Second World War, the Labour Party had its industrial outlook and priorities clear.

(3) *Workers' control*. Before the Labour Party could be sure of the type of socialism it wished to promote, however, it had to consider the currents of opinion among its likely supporters. Capitalism was a system under which labour was hired by capital-owners – and it was natural, since this was the system under criticism, that a simple reversal of control should be considered.

The most elaborate doctrines of workers' control were developed on the Continent, where they were known as syndicalism. In Britain the principle became best known in the form of guild socialism. There was a movement of militant shop stewards, mainly in the engineering industry, during and just after the First World War which proclaimed workers' control as its objective; but this was short-lived. Guild socialism itself was advocated by A. R. Orage (in a magazine called *The New Age*), and by A. J. Penty, S. G. Hobson and G. D. H. Cole in various books and pamphlets. It envisaged a system whereby each industry was controlled by a workers' guild. Direction, at any rate in later versions, would have been in the hands of elected workers' representatives and of Government nominees charged with the duty of protecting the consumers.[3]

Two themes animated the proposals of guild socialists. The first was the need to liberate workers in their daily routine in the factories. Changes, such as Government ownership, which made no immediate change in the relations between employer and employee, were condemned as inadequate. A transformation in the direct control of the workers' lives was needed. Secondly, the guild socialists were strong advocates of the representation of interests and were distrustful of assemblies (like the House of Commons) based on geographical constituencies. An employer, in their view, whether he was elected or not, could not possibly represent a working man. They therefore proposed schemes for national assemblies elected by occupational constituencies.

Guild socialism as such faded quickly after the end of the First World War. Its institutional proposals were at once crude and idealistic. They had little appeal to the militant yet hard-headed and experienced socialist leaders of the time, who saw in the existing political machinery opportunities for achieving effective power. Among the intellectuals the preference of Fabians like the Webbs for Government or municipal ownership (or consumer control) was not to be overcome. But among trade unionists there persisted – certainly until the 1930s and to some extent beyond – a demand for workers' *participation*, at least. Some share in control, that is to say, was desired; and this feeling was not easily denied. In the end, only minimum concessions to this point of view were made; what they were will emerge later in the chapter. In fact, there is a sharp difference of principle between concepts of workers' control, concerned with power within industry, and public ownership aiming at the well-being of the whole community. The 1960s saw a revival of workers' control as a programme among militant trade unionists.

(4) *The need for national economic planning.* The idea of economic planning by central authorities is a comparatively new one. It was not much discussed by Marxists or by Fabians before the First World War. When the Communists came to power in Russia, however, they were faced with the problem of running a collectivized economy, and it was by a series of five-year plans that they imposed order and direction on economic activity. The notion of a centrally directed economy came under strong attack by anti-socialist economists between the wars.[4] It was argued very strongly that without a free market from which freely negotiated prices could emerge, the controllers of enterprises (publicly or privately owned) would have no guide by which to make rational production decisions. Nor would a central directorate have any means of relating their programmes to what people actually wanted.

The socialist response to these criticisms varied. But those whose views were influential in the British Labour Party accepted the necessity for free consumer demand and tried to devise methods by which publicly owned enterprises (i.e. those without the desire for profit) would respond to it. To do this a considerable degree of autonomy had to be granted to public enterprises, and – as described later in this chapter – this requirement favoured the public corporation as the vehicle of nationalization.

In the same period between the wars, however, some industrialists and some economists were beginning to doubt whether free competition was sufficient by itself to ensure economic welfare. The National Government abandoned free trade in 1933, and numerous schemes of regulation were promoted by Government and businessmen alike. The decisive change for non-socialists came, however, with the publication and acceptance of J. M. Keynes's *General Theory of Employment, Interest and Money* in the years before 1939. This provided what had been lacking, to some extent in socialist as well as non-socialist ideas: an economic rationale for general Government control, as distinct from piecemeal intervention.

Socialists believed that Keynesian planning reinforced their case for public ownership in industry. Only if major industries were owned and directly controlled, they argued, could investment be stimulated and the public sector exert a steadying influence on the economy. The inter-war depression, and the belief that central planning might relieve it, helped to reconcile many people to the idea of a controlled economy. And, in the 1930s especially, there was a strong feeling on the left that private enterprise would not co-operate with a Labour Government. The degree of control needed for planning would therefore necessitate nationalization – perhaps on a greater scale than that originally envisaged.

Many believers in central economic planning, of course, were not socialists and did not accept the need for widespread public ownership. Indeed, the acceptance of Keynesian economic ideas did not seem to everyone to involve planning as such, and the post-war years in Britain saw much controversy about the best type of full-employment measures to adopt. But by this time the Labour Government had established the basic nationalized industries.

(5) *Non-socialist influences.* At all times there have been people who would not accept any general socialist doctrines but were nevertheless prepared to advocate nationalization of particular industries or services. Joseph Chamberlain promoted a great deal of municipal enterprise in Birmingham. Mr Gladstone nationalized telegraphs in 1869 and at one time contemplated railway nationalization. Mr Winston Churchill declared in 1918, 'The Government policy is the nationalization of the railways. That great step it has at last been decided to take.'[5] In fact, the Government contented itself with amalgamation. But between the wars there was a slow spread of *ad hoc* public ownership – the B.B.C., London Transport, the electricity grid and coal royalties are examples. There were also reports between 1936 and 1945 on certain industries – MacGowan on electricity, Heyworth on gas and Reid on coal – which recommended action so drastic that many thought it would not come about without nationalization.

Perhaps the argument that appealed most strongly to non-socialists was the monopoly one. In cases where monopoly was natural or desirable, then public ownership might provide necessary safeguards. This was not incompatible with belief in a generally competitive system or in the greater drive and initiative of private enterprise.

The development of these sorts of opinions, together with the isolated acts of public ownership by non-socialist governments, seemed to many observers to confirm the existence of an irreversible trend. There was much talk of inevitable Government control and ownership 'whatever party is in power'. Marxists of course believed in general historical laws, by which broad future developments could be predicted. But those who rejected this outlook found the pressure of twentieth-century developments impressive, and the belief that increased collectivism was in some sense an unavoidable trend of the times was very fashionable until about 1950. The Conservative Governments of the 1950s managed to check the spread of collectivism; but it was no more than a check, not a reversal, and there were further extensions of Government activity in the 1960s.

It is easy to regard the growth of public control and planning entirely in intellectual terms – as a change in both academic and popular ideas about the economic role of Government. There is of course a good deal of truth in this. There has been a considerable movement of opinion. But the change was not merely a matter of people revising their views: there has been a transformation in the nature of the economy and of society. It is not a case of new ideas being applied to old situations and unchanged industries. Rather, the development of the structure and industrial content of society has led partly to a revision of doctrine, and partly to different results from the application of old criteria.

Thus among the publicly organized activities of today there are many that scarcely existed at all at the turn of the century. Some of them, such as electricity and air transport, began as private enterprises under public regulation. Radio and television have been, in Britain, predominantly public enterprises. Atomic energy has always been a Government concern. The internal-combustion engine has led to great public concern with roads and road haulage. Some existing Government activities, such as telecommunications, have enhanced importance through technological development.

During the period between the two world wars, the forces that shaped British nationalization were built up. The experience of the inter-war period was in the minds of the Labour Party politicians who carried out the main nationalization measures after the Second World War. So far, however, this chapter has dealt with the growth of the *desire* to nationalize. To some extent the rejection of consumers' or workers' control decided the character of non-capitalist enterprise: the only other possibility was ownership by the community as a whole, through the machinery of government. But the form taken by common ownership – the institutions necessary for its embodiment – were matters of vital importance. It is to the evolution of the public corporation, therefore, that attention must now be given.

RISE OF THE PUBLIC CORPORATION

In the nineteenth century the foundations of the modern British administrative system were laid. The dominant reforms of the period were liberal and utilitarian in spirit. They aimed at efficiency, honesty and impartiality. It was not envisaged that many trading activities would be carried on by the Government; fairness and economy would be the guiding principles of those that were.

Government departments were in origin the offices of ministers, and until the middle of the nineteenth century they were staffed in a haphazard way. In 1854 a report by Sir Stafford Northcote and Sir Charles Trevelyan set out a scheme for a new unified Civil Service. It was to be a permanent career service, working loyally and impartially for changing political masters, and was to be divided between clerical and superior positions. These principles were gradually put into effect, and by the end of the century they dominated the administrative structure of the central government. Departments are under the direct control of Ministers, who are responsible for all that their departments do – they must answer in Parliament for minor details of administration as well as major policy.[6] Civil servants influence policy by advising ministers: they have no authority of their own, and act always in the name of the Minister. In dealings with the public their discretion is usually limited, and in their striving for impartiality there is, traditionally, fairly close conformity to rules and precedents. Money is provided annually by Parliament and must be spent on the purpose for which it has been authorized.

The main trading organization of the Government in the nineteenth century was the Post Office. This was a Government department like the others, staffed by civil servants and controlled by a responsible Minister, the Postmaster-General. Until 1933 it was operated virtually like any other department. Since then there has been an increasing adaptation to commercial practice, culminating in 1969 in the adoption of public-corporation form.

There was one other nineteenth-century administrative body of importance: the local authority. This consists of an elected council controlling a variety of departments, many of which have large staffs. Thus local services, including trading services, are under the direct supervision of elected politicians. At one time the extension of municipal trading was regarded as a main route for public enterprise,[7] but in the twentieth century the urgent problems of coal-mining, railways and electricity demanded national solutions. Municipalization has therefore been overshadowed by nationalization.

The principle that all public administrative bodies should be directly subordinate to elected authorities was firmly maintained between 1855 and 1905.[8] In this period the experience of the Poor Law Commission set up in 1834 was held to be decisive. Widespread criticism of the Commission had had little effect on its administration, and no Minister had been able to control its actions or, when necessary, defend them. The Commissioners were stigmatized as 'The Three Kings of Somerset House', and after the replacement of the Commission in 1847, the idea of independence or autonomy in administration was under a cloud for the rest of the century.

The growth of Government activity in the twentieth century has involved the abandonment of this principle. There were one or two examples of new non-departmental authorities before 1914; after the First World War, however, the number of such bodies grew steadily. The changes were not unforeseen, or unopposed. In 1918 a Government committee under Lord Haldane declared:

> We are so far from thinking that the importance of a service to the community is *prima facie* a reason for making those who administer it immune from ordinary parliamentary criticism, that we feel all such proposals should be most carefully scrutinized, and that there should be no omission, in the case of any particular service, of those safeguards which Ministerial responsibility to Parliament alone provides.[9]

This opposition, however, had little effect.

It cannot be stressed too strongly that the growth of non-departmental administration has resulted in a great *variety* of institutions. Once the fixed principles of the Government department and full ministerial responsibility are abandoned, many degrees of control and many special relationships become possible. Some autonomous institutions, such as the British Council, are only a little different from departments. On the other hand there are bodies like the British Standards Institution, formally private and independent, which receive large, regular grants from the Government. Their purposes also vary greatly: some administer services, some regulate industries, some disburse funds, some are advisory, some quasi-judicial.

Nevertheless, among these twentieth-century autonomous institutions there can be no doubt that the public corporation is preeminent. Moreover, there lies behind the public corporation a theory and a fairly definite set of principles; the other autonomous bodies have developed in a much more confused and pragmatic way, with little background of deliberate principle.

The beginnings of the early public corporations – the forerunners of the present nationalized industries – can now be traced.

It is usual to begin with the Port of London Authority. At the beginning of the century the need for some reform was evident, and in 1902 a Royal Commission under Lord Revelstoke recommended placing the docks in the hands of a non-profit-making public trust. This was to be elected by port users, on the model of the Mersey Docks and Harbour Board of 1857. After attempts to legislate in 1903 and 1905 failed, the Port of London Act was finally passed in 1908. This provided for a Board with eighteen members elected by port users and ten appointed by public authorities, including Government departments and local authorities. The Authority owns and runs the docks and has powers of river conservancy. Representatives of labour serve on the board among the nominees of public authorities, but owners of Port of London stock have no share in control. In so far as the Authority was similar to other port trusts, its establishment could not be regarded as an unprecedented move. The Liberal Government of the period set up other non-departmental bodies, however, in the Road Board (1909) and the Insurance Commissions (1911), and though these were short-lived, it was clear that new (or revived) types of institutions were being sought for new Government activities.

In 1919 the Forestry Commission was established, modelled on the Ecclesiastical and Charity Commissions. Its duties are to maintain national forests and to carry out a programme of afforestation on waste land, for which powers of compulsory purchase are available. Its employees are civil servants; it is supported by Treasury grants, since sales of timber cannot yet cover its costs; and since 1945 the Minister of Agriculture has had power to give general directions to it. Nevertheless it retains considerable operational independence from the Government machine. Also in 1919, a supervisory body for the electricity industry, the Electricity Commissioners, was set up. It had judicial and administrative duties, but power to reorganize the industry was struck out of the Bill by the House of Lords, which was to mean that structural changes in the industry were later necessary.

These developments were merely preliminary. The establishment of the public corporation in the form in which we now know it came in the late 'twenties, with the British Broadcasting Corporation and the Central Electricity Board, followed by the London Passenger Transport Board in the early 'thirties.

Between 1922 and 1926 broadcasting in Britain was in the hands of the British Broadcasting Company Ltd, owned by radio-manufacturing companies. After the report of the Crawford Committee on broadcasting in 1926,[10] it was decided to replace this by a publicly owned but independently managed body, the British Broadcasting Corporation. It was clear by this stage that the new medium of communication had potentialities of great social and political consequence. Dislike of commercial radio as it was emerging in other countries, and the desire to establish a responsible and impartial source of public information, led many sections of opinion to favour a Governmental body. Nevertheless, close control by the Government of the day was unacceptable for political reasons, and it was doubted if an ordinary department would show adequate understanding of entertainment or cultural matters. The B.B.C. was thus essentially an attempt to insulate a public institution from partisan political interference; and it was designed – unlike most other public corporations – to avoid commercial operation. There was to be no advertising, and revenue was derived from the proportion of licence fees that the Government handed over to the B.B.C. A board of governors exercised general supervision, but real power lay with the Director-General. The first of these, Sir John Reith, was a man of determination and strict principle who imparted a good deal of his own austere character to the corporation. The Postmaster-General was responsible in Parliament for Government broadcasting policy and had substantial reserve powers, but he did not interfere in the ordinary running of the B.B.C.

The first attempts to establish a national grid for electricity supplies after 1918 failed,[11] and the Weir committee reported in 1926 in favour of a new authority to control generation and main transmission. This was accomplished by an Act passed the same year, and the Central Electricity Board began operation in 1927. The Board was appointed by the Minister of Transport after suggestions from various interested groups; but members had to sever all connection with bodies whose interests might conflict. It built and owned transmission lines, had full control of the main generating stations and sold electricity to private and municipal distributors. Supervision was exercised by the Electricity Commissioners, but the Board was very largely autonomous in practice. In Parliament the establishment of the Board was supported by the Labour Party and criticized by some Conservatives as 'socialistic'. Nevertheless it was carried through by the Government as the only effective way of advancing the progress of the industry. Its monopolistic character made public responsibility desirable, but its independent management made it possible to combine this with business methods of operation, free from close political interference.

The reorganization of public transport in London was a difficult and controversial matter. Since the beginning of the century, rising demand, lack of co-ordination and shortage of capital had prompted several mergers among the private-enterprise firms concerned. By the middle of the 1920s a combine, including the tube railways and most of the buses, had been built up under the control of Lord Ashfield. In 1928 a scheme for the co-ordination of London transport under private ownership was pressed forward.

When Mr Herbert Morrison became Minister of Transport in the minority Labour Government of 1929, however, he decided on a policy of public ownership and unified control. Eventually an agreed scheme on these lines was negotiated with the existing undertakings, but the Labour Government fell before it could be enacted. With some modifications, however, it was put into effect by Liberal and Conservative ministers in the succeeding National Coalition Government.

The Act set up the London Passenger Transport Board. It consisted of seven members, who were appointed, not by the Government, but by a body of trustees – in fact, holders of important non-political public offices. The first chairman was Lord Ashfield, and an officer of the Transport Workers' Union was made a part-time member, after relinquishing union duties. The L.P.T.B. took over all buses, trolley buses, trams, tubes and underground railways in London in July 1933, with monopoly powers and the object of providing an integrated service. The Board was financially independent, and supervision by either the Minister or Parliament was minimal.

With the establishment of these three bodies, the lines of the new type of institution were clear. The 'public service board', as it was usually called before the war, had emerged as an alternative public institution to the central department and the local authority. The challenging task – fundamental to public ownership of industry – of combining public responsibility with business-style management had begun.

The new corporations were essentially designed to meet particular circumstances, and for the Conservatives especially, who set them up, exceptional arguments were needed to justify the element of public ownership. Nevertheless, there was some theoretical commendation of these innovations. In 1926, in 'The End of Laissez-faire', J. M. Keynes noted that:

... In many cases the ideal size for the unit of control and organization lies somewhere between the individual and the modern State. I suggest, therefore, that progress lies in the growth and the recognition of semi-autonomous bodies within the State – bodies whose criterion of action within their own field is solely the public good as they understand it, and from whose deliberations motives of private advantage are excluded ...[12]

In 1928 the Liberal Party issued its famous Yellow Book, entitled *Britain's Industrial Future*. This stressed the need 'to find room for various types intermediate between the Public and the Private Concern'. Existing public boards had crept into the system without sufficient criticism or consideration. Nevertheless, the *ad hoc* public board was a better model to follow than that of direct public trading.

Some other independent bodies, such as the Agricultural Marketing Boards and one other public corporation, the British Overseas Airways Corporation of 1939, were created by the pre-war Conservative-dominated Government. But in the end it was the Labour Party that was to make most use of the public corporation, and their acceptance of it deserves special attention.

It is convenient at this point, however, before turning to the Labour attitudes, to establish clearly what a public corporation is. There is much discussion of the 'theory of the public corporation' or the 'concept of the public corporation', and a summary of the main features of the institution will enable us to discern the issues more accurately.

(1) The term 'public corporation' describes a specific *legal* form, as public companies and industrial and provident societies are legal forms. The expression 'nationalized industry' is not a legal term. The public corporation is a corporate body – that is, it can trade in its own name, sue and be sued, own property, and so on.

(2) It is a statutory body; its constitution, powers and duties are prescribed by law and can be modified only by legislation.

(3) It is publicly owned; any securities it may issue give no powers of control to lenders and usually pay a fixed rate of interest.[13]

(4) There is some degree of Government control. This normally includes the appointment of a corporation's governing board, and

may include by statute various policy and financial matters. In the post-war British nationalized industries the degree of control is considerable in practice.

(5) The corporation is independent in respect of its actual operations and management and has some degree of policy discretion. Its personnel are not civil servants, and its finances are separate from those of the Government.

There are in addition other practical rules that the British nationalized industries have in common – about pricing, accountability, finance and so on. Most public corporations are financially autonomous in that they exist largely on trading revenue. The principle of Government-appointed boards excludes direct sectional representation. Out of the principles, however, some general themes emerge. The public corporation is disinterested in the sense that its controllers do not reap personal advantage from its activities; it does not operate for its own benefit, and it has no inherent self-regarding motives for choosing one policy rather than another. Public responsibility can be expected of it because it has no reason to evade it.

The dominant idea of the public corporation, however, is undoubtedly its combination of business management with public accountability and control. It is on this combination that the concept centres. It is here that the success of the public corporation, as a distinct type of institution, must be judged. The proper phrase to describe its administrative status is undecided: autonomous, semi-autonomous, independent, semi-independent and quasi-governmental have all been used. Provided the principle is correctly understood, they need not be misleading.[14]

Contemporary political beliefs in Britain imply that public institutions must ultimately be subject to popular control. For the public corporation that control is exercised (whatever advisory or consultative arrangements there may be) only through the national machinery of Government. It thus aims to be a system of *indirect* control by the *whole community*, and not direct control by any sections of it.

The Labour Party and the public corporation

The creation of the public corporations between the wars, as just described, was the work of Conservative or Conservative-dominated Governments. Only in the planning of the London Passenger Transport Board did the Labour Party have any influence. It was not clear, therefore, whether the public corporation was a suitable instrument for nationalization as the Labour Party envisaged it. There were at least two reasons for suspecting that it might not be. First, one of its main attractions for Conservatives was the possibility of minimizing political interference and applying the methods of business management. The Labour Party, on the contrary, was dedicated to industrial change by political means, and the idea of making nationalized bodies as much like private business as possible had no natural appeal. Secondly, the Labour Party was the party of the trade unions and of employees generally. The new public corporations gave the trade unions no share in industrial policy-making and did nothing to modify the employer-employee relationship.

The objections to the public corporation's autonomy were the first to be overcome. Members of the Labour Party had little faith in the general run of businessmen, it is true; but they accepted that some independent and experienced managers, freed from the profit motive, would be of service. The alternative of control by Government departments was no great counter-attraction to the politically minded, for the reputation of the Civil Service between the wars was one of conservatism and timidity.

The place of the workers in a nationalized organization, however, took longer to settle, and it was discussed against a background of industrial conflict in the 1920s that contributed to trade union militancy. The situation in the coal industry led to a commission of inquiry in 1919 under Sir John Sankey; and this, by a narrow majority, recommended nationalization. The trade unions proposed to this commission that the mines should be owned by an independent Mining Council, with a Minister as chairman. Half the members were to be appointed by the Government and half by the mineworkers' union. The plan thus embodied the doctrine of 'joint control', and similar plans were put forward at various times in the 1920s. In specifying an independent body, the miners had clearly abandoned the idea of administration through a Government department, but they were determined at this stage on sharing control themselves. The Minister's role in these plans – as a responsible member of Government as well as a member of a council that he could not control – was obscure, and his position probably untenable.

It was not possible, in the event, to nationalize the mines at this time, and the dispute in the industry led to direct action and the General Strike of 1926. It was not until the early 1930s that the question of the technique of nationalization came to the forefront again. By this time the Conservatives had established the British Broadcasting Corporation and the Central Electricity Board.

In the 1929–31 Labour Government, which had no House of Commons majority, the Minister of Transport was Mr Herbert Morrison. In this capacity he was responsible for dealing with the C.E.B., and he prepared legislation designed to reorganize London Transport as just described. This was enacted, in a modified form, by the subsequent Conservative-dominated Government. (In general, Mr Morrison played a great part in persuading the Labour Party to accept the public corporation, as well as in helping to create several such bodies. In consequence there is a practice of referring to them as 'Morrisonian public corporations'.)

The absence of workers' participation in the management of the L.P.T.B. was therefore the occasion of renewed controversy in the Labour Party. The leader of the Transport and General Workers' Union, Mr Ernest Bevin, condemned the arrangements. At the 1932 Trades Union Congress a report which generally endorsed the idea of the independent public corporation was passed, but opposition from the T.G.W.U. led to the omission of the section that denied workers direct representation. In the same year Mr Bevin attacked the L.P.T.B. arrangements at the Labour Party Conference.

In the following years, however, agreement was reached on the necessary principles. The opponents of direct trade union representation pointed out that it would lead to pressure for other sectional representation, possibly from hostile groups. Management was becoming a highly skilled profession and should be as efficient as possible. The direction of big industrial concerns could not be carried on as a bargaining process between groups, and it was vital that nationalization should be seen to be a success, or the public would lose faith in it. Moreover, the trade unions themselves would be placed in a false position if, because they were involved in management, they could not effectively represent the workers' interests. In the outcome of these arguments it became accepted that workers' participation would mean that some trade unionists would be appointed to management boards, and that the trade unions might suggest who these should be. But they would nevertheless be chosen by the Government and would retain no ties with their unions. They would not act as spokesmen for union policy. Instead, trade union views would be pressed through compulsory advisory and consultative machinery.

The settlement of this issue after 1935 meant that the main lines of nationalization methods were decided. In principle, the Labour movement had accepted the public-corporation model recommended by the Liberals and initiated by Conservative Governments. There were some modifications in practice – such as the rights of trade unions to consultation, and more explicit powers of control by the Government – but the main structure of the new institutions was clear and widely accepted by all parties. A current of opinion in favour of more direct representation of workers in management has continued, but so far it has had little effect.

It should be remembered that in the 1930s and 1940s the Labour Party was much influenced by the ideas of economic planning previously mentioned. The public corporation seemed to fit the needs of planning in two ways. It embodied strong managerial authority, so that it could ensure that agreed central plans were carried out; and yet it was sufficiently independent to be able to respond to market pressures and so enable consumer demand to affect future plans. To some extent, therefore, the decline of ideas on workers' participation and joint control should be seen as consequences of the rising belief in the need for a centrally planned economy. Theoretically, however, the distinction was between community control in the public interest, and workers' control in their interests as producers.

In retrospect, three main periods can be distinguished in Labour Party thinking about control of public enterprise. In the first, before the First World War, it was assumed (rather than explicitly argued) that the Government department, such as the Post Office, provided the model for a public enterprise. Secondly, in the 1920s joint control was favoured. Thirdly, the managerial public corporation was accepted, after argument, in the 1930s. Though the public corporation still continues in favour for major industries, it is possible to distinguish a fourth period, after about 1955, when a variety of schemes for promoting public enterprise were advanced.

3 The Major Nationalized Industries

MOST nationalization as we now understand it dates from the years 1946–9; there has been a secondary period of growth in the 1960s.

As indicated in Chapter 2, there was by this time some growth of public ownership, partly associated with the new public corporations, partly with local authorities, and partly with other bodies. Thus public corporations of an industrial character existed in electricity and in London passenger transport. In 1939 an Act was passed setting up a new air-transport organization, the British Overseas Airways Corporation, but the war prevented its coming into operation. There was much municipal enterprise that could be considered industrial. About one-third of the gas industry was in municipal ownership, and so were two-thirds of electricity distribution. City bus services were typically owned by local authorities. A few large towns had also begun to operate municipal aerodromes. Manchester shared the ownership of the Manchester ship canal, and Hull owned the local telephone system. Bristol owned docks, and Birmingham a municipal bank. The central Government operated industrial undertakings like naval dockyards, the Royal Ordnance factories and the Royal Mint. The public houses of Carlisle and nearby districts had been Government-owned and -managed since the First World War. With the growth of telephone and telegraph communications, the Post Office had become in part an engineering service. In 1938 the right to receive royalties on coal mined was transferred from the landowners to a public Coal Commission. In addition, of course, there were numerous non-industrial activities in public ownership, controlled directly or indirectly by the Government – from the British Broadcasting Corporation and the Forestry Commission to the Racecourse Betting Control Board (running the totalizator) and the National Stud.

The war of 1939–45 diverted the normal progress of industrial organization. In these years industry generally was subjected to a system of close control involving the rationing of scarce materials, the allocation and direction of labour, and in many industries the concentration of civil production in a limited number of firms. The railways were taken over and operated on behalf of the Ministry of War Transport. Road haulage, coastal shipping and canals were likewise closely controlled. But all these measures, drastic as they were, consisted of controls imposed without disturbing the existing ownership.

A few highly specialized firms – S. G. Brown Ltd (precision instruments), Power Jets Ltd (jet-propulsion engines) and Short Brothers (aircraft) – ended the war in public ownership. The case of Short Brothers was the most significant. The Government took the firm into public ownership in 1943 and then replaced the existing management by directors of its own choice. Even the powerful wartime controls were found inadequate and had to be surpassed in this case at least. But in the general story of wartime industry this was a mere incident.

PARTY PROGRAMMES IN 1945

This is not the place to analyse the causes of changes in political attitudes. It is important to note, however, that the reforms in the air at the end of the war were overwhelmingly of an economic character. By this time there had arisen a general popular demand for change in the economic system. The great evils of the inter-war years had been depression and unemployment; and no politician doubted that, somehow, they had to be conquered. The publication in 1936 of J. M. Keynes's *General Theory* provided a theoretical basis for controlling the economy, and in 1944 the Coalition Government published a White Paper making proposals on *Employment Policy* which embodied some of Keynes's ideas. There was in addition great political controversy at this time about social security, dominated by Sir William Beveridge's report on *Social Insurance and Allied Services* of 1943.

But underlying these discussions were more deep-seated political attitudes, and the parties made their responses to the needs of the period in accordance with philosophies shaped over many years. As we have seen, the Labour Party had long declared itself a socialist party, and though this meant many different things to different people, none in the Party doubted that measures of public ownership would be involved. The Conservative Party was not prepared to advocate any such measures. In the past it had carried through many schemes for the regulation of industry and had set up public corporations in special fields; and by 1945 it was ready for further economic and industrial reform. But nationalization or other public ownership was regarded by Conservatives as unnecessary, bureaucratic and possibly totalitarian.

The Labour programme for the 1945 election was called *Let us face the future*. It included a large variety of proposals – on planning for full employment, on social security, on housing – and it stated clearly:

> There are basic industries ripe and over-ripe for public ownership and management in the direct service of the nation. There are many smaller businesses rendering good service which can be left to go on with their useful work.
>
> There are big industries not yet ripe for public ownership which must nevertheless be required by constructive supervision to further the nation's needs ...
>
> In the light of these considerations, the Labour Party submits to the nation the following industrial programme:
>
> (1) *Public ownership of the fuel and power industries* – For a quarter of a century the coal industry, producing Britain's most precious national raw material, has been floundering chaotically under the ownership of many hundreds of independent companies. Amalgamation under public ownership will bring great economies in operation and make it possible to modernize production methods and to raise safety standards

in every colliery in the country. Public ownership of gas and electricity undertakings will lower charges, prevent competitive waste, open the way for co-ordinated research and development and lead to the reforming of uneconomic areas of distribution. Other industries will benefit.

(2) *Public ownership of inland transport* – Co-ordination of transport services by rail, road, air and canal cannot be achieved without unification. And unification without public ownership means a steady struggle with sectional interests or the enthronement of a private monopoly, which would be menace to the rest of industry.

(3) *Public ownership of iron and steel* – Private monopoly has maintained high prices and kept inefficient high-cost plants in existence. Only if public ownership replaces private monopoly can the industry become efficient.

These socialized industries, taken over on a basis of fair compensation, to be conducted efficiently in the interests of consumers, coupled with proper status and conditions for the workers employed in them.

An earlier passage in the manifesto stated:

... the Bank of England with its financial powers must be brought under public ownership, and the operations of the other banks harmonized with industrial needs.

And in the section on the land:

Labour believes in land nationalization and will work towards it, but as a first step the State and the local authorities must have wider and speedier powers to acquire land for public purposes wherever the public interest so requires.

To the careful reader this indicated that land would not be nationalized, but that public authorities would have powers of compulsory purchase.

These declarations indicated the scope of the nationalization programme of the Labour Party at its zenith; and they were reflected in the legislation of the Attlee Government of 1945–51. In retrospect, it can be seen that they embodied a distinctive political outlook. Practical reasons, of some sort, related to the public welfare, were given for each proposed measure; and each proposal related to a whole industry, not to particular firms. There was no suggestion of expropriation, or that large profits were available for redistribution to exploited workers. When the Labour Party returned to office in 1964–70, under the leadership of Harold Wilson, its public-ownership programme was – in terms of legislation – much modified. The changes of both these periods, and those of the intervening Conservative regime, are described below.

THE PROCESS OF LEGISLATION

The Labour Government that took office in August 1945 was heavily occupied by general problems of demobilization and reconstruction, the balance of payments and social-service reform. There was, however, a feeling in the Party that the long-heralded opportunity given by its electoral success should not be missed. Other parties, and previous Labour minority Governments, had been accused of disappointing expectations, of betraying promises when power had been achieved. The feeling of the time, especially on the left, was that the least that could be done to avoid a repetition of such charges was to carry out the declared programme to the full.

At all events, nationalization plans were not delayed. There seems to have been some rough order of priority in that the Bank of England (the simplest) and the coal industry (the most urgent) came first, and the steel industry (the most doubtful) was left until late – perhaps too late for its effective accomplishment. There was a Cabinet committee on the socialization of industry, and the Cabinet committee on future legislation provided places for nationalization measures in the long series of Government Bills that were carried through Parliament.

For most Bills a 'guillotine' motion was passed, providing a timetable for the committee stage, when detailed amendments could be considered. This practice limited discussion, and some clauses were passed through the Commons undebated; but it made sure that reasonable progress was achieved and that effective obstruction was not possible. The House of Lords, where the Conservative Party has a large permanent majority, acquiesced in nationalization Acts, as it did in other Labour legislation, until the presentation of the Parliament Bill and the Steel Bill. Guided by Lord Salisbury, then Conservative Leader in the Lords, peers proposed amendments to legislation but did not insist on the acceptance of their views while, in their opinion, the mandate of the Labour Party held good. In 1949 events took a different turn, as is explained below.

Most of the main Acts have a similar form. They begin by prescribing the position of the new corporation and its governing board, its powers and duties. Then the terms of compensation are set out, followed by the financial arrangements of the new body. The principle of full compensation had been accepted, after some argument, by the Labour Party between the wars. The Acts provided for the compulsory replacement (usually at market value on a certain day) of existing stocks and shares by new fixed-interest stock, which carried no ownership rights but which could be bought and sold like other Government securities. The meeting of interest charges on this compensation stock became a statutory duty of the new corporations. The Acts also gave the relevant Minister the power to nominate the actual time of take-over. There was thus an interval of a few months between the final passing of an Act and 'vesting day', in which the first boards could be appointed and preliminary administrative arrangements made. Generally speaking, these principles survived through the 1960s.

The Bank of England

The first nationalization measure, the Bank of England Act, was passed by February 1946. This was a simple move designed to prevent the Bank from pursuing policies different from (and perhaps in opposition to) those of the Government. The assets were transferred to the Treasury, and the Court of Governors was reduced in size, but the structure of the Bank's organization remained as before. Formal power of direction over the Bank, after consultation, was given to the Chancellor of the Exchequer; and the Bank in turn has power, with Treasury consent, to give directions to commercial banks. (Neither power has been used.) The existing Governor, Lord Catto, was reappointed and remained in office until 1949.

The independence of the Bank has remained a matter of some controversy. In 1957, during the controversies surrounding the Bank Rate Tribunal, critics alleged that the Bank of England was the effective source of monetary policy, and that it reflected the opinion of the City of London rather than that of the Treasury and the Government. After the report of the Radcliffe committee on the working of the monetary system in 1959,[1] some formal changes were made, but the realities of the situation remain. The Bank works with the Treasury but develops its own views, based on its contracts with industry and financial circles. The Government is legally in a position to impose its will, but normally the relationship is one of collaboration and consultation.

Coalmining

A much more significant step was taken in 1946 with the nationalization of the coalmining industry. For many supporters of the Labour Party this lay at the centre of their plans and at the heart of their emotions. There was a long and bitter history of bad labour relations in the industry, and in many places the miners formed a closed community entirely dependent on the local pits. Industrial strife and economic depression had brought poverty and despair to these communities, and hence a feeling that not mere amelioration but a fundamental change in the order of things was required. Moreover, the years of depression had starved the industry of capital and of technical progress; and there had been insufficient reorganization and amalgamation, in spite of Government attempts to promote them.

Mr Emanuel Shinwell, the Minister of Fuel and Power in charge of the Bill, complained afterwards[2] that he had only a few pamphlets and private memoranda to guide him in fashioning the new structure. But there were at least some preparatory ideas, from the

Sankey Commission onwards: and one of the private memoranda had been drawn up by Mr Shinwell himself, with Mr John Strachey. In the event, the Coal Industry Nationalization Act of 1946 set up a public corporation on lines foreshadowed by pre-war experience.

The case for the Bill, as presented, was more practical and less dogmatic than might have been expected. The sad state of the industry needed no elaboration. The technical failings of British coalmining had just been set out in the report of a Government committee under the chairmanship of Sir Charles Reid.[3] This did not actually recommend public ownership, but stressed the cardinal necessity for 'a comprehensive scheme of reorganization' under an Authority which would ensure that the existing companies (whose pattern was often ill suited to the mining of coal-measures in particular areas) were merged into effective units. Taken with the general social situation in the coalfields, there was an overwhelming incentive, for any Government not ideologically opposed to it, to proceed with nationalization. The Conservatives, who had some grounds of principle for resisting public ownership, in fact criticized particular points in the Bill and voted against it on the grounds that it failed to solve specified problems of the industry. The Liberals supported it, their Leader (Mr Clement Davies) declaring that it would be 'one of the most epoch-making Acts of Parliament in our history'.

The Act set up the National Coal Board, which, since vesting day (January 1st, 1947), has owned all the mines in Great Britain. It has a right to a monopoly of 'working and getting the coal', but small mines may be operated by private enterprise under licence from the Board. In 1970 these mines produced about 0·7 million tons of coal. Coal distribution remains in private hands, except for some arrangements in the Midlands, where the old colliery companies had also been distributors. In taking over the old companies, the Board also acquired various ancillary activities, such as coke ovens and tar-distillation plant, and enough brickworks to make it the country's second largest producer. Compensation to the coal-owners was on a 'net maintainable income' principle, not (as with later measures) on Stock Exchange values.

The first Coal Board consisted of nine members under the chairmanship of Lord Hyndley. The actual take-over was smoothly effected, but the coal shortage in the very cold winter of 1947 brought early sharp criticism. Despite the establishment of divisions and areas for administrative purposes under the Board, there were many accusations of over-centralization. A new Coal Industry Act of 1949 increased the size of the Board and introduced part-time members. The chairmanship of Sir Hubert Houldsworth (1951–5) was marked by strenuous efforts to raise production, but under Sir James Bowman (1955–60) there was a check to demand that brought about large stocks of small coal. Further reorganization was carried out after the Fleck report of 1955, discussed in Chapter 5. The fourth and most spectacular chairman of the Coal Board was Lord Robens (1960–71). He succeeded in raising the productivity and in sustaining the morale of the industry through a deep crisis in its fortunes, which necessitated more reorganization and brought about a big reduction in the size of the industry.[4] Mr Derek Ezra became chairman in 1971.

Civil aviation

Before 1939, commercial air transport was in its pioneering days. Imperial Airways, a subsidized company, had opened many Empire routes, and British Airways, also subsidized, was doing the same in Europe. The Conservative Government amalgamated these into a publicly owned corporation just before the war. The technical progress of aviation during the war was enormous, but the total neglect of civil flying meant that a new start had to be made after 1945.

The Labour Government decided to continue the British Overseas Airways Corporation, nominally in existence, and to set up two new ones, British European Airways and British South American Airways, all being independent public corporations. These three were to be the only British airlines to provide regular services; but privately owned companies would be allowed a subordinate place.

In the main debate on the Bill, Labour spokesmen stressed that subsidies would be necessary at first to any airline, and that nationalization by public corporation would enable these to be used effectively and without meddlesome supervision. The Conservatives criticized the monopolistic features of the plan – that is, the restrictions on the scope allowed to private-enterprise companies – and alleged that excessive powers had been given to the Minister. The Bill was passed as the Civil Aviation Act 1946.

In 1949 British South American Airways was merged with the British Overseas Airways Corporation. In 1952 the Conservatives began a process of giving greater scope to private airlines. Since 1960 these have been able to compete for any service, including regular scheduled services. In practice, all services need the permission of the licensing authority, and this is what determines the opportunities of the various operators.

Major changes in the control of air transport followed the publication in 1969 of the Edwards report *British Air Transport in the Seventies* (Cmnd. 4018). Though it found nothing radically wrong in British civil aviation, 'nothing calling for really urgent surgery', it did recommend some institutional changes. The Conservative Government put these into effect in the Civil Aviation Act of 1971. A supervisory Civil Aviation Authority was set up (with Lord Boyd Carpenter as first chairman), which took over the functions of licensing, safety and general regulation and control from various other bodies. It controls some aerodromes, and operates the national air-traffic control jointly with the Ministry of Defence. One of the recommendations of the Edwards committee had been that a private-enterprise 'second-force' airline should be maintained, and the Civil Aviation Authority has a statutory duty in its licensing policy to make a place for such an airline – in practice, British Caledonian Airways.

The second new body established by the 1971 Act was the British Airways Board (of which Mr David Nicholson was the first chairman). On many occasions in their history there had been rumours of the unification of the two main corporations, although they provide very different services – B.E.A. is a 'short-haul' operator, and B.O.A.C. flies on long transatlantic, Commonwealth and other world-wide routes. At first, following the Edwards report, the Government rejected unification; but in fact the British Airways Board now has strong control over the two corporations and their subsidiaries, including appointment of their Boards, and it will operate them as a group. In July 1972 it was announced that the two air corporations were to be regarded as operating divisions of a unified British airways group.

Nearly all civil airports providing regular services were owned and run directly by the Ministry of Aviation after the war, and Mr Herbert Morrison declared in 1946 that 'if ever there was a service which is not fit for municipal enterprise, it is the provision of airports.'[5] The growth of private-enterprise flying has encouraged the growth of the lesser airports, however, and there has been in fact considerable growth in municipal provision since 1955; this was accelerated in 1961, and in 1965 a British Airports Authority was created to run four main airports. Landing charges for use of airfields, and it is hoped that eventually airports will be financially self-supporting.

The growth of air traffic led the British Airports Authority to insist that a third large London airport would be needed at an early date. From this plea there stemmed a very deep controversy over the site, an elaborate inquiry under Mr Justice Roskill which recommended Cublington, and eventually a Government decision to build an airport at Foulness.

Aircraft construction is a private-enterprise industry, though the Royal Air Force and the nationalized airlines buy most of its output. In consequence the Government is in a strong position to deal with it, and in 1959–60 Mr Duncan Sandys, then Minister of Aviation, was able to impose drastic amalgamations. A committee of inquiry into the aircraft industry, under the chairmanship of Lord Plowden,[6] recommended in 1965 that the Government should purchase a financial share in the two largest construction companies, the British Aircraft Corporation and Hawker Siddeley; and a majority of the committee believed that this should be a majority holding, in order to give effective control. Nothing came of this proposal. Unexpectedly, however, public ownership came to the aircraft engine industry in 1971, when the disastrous financial condition of Rolls-Royce Ltd led to it being taken over by the Government.

Cable and Wireless

Cable and Wireless Ltd was a firm established in 1929 which operated various international telecommunication links, particularly between Britain and countries in the Commonwealth. In 1938 the British Government acquired a minority of the shares, in 1946 the Labour Government decided on the compulsory transfer of the rest, and this was achieved, under the Cable and Wireless Act, on January 1st, 1947. In 1948 the property of the company and its subsidiaries was divided among member-states of the Commonwealth.

Public ownership in this case has not meant the creation of a public corporation, and the usual forms of control and accountability do not apply. The company now operates foreign and Commonwealth communication services, and owns submarine cables and cable ships.

Transport

In some ways transport was better prepared for nationalization than any other industry, and yet it has maintained a persistent air of crisis, punctuated by drastic reorganizations. Preparation was helped by the fact that the railways had been subjected to detailed Government regulation from the beginning, and in 1921 the system had been recast into four main companies by the Railways Act. Transport in London was unified under public ownership by the London Passenger Transport Act of 1933. His experience in the preparation of this Act inspired Mr Herbert Morrison to write *Socialisation and Transport*, thus providing the most considerable practical scheme of nationalization to be prepared in advance. Road haulage was in private hands but controlled by a licensing system established by the Government in 1933. A high proportion of bus services were municipally owned; all were regulated by licence. The roads themselves, of course, are publicly owned; but no one has ever seen fit to administer them as part of the transport industry.

The Transport Act of 1947 was a nationalization measure with a policy. The structure of the new public corporation was deliberately designed to bring about the integration of the country's transport. That is to say, competition between the different *forms* of transport (particularly between road haulage and the railways) was to be minimized, and each type fitted into a unified system. The Act itself did not bring this about directly, but it created the British Transport Commission, a small board of five full-time members, for the purpose; Lord Hurcomb, a former civil servant, was the first chairman. The B.T.C. itself became the owner of all transport property specified in the Act, and it had complete control over policy. Nevertheless, the actual management of the undertakings was in the hands of a series of Executives – a Railways Executive, a Road Haulage Executive, a Road Passenger Executive,[7] a Docks and Inland Waterways Executive, a Hotels Executive and a London Transport Executive. These comprised small boards appointed by the Minister but regarded essentially as agents of the Commission.

The proposals concerning road transport need further explanation. Since 1933, goods transport by road has been controlled by a system of licences – 'A' and 'B' for haulage firms and 'C' for those carrying only their own goods. The 1947 Act used the restrictions possible through the operation of this system to check competition against nationalized services. In particular, private road-haulage firms (holding 'A' and 'B' licences) were confined within a twenty-five-mile radius; and 'C'-licence vehicles were still forbidden to work for hire. For road-passenger services the Commission was to prepare schemes for specified areas which would co-ordinate the services with one another and also with rail provision. Within this framework the Commission would acquire bus services and long-distance road haulage – that is, the hauliers whose business was predominantly over a forty-mile radius. Prices charged by the Commission would be supervised by a transport tribunal, described in Chapter 6.

In the Commons the Conservatives totally opposed the Bill. The Liberals also decided against it, though they would have accepted nationalization of railways and canals in another form. Critics condemned both the prospective lack of freedom for transport users to choose their own form of transport, and the restrictions placed on the use of a firm's own transport. There was also some displeasure over the terms of compensation, and a Member quoted *The Economist*'s declaration that '... it is the widow and the orphan, the patient and the pensioner, who will mainly suffer.'[8]

In spite of criticism and campaigns the Bill was passed, and the Act received the royal assent in August 1947. The railways, canals and London Transport were taken over on vesting day (January 1st, 1948), but other parts of the industry were acquired gradually. For several years the Commission was busy taking over road-transport firms, both passenger and goods-carrying, and there was slow progress in carrying out the policy of integration. In 1948 the provincial bus group of Thos Tilling was acquired, and in 1949 that of Scottish Motor Traction. In addition, the Commission had a minority shareholding in a holding company called British Electric Traction Co. Ltd, which owns most of the private-enter-prise bus companies of any size. Road-haulage companies were also taken over, and by 1952 the Commission owned 42,000 lorries.

Various other enterprises came into public ownership with the Transport Act, often because they had been previously owned by the railway companies, rather than through deliberate policy. The railway hotels form a substantial concern. Pickfords road services and Carter Paterson road-parcels services are publicly owned, and so, until recently, were two well-known travel agencies, Thomas Cook and Dean & Dawson. Docks owned by the railways came under the Commission. Shares in some shipping companies were also acquired.

Less than four years after nationalization, the Conservatives came to power, with a different set of transport policies. They quickly called a halt to further acquisitions by the Commission, and they ended the integration policy. The 1952 annual report of the Commission sets out some projects that were abandoned. For example, the railways' collection-and-delivery services were to be combined with local services of the Road Haulage Executive; motor engineering and stores were to be unified; some road-haulage traffic was to be carried on rail trunk lines; and some cross-country rail parcels were to go by road.

Conservative policy was embodied in the Transport Act of 1953. This first set out to denationalize long-distance road haulage; and it required the British Transport Commission to reorganize its administrative structure. The system of Executives was abolished, and the Commission's tasks of preparing co-ordination schemes and taking over docks and harbours were cancelled. The denationalization of road haulage was no great success: it proved impossible to sell all the vehicles down for disposal, and in 1956 a further Act put a road-haulage organization, British Road Ser-Services, on a permanent basis as a subsidiary of the British Transport Commission. An attempt to revive the railways largely by technical development was begun in the British Railways Modernization Plan of 1955, at a cost then estimated at £1,660 million.

Continued financial difficulties of the railways led to further proposals by the Conservative Government in December 1960. After an unpublished report by a committee under Sir Ivan Stedeford, the Government decided to put an industrialist from the chemical industry, Dr Richard Beeching, in charge of a new drive for financial viability, replacing Sir Brian Robertson, who had been chairman in the years 1953–61. By the Transport Act 1962 the British Transport Commission was abolished and a British Railways Board set up with great responsibilities transferred to regional railway boards.[9] Road haulage, road-passenger services, Cook's travel agency, and other interests were transferred to a holding company in public ownership; canals to a new British Waterways Board; and nationalized docks to a British Transport Docks Board. General transport supervision was retained only in the form of an advisory council to the Minister of Transport. At the new Railways Board Dr Beeching set out to achieve commercial success. A report on *The Reshaping of British Railways* in 1963 set out plans for doing so by introducing new freight services (liner trains), by closing many non-paying lines, and by other means; and another report in 1965, *The Development of the Major Railway Trunk Routes*, described proposals for streamlining trunk services. In 1965 Sir Stanley Raymond succeeded Dr Beeching as chairman.

However, by this time, a Labour Government was in office, and the Minister of Transport, Mrs Barbara Castle, had extensive plans for reforming the industry. The preparations were aided by the strengthening of the economic planning staff at the Ministry. A general outline of intentions was set out in a White Paper on *Transport Policy* (Cmnd. 3057) in July 1966, and a series of White Papers on particular subjects followed. The bulk of these policies were embodied in the long Transport Act of 1968.

The Act established a number of new organizations. First, it created the National Freight Corporation to promote an integrated service for goods transport by road or rail, concerned particularly with general merchandise, sundries and parcels. This took over road services from the Transport Holding Company and responsibilities for sundries traffic from British Railways. The Act also established a Freight Integration Council as a co-ordinating body with a wide concern, including both the new Corporation and the Railways Board.

Secondly, the Act established new bodies in passenger road transport. In major conurbations (in practice Tyneside, Merseyside, Selnec and the West Midlands) new public corporations known as Passenger Transport Executives were set up with general powers to produce integrated passenger transport, and operate bus services formerly run by local authorities. To begin with these were supervised by Passenger Transport Authorities, bodies appointed by the various local councils in the areas, and in fact consisting largely of councillors. These Authorities had financial powers and duties, as well as the right to appoint members of the Executive; but as part-time bodies they were dependent on the full-time Executives for expert advice and guidance. In the recasting of local government in the early 1970s the functions of the P.T.A.s are being transferred to the new metropolitan authorities. The Executives will continue as autonomous corporations, but in some cases the area they cover is being altered.

A third public corporation created by the 1968 Act was the National Bus Company. This took over the bus interests owned by the Transport Holding Company, including some that it had recently acquired. The buses are operated commercially through about sixty local or regional subsidiary companies, and in fact the N.B.C. runs the bulk of the stage-bus services in England and

Wales (apart from London, the conurbations and municipal services), including such well-known names as Crosville, Trent, Midland Red, Southdown, United Counties and Western Welsh. Some of these of course run in the P.T.E. areas, and there is a statutory obligation on the N.B.C. to co-operate in the reorganization of services within these areas.

The Scottish Transport Group is the fourth public corporation created by the Transport Act. This includes not only bus companies but the Caledonian Steam Packet Company, David Mac-Brayne Ltd and other businesses concerned with insurance and tourism in Scotland. It can provide ancillary services and must co-operate with other transport bodies. It is responsible to the Secretary of State for Scotland.

Besides restructuring these public corporations, the 1968 Act also made important financial changes. For the first time support was provided not to meet deficits but to further stated policy aims, declared necessary on social grounds. The best-known of these is the system of grants for unremunerative passenger services on the railways. The Minister, if satisfied that the services are desirable for social or economic reasons, may make grants for specific lines, for a maximum of three years at a time. There are also some additional grants to relieve the Railways Board of the cost of maintaining redundant track and signalling, pending its removal.

There are also grants to help road passengers. Capital grants may be made towards improved facilities for passengers – bus stations and so on. Grants can be made for transport research. The Act established, moreover, a system of financial support for bus services through grants of 25 per cent of the cost of new buses; grants towards the duty charged on bus fuel; and grants or loans in support of rural bus services.

The Act made numerous other provisions including restrictions on the hours of work of drivers of buses, lorries and other vehicles. It also made a division of the undertaking of the British Waterways Board into commercial waterways and cruising waterways, with different standards of maintenance; and it established an Inland Waterways Amenity Advisory Council. A later measure, the

Transport (London) Act of 1969, transferred the control of London Transport from the Ministry of Transport to the Greater London Council; with the exception of the green bus services, which became, as London Country Bus Services Ltd, a subsidiary of the National Bus Company. Another item in the Labour Government's transport plans – the nationalization of the ports – was left for later legislation, and the Government fell before it was enacted.

At the end of 1967 Mrs Castle, the Minister of Transport, removed Sir Stanley Raymond from the chairmanship of the Railways Board, and replaced him by Sir Henry Johnson. When Sir Henry retired in 1971, the Conservatives were in office, and they appointed Mr Richard Marsh to the chairmanship – Mr Marsh having served as Minister of Transport (in succession to Mrs Castle) in 1968–9. The financial circumstances of the railways improved for a time, but the price-restraint policies of the early 1970s hit them very hard, and special additional grants from the Government were necessary. Doubts as to the adequacy of the specific supports of the 1968 Act began to appear.

In pursuance of their general philosophy of minimizing Government commitments, the Conservatives in 1972 arranged to sell the travel agents, Thomas Cook Ltd (hitherto the only remaining significant asset of the Transport Holding Company), to a consortium of private organizations which included the Midland Bank, Trust Houses Forte and the Automobile Association. In 1972 proposals were made to break up the British Waterways Board, and distribute the waterways among a number of Regional Water Authorities.

Electricity

The nationalization of electricity was preceded by the report of a committee on electricity distribution (the McGowan committee), which in 1936 recommended considerable amalgamation among the existing undertakings. The generation of electricity was already in the hands of the publicly owned Central Electricity Board, which operated the grid. It was clear that the need for electricity would rise considerably, and that there would be great economies from the use of larger power stations and general standardization of methods. There was, therefore, a case for nationalization on technical and organizational grounds.

In the debates in 1947 the Conservatives opposed the Bill on the grounds that it would cause great dislocation and that the position of consumers would be damaged. The Liberals voted for it.

As a result of the Act, the whole industry was owned and controlled by the British Electricity Authority (called the Central Electricity Authority after 1955), though distribution was organized by a number of regional boards. The whole system was reviewed by an official committee, which in 1956 produced the Herbert Report, one of the most important documents in the story of British nationalization.[10] The general implications of the doctrines advanced in this report will be discussed later, particularly in Chapters 5 and 7. For electricity the consequence was the break-up of the unified structure over which the first chairman, Lord Citrine, had presided between 1948 and 1957. There are now twelve Area Electricity Boards, concerned with distribution; a Central Electricity Generating Board (chairman, Sir Stanley Brown); and an Electricity Council with certain general and supervisory duties (chairman, Sir Peter Menzies). All these have an autonomous statutory existence, and their members are appointed individually by the Secretary of State for Trade and Industry.

In Scotland there are different arrangements. The 1947 Nationalization Act excluded the North of Scotland from its general provisions, and this region was served by the North of Scotland Hydro-Electric Board. This body had been established in 1943, and in 1947 it was necessary only to modify its constitution slightly. In 1954 the South of Scotland Electricity Board (which does not use water power) was also made independent. Both are public corporations of the normal type, supervised by the Secretary of State for Scotland.

The post-war history of electricity has been marked by a steep and steady rise in demand, and its main problem has lain in keeping pace with growing requirements. Generation is now effected by burning heavy oil as well as coal, and a small contribution is made by nuclear power stations.

Gas

In 1948 the Labour Government began to nationalize the gas industry. Again, there was a preceding inquiry by an official committee, resulting in the Heyworth report of 1945.[11] This proposed that regional boards, set up by Act of Parliament, should acquire all the undertakings in their own areas. Larger units in the industry were necessary, it claimed, to lower production costs, to develop research, sales and distribution, and to eliminate inefficient plant.

The Bill provided for the transfer of all gas undertakings – whether municipally or privately owned – to twelve Area Gas Boards. It was steered through the Commons by Mr Hugh Gaitskell, then Minister of Fuel and Power, against vigorous opposition. The Government argued, mainly on the lines of the Heyworth report, that larger units with predetermined boundaries were necessary; and only nationalization could ensure speedy action. The Conservatives suggested that nationalization was unnecessary, and that (with coal and electricity) a dangerous fuel and power monopoly was being created. The Liberals supported the Bill.

The provisions of the 1948 Act gave each Area Board a monopoly of the manufacture and supply of gas within its boundaries; some ancillary activities – coking, tar distillation and chemical by-products – were inherited from the companies taken over, but no attempt was made to acquire such activities deliberately. At first these Area Boards were undoubtedly the main management bodies of the industry. They were co-ordinated to some extent, however, by a Gas Council which consisted of the chairmen of Area Boards but had a full-time chairman and vice-chairman. This highly decentralized structure was modified over the years, and in 1972 it was replaced by the British Gas Corporation.

The need for structural change was determined by the technological revolutions of the 1960s. The first change was brought about by the development of methods of producing gas from fuel oil or naphtha, and by the importing of natural gas (methane) from the Sahara. Both these promised more economic supplies than could be expected from the development of methods of producing town gas from coal. After a year or two in which progress towards these techniques was made, however, a second revolution was brought about by the discovery of quantities of natural gas under the North Sea. The consequence of these changes was to make the bulk supply of gas largely a national operation, and a system of trunk pipelines was built.

The British Gas Corporation is itself the owner and controller of the whole gas industry. By the 1972 Act the Area Boards lost their statutory independence, and though they continue as administrative units concerned mainly with gas distribution, they are now appointed by and can be redeployed by the Corporation.

Steel

The story of the nationalization and denationalization of the iron and steel industry reflects a clash of principles more clearly than does any other major episode in post-war politics.[12] The Labour Party was sharply divided from Conservatives and Liberals on the issue; nationalization was forced through against bitter and determined resistance; compromises were rejected; it was reversed as soon as its opponents had power to do so; and eventually it was restored.

Government intervention in the steel industry began in the 1930s. Technical progress had been lagging and investment was inadequate. The Government of the day agreed to give tariff protection provided that steps were taken to reorganize and modernize the industry. The Import Duties Advisory Committee, a body whose general duty was to decide tariff changes in the national interest, was thus given a supervisory role over the steel industry, in that it had to be satisfied that protection was being used to secure improved efficiency. A new trade association, the British Iron and Steel Federation, was set up, and machinery for collective policy-making by the industry was developed to a greater degree than in any other private-enterprise industry. During the war an Iron and Steel Control was established with full powers over production and distribution, with many of its personnel recruited from the B.I.S.F. The importance of steel in armament production made strict control of the allocation of supplies essential, and continued shortage relative to demand meant that steel rationing was needed for many years after the war. In 1946 an interim system of public control was established through an Iron and Steel Board, which comprised two independent members (including the chairman), two employers, two trade unionists and a representative of steel-using firms.

However, the steel industry had been scheduled for nationalization in 1945 in *Let us face the future*. The leaders of the steel industry were prepared to accept strong public control, and they hoped that a system could be arranged which would satisfy the Labour Party without entailing full public ownership. Private discussions between the industry and members of the Government took place in the summer of 1948, and a tentative agreement was reached with Mr Herbert Morrison. The idea of compromise did not please many Labour politicians, however, and the agreement (whose contents are still secret) was not accepted by the Cabinet.[13]

The decision of the Government to proceed with nationalization brought many problems. Relations with the industry deteriorated rapidly and its representatives on the Iron and Steel Board withdrew, making the work of that body impracticable. Vehement political opposition was aroused, and the Conservative majority in the House of Lords seemed likely to show its strength at last and reject the Bill. Moreover, the iron and steel industry was a very complex one with many ramifications, and the technique of nationalization was more difficult to apply than before.

The Government tried to forestall the action of the House of Lords with a new Parliament Act. The first Parliament Act of 1911 had limited the powers of the Lords, so that they could delay legislation for only two years. The new proposal shortened the delay to one year. The Lords opposed this curtailment, and so the Bill had to be passed under the terms of the 1911 Act.

The Nationalization Bill had a stormy passage through Parliament, guided by the Minister of Supply, Mr George Strauss. The Government claimed a mandate, and argued that the industry was monopolistic and not very efficient; as a basic industry, it needed full public responsibility. The Opposition denied all such contentions:

the industry was, in its view, competitive, efficient, progressive, and had good labour relations. The motives for nationalization, alleged the Conservatives, were clearly ideological and political. The fact that the controversy of that time centred on the appropriateness of public ownership as such rather than on the reconstruction or rehabilitation of the industry accounted for much of its bitterness.

Eventually, however, after much difficulty, the Act was passed, though it could not be made operative before the General Election of February 1950. The Labour Party won this election by a very small majority, but nevertheless declared its intention of implementing the Act, and it began to make the necessary administrative arrangements. The leaders of the steel industry and the Conservative Party refused to resign themselves to nationalization, however: they felt that the Government's majority was so slender and its prospects so insecure that delay might still bring some success. No prominent businessmen in the steel industry agreed to serve with the new Iron and Steel Corporation, and any steel industrialist who consulted the B.I.S.F. about service with the corporation was advised not to join it. In other words, the existing managers of the industry boycotted the new structure.

On February 15th, 1951, the industry passed into public ownership, and the Iron and Steel Corporation began its work under the chairmanship of Colonel Steven Hardie, who had previously been chairman of the British Oxygen Co. Ltd. Nevertheless, no immediate change took place in the management of the companies, who continued to consult together and to co-ordinate policies in their trade association, the British Iron and Steel Federation. The corporation made some changes in the boards of directors of the companies, and prepared consolidated accounts. Eventually its legal authority must have prevailed.

In October 1951, however, there was another General Election, and the Labour Government fell. The new Conservative Minister of Supply, Mr Duncan Sandys, issued a general directive under Section 4 (1) of the Act, prohibiting further changes in the industry's financial or management structure. In February 1952 Colonel Hardie resigned as chairman of the corporation after a confused dispute with the Minister about steel prices. Progress by the nationalized corporation had come to an end, and in 1953 the Conservatives passed the Iron and Steel Act providing for the denationalization of the industry.

This abolished the Iron and Steel Corporation and set up a regulatory Iron and Steel Board with functions relating to raw materials, prices and industrial development. The actual ownership of the steel companies passed to the Iron and Steel Holding and Realization Agency (ISHRA), a small, independent body with the duty of selling the companies to private owners. Preference was given to previous owners of steel shares willing to buy, but many were sold to the public. In its first five years ISHRA succeeded in disposing of most of the companies on its hands, regrouping some units and reorganizing the structure of the stock in the process. But the process has since slowed down, and in 1964 one very large company (Richard Thomas & Baldwins Ltd) and a number of smaller enterprises remained with ISHRA. Ten years after the denationalization Act, that is to say, they remained in public ownership.

In 1959 some substance was given to the Labour Party's contentions about the inadequate expansion of the industry. Following criticisms by the Iron and Steel Board of the development plans put forward by the companies, the Government authorized special loans of £120 million to two firms, Richard Thomas & Baldwins and Colvilles, to build new continuous-strip-rolling mills. The question of location (in order to provide employment in South Wales and Scotland) was important, as well as that of the future capacity of the industry, and it was demonstrated that means of securing expansion – admittedly highly controversial ones – could be found without nationalization.

The question of steel nationalization remained politically alive, however, and was still part of the Labour Party programme when it returned to office in 1964. Controversies about the efficiency, the capacity and the modernization of the industry continued. In the middle 1960s the industry set up its own investigation into the possibilities of reorganization.[14] This was overtaken by political events, however, and in April 1965 the Labour Government published its plans in a White Paper on *Steel Nationalization* (Cmnd. 2651). A national steel corporation was proposed, to take over fourteen large companies, which in practice dominated the industry – they were responsible for over 90 per cent of most of its major products. The Government survived a debate on these proposals very narrowly, but it was not possible to enact them until after the election of 1966, when the Government had a larger majority.

The Iron and Steel Act of 1967, piloted through Parliament by Mr Richard Marsh, created the British Steel Corporation, which began operations in July 1967. The Iron and Steel Board was abolished. The method of nationalization itself implied two things: first, that an appreciable private sector would remain, in competition with the nationalized corporation; and secondly, that the firms taken over would have interests in other products besides steelmaking: in fact in wire, tubes and structural steel. It was intended moreover that, with Government approval, the B.S.C. would diversify further as its commercial advantage might indicate. Most of the standard concepts of the public corporation were applied to steel, but the notion of a 'public firm' operating in the economy with some autonomy had clearly overtaken the idea of 'administering the industry' as a predefined monopoly. The Corporation, under its first chairman, Lord Melchett, soon found itself with serious problems. It formulated and carried through two reorganization plans, discussed in Chapter 5. Its finances were in difficulty, and it needed to carry out a large investment programme if the rationalization and modernization which public ownership implied were to be carried through. Its most notable experiment was the establishment of part-time worker-directors on its divisional Boards, discussed in Chapter 4.

The Post Office

Postal and associated services constitute one of the most substantial of any modern government's trading services. The British Post Office can trace its origin to the sixteenth century, and in the nineteenth century its activities underwent a great expansion with the introduction of cheap postage. In 1869 the inland telegraph service was nationalized (probably the first use of the word), and in 1912 the telephone service was taken over completely, apart from the local-authority system in Hull. The Post Office also operated a banking service, from 1861 to 1969, and it still acts as an agency for other Government services, such as the payment of old-age pensions.

Up to 1933 the Post Office was run like any other Government department. Since then, there has been a series of changes, culminating in the Post Office Act of 1969, which converted it into an independent public corporation. An Act of 1961 had already separated the finances of the Post Office from those of the rest of the Government, and they were reported to Parliament by commercial accounts only. The system of financial targets had already been applied to the Post Office. The creation of the public corporation from October 1st, 1969, was therefore a final step in a long procession. The new corporation is under the supervision of a new Minister of Posts and Telecommunications, who is also concerned with broadcasting policy. Post Office Savings were renamed National Savings and retained as a Government function. Though there are some common services at headquarters, the work, organization and finances of the Post Office are divided into a postal side and a telecommunications side. The postal side is also concerned with the national Giro, and through local post offices provides the agency services for other Government departments. The telecommunications side is, in the early 1970s, engaged in a large programme of investment and re-equipment. Post Office staff are, of course, no longer civil servants. The first chairman, Lord Hall, was replaced, after a dispute with the Minister in 1970, by Mr A. W. C. Ryland.

Common characteristics

It is worth noting some features that the various nationalization Acts had in common. First and most obviously, with minor exceptions they all set up public corporations on the model described in Chapter 2. There were no concessions either to workers' control or to direct administration by Government departments.

Secondly, the Acts contained stronger provision for control by

Ministers over the corporations than did pre-1939 legislation. A clause giving the relevant Minister power to issue 'directions of a general character' was included in all post-war Acts but in none of the earlier ones. Again, the later Acts gave Ministers the power to dismiss members of the boards (except those of the Bank of England), and their period of office is a maximum, not a fixed, one. Powers of Ministers to intervene in the financing of the corporations are also stronger in post-war legislation.

Thirdly, all the Acts made some provision for the representation of consumers – by establishing special councils or committees for the purpose. (These bodies are discussed in Chapter 6.) The boards were also obliged by all the Acts to establish machinery with the unions for settling pay and conditions, and to set up machinery for 'joint consultation' on matters affecting the industry generally.

Fourthly, all the Acts made similar statements about the obligation of corporations to cover their costs 'taking one year with another'. The elaboration of doctrine around this principle will be considered in later chapters.

Finally, the detail in which the structure of the corporations was set out in the Acts increased between 1946 and 1949. This may have been due to a desire to ensure decentralized organization, but it also relates to the character of the various industries.

The Acts make it clear that public corporations have no power to commit unlawful acts, although they have wide freedom to pursue any activities that seem to them helpful to their duties. The corporations pay taxes (mainly corporation tax) in the same way as other businesses. They are also liable for local rates, though in many cases there are special arrangements whereby they meet this obligation.

OTHER NATIONALIZATION

The account given so far in this chapter excludes many public corporations and other government trading bodies.

A number of additional moves towards public ownership were made by the Labour Government. The centralized buying of

C

supplies for the cotton industry begun during the war was continued by the Raw Cotton Commission, set up under the Cotton (Centralized Buying) Act of 1947. This was repealed by the Conservatives in 1954 and the market in cotton futures in Liverpool restored. The Licensing Act of 1949 provided for the state management of public houses in the new towns, but no progress had been made when the Conservatives repealed this provision in 1952. In 1972 they took steps to abolish the existing State Management Districts in Carlisle, Gretna and Cromarty.

By the Overseas Resources Development Act of 1948, two public corporations were set up – the Overseas Food Corporation and the Colonial Development Corporation. The first sponsored the ill-fated scheme to produce vegetable oils by growing groundnuts in undeveloped areas in Africa, and it was wound up in 1955. The C.D.C. finances, preferably in collaboration with other bodies, a variety of projects for which capital cannot be found elsewhere. The White Fish Authority (1951) and the Herring Board (1935) are public corporations that regulate and support the sea-fishing industry, which is not publicly owned. The Sugar Board is a public financial agency for subsidizing and regulating the British Sugar Corporation.

A full catalogue of Government bodies engaged in trade, and of public corporations and public authorities regulating or supervising industry, would be long and tedious. Its presentation would emphasize the variety as well as the extent of the Government's economic activities, and it is important to appreciate the many-sided character of the Government's concern. But for the aspects of the subject dealt with in this book, the dominant role of the public corporations in the basic industries is clear. For the most part, therefore, succeeding chapters will concentrate their attention on the coal industry, the electricity industry, the gas industry, the railways and other inland transport, and the airlines. These fall into two groups, the power industries and transport. The developments of the 1960s have added steel and the Post Office to the list of major corporations.

First, however, the position of three further public authorities deserves special explanation. These are the National Research

Development Corporation, the Atomic Energy Authority and the Industrial Reorganization Corporation of 1966–71.

The National Research Development Corporation is perhaps a special case. It is a public corporation set up by the Development of Inventions Act of 1948, and though clearly not an 'industry' in the usual sense, it was noted in the Labour Party's programme of 1961, *Signposts for the Sixties*, as a possible channel for the encouragement of further public ownership. Its role so far has been to examine new inventions and to consider their value for development and commercial exploitation. Some of these arise in Government or Government-sponsored research, and it may be inconvenient for the discoverers to pursue them further. The N.R.D.C. tries to arrange for them to be carried forward by other bodies, and it eventually offers them for commercial use. It also investigates the merits of inventions submitted to it by the public, and tries to ensure that no chance is lost of putting these to practical use: that is, in suitable cases it again tries to arrange for further development and commercial application. It can help with finance for these purposes. The corporation consists of ten members – scientists, industrialists and financial experts. It is financed by loans from the Government and by royalties on the patented inventions it has made available to industry.

The N.R.D.C. does not itself originate much; it is mainly concerned with development. Its function is to make sure that, as far as possible, no innovation that is commercially viable is suppressed, ignored or neglected. Among the projects it has helped to promote are the Hovercraft, 'dracones' (long flexible containers for towing oil across the sea), printed electrical circuits, carbon fibres, and the Cephalosporin antibiotic drugs, which are likely to have important uses in conditions where penicillin is not effective. Further Development of Inventions Acts in 1965 and 1967 helped the Corporation towards a considerable expansion of its activities.

Atomic energy

The atomic-energy industry differs in many ways from the other nationalized concerns. It is a completely new industry and has never been run by private enterprise. Its origins lie entirely with the wartime developments that began in Britain and led to the construction in the United States of the first atomic bombs. For many years all atomic-energy projects were carried out under direct Government control, through the Department of Scientific and Industrial Research and the Ministry of Supply.

Since the war there have been two sides to the atomic-energy programme: first, the development and manufacture of nuclear weapons; and secondly, the furtherance of civil uses of atomic energy. The principal application on an industrial scale has been the building of power stations for the generation of electricity. Both sides of the programme are sustained by the Atomic Energy Research Establishment at Harwell, in Berkshire, set up in 1946.

By the Atomic Energy Authority Act of 1954, the Conservative Government transferred management to a new public corporation. This move was opposed by the Labour Party at the time, on the grounds that the arrangements would be cumbersome and that atomic energy was so vital that direct Government responsibility was needed. The Authority consisted at first of five full-time and five part-time members; the numbers have varied slightly since. It has extensive powers over the whole field of atomic energy. Since 1964 it has been under the supervision of the Ministry of Technology, and since 1970, of the Department of Trade and Industry.

There are thus three features that distinguish atomic energy from the other nationalized industries. First, it was not nationalized as part of the great Labour programme of 1946–9, and its public-corporation form is due to Conservative action. Second, though it manages its own finances, most of its income is derived from public funds, and its accounts are similar to those of Government departments. It provides power stations (for the Central Electricity Generating Board)[15] and nuclear weapons (by contract with the Ministry of Defence), and it sells isotopes and some other products, but it is very far from being a commercial body. Along with this financial dependence goes close policy control by the Government. Third, much of its activity is still secret, and its employees, like civil servants, are subject to the Official Secrets Acts.

The industrial progress of atomic energy has been bedevilled by economic difficulties. At first it was hoped that electricity generated by nuclear stations would be cheaper than that from conventional (principally coal-fired) ones. But for many years it was in fact much more expensive. The capital cost of a nuclear power station is still several times that of a conventional one, and only in the latest designs is the cost of electricity generation down to that of conventional stations. Delays in commissioning power stations using the advanced gas-cooled reactor in the late 1960s further handicapped the economic progress of the industry.

INDUSTRIAL REORGANIZATION

In 1966 the Labour Government set up the Industrial Reorganization Corporation, to further its policy of 'restructuring' British industry.[16] The function of the I.R.C. was to advise, encourage and if necessary assist mergers or regrouping of firms which, in its judgment, would further industrial efficiency. It had very large funds at its disposal which it could if necessary lend to firms, or it could itself hold equity shares, at least temporarily. It operated in collaboration with and through the normal mechanisms and institutions of the stock market, but its expertise, prestige and financial resources enabled it to play a major part in important mergers. Its preferences could be decisive in putting developments in train, or in determining the outcome of rivalry in the take-over field. By 1971 it had been involved in about ninety projects, of which seventy-five were successful. Its ability to hold shares gave it some resemblance to the Italian holding company mentioned below, but its role was not extensive and its actual shareholding temporary. It was abolished by the Conservative Government in 1971.

It is convenient to mention here another Labour experiment, the Industrial Expansion Act of 1968,[17] if only to distinguish it from the I.R.C. This Act enabled the Government to give financial support to firms in the form of loans, grants, guarantees, the underwriting of losses or the subscription of share capital. This last meant that shares – perhaps the whole of the equity – in industrial companies could be secured by the Government without further recourse to Parliament. This could only be done by agreement with the firms concerned, and in fact few opportunities were found to make use of the Act. It was, nevertheless, vigorously attacked by the Conservatives, as opening the way to 'backdoor nationalization', and was substantially repealed in 1971. It had brought about a Government equity holding of £3 million in International Computers Ltd, as well as a grant of over £13 million; and loans for aluminium smelters at Invergordon and Anglesey had been made. Another concern of the Labour Government was an attempt to use the purchasing power of the public-sector in order to promote rationalization among suppliers, and hence efficiency. This did not get much beyond some co-ordination of central Government departments.[18]

NATIONALIZATION ABROAD

There is no space here to give any proper account of public enterprise in other countries. The amount of nationalization varies enormously, since it has been determined by the great political issues of the century. In Communist countries, of course, virtually all enterprise is publicly owned, though the system of direction and management bears little resemblance to the public-corporation method. There are wide variations in the amount of nationalization in more comparable countries, reflecting their political temper in recent years.

France offers the greatest similarities to Britain. Railways were nationalized in 1936, and the coalmines, electricity, gas, the Bank of France and some other banks were all nationalized in the post-liberation period, 1944–6, in an even sharper burst than the British process. In addition, about half the French insurance business is publicly owned; and some enterprises (the Renault motor firm, for example) were nationalized because their owners had collaborated with the Germans during the war. Since 1948, Air France has been a company in which the Government holds the majority of shares.

The major enterprises form distinct concerns similar to our public corporations, but the direction of each has been put in the hands of a tripartite body. These boards consist of representatives of the personnel, of consumers and of the Government, all serving part-time. There have been difficulties in working this system, partly because in France there are strong financial controls and economic planning systems, and partly because there is an inherent conflict between the groups represented. In consequence, these boards have found their position gradually weakened, and much power has passed to the ministries that supervise them and to the full-time professionals who manage them.

In West Germany there is less public ownership, though the railways have long been nationalized and there is much public enterprise in gas and electricity. For many years after the war the Volkswagen car firm had no shareholders and seemed to thrive without them, though a measure of private ownership has now been instituted.

West Germany has experimented with another approach to industrial control – *co-determination*. Under the law of May 1951, which applies to the steel and coalmining industries, each firm in these industries has two-tier control: there is a supervisory council and a managing board. On the supervisory council there are five representatives of the shareholders, five of the employees, and one public figure chosen by these ten; and the council appoints the managing board. Members of the management cannot be members of the council, though they may attend its meetings. The law of October 1952 on the constitution of the enterprise applies to other industries. All firms with more than five employees must have a works council, with from three to thirty-five members. These systems mean that the control of German enterprise is closely regulated by law, but there is no direct ministerial supervision as with Britain's public corporations.

Italy has publicly owned railways, gas and some other enterprises. Two large organizations (the Instituto per la Ricostruzioni Industriale and the Ente Nazionale Idrocarburi) act as publicly owned holding companies with shares in many firms, sometimes amounting to a controlling interest and sometimes not. This provides an extensive public-enterprise system of great flexibility (but doubtful accountability) which has attracted wide attention in recent years. In Scandinavia and the Low Countries there is rather less nationalization than in the other three.

In all countries mentioned, telecommunications and railways are publicly owned, and there is some degree of public ownership in the fuel and power industries. Iron and steel are publicly owned in Austria and to some extent in Norway and Sweden. Many other industries are either part or wholly state-owned, including cigarettes (France), tobacco (West Germany) and matches (both). In many countries the state participates in business through joint enterprises, and a wide variety of industries are affected in this way.

The United States of America maintains private enterprise in fields where most other countries have abandoned it: airlines, railways, radio and television, and even telephones, are all privately owned. Nevertheless, there is considerable public intervention, through independent regulatory agencies and otherwise. The Tennessee Valley Authority was established in 1933 as an agency 'clothed with the power of government, but possessed of the flexibility and initiative of a private enterprise', according to President Roosevelt. It has been largely responsible for the development of a whole region, based on hydro-electric and other power installations.

Though the degree to which Western countries have adopted nationalization varies, there are similarities in the general pattern. British nationalization is comparatively extensive in the basic industries – sometimes called the 'infrastructure' of the economy. It is not particularly widespread in other industries, where there are comparatively few examples of publicly owned firms or special monopolies.

4 The Practice of Nationalization

BRITAIN has now had over twenty years' experience of nationaliz-ation. There have been important changes and some considerable recasting of the structure of the corporations in that time, as described in Chapter 3. In this chapter the aim is to describe some of the main features of the experience of the various corporations. It is not possible to give economic or technical analyses of the pro-gress of the industries in any detail. This book considers the prob-lems of nationalization as such, and the economics of power or of transport need separate treatment. It is necessary, however, even for those whose main interest is in politics and administration, to have some understanding of the industrial record of the corpora-tions. This chapter therefore sets out some of the facts about their performance.

It will not be possible, here or elsewhere, to answer questions about the general 'success' of nationalization. There is no obvious criterion of success; possible tests are vague and disputed, and in the past even the economic standards laid down by the Govern-ment were far from clear. It should also be borne in mind that the corporations have not been free agents. These questions of control and objectives are discussed in Chapters 6 and 7. Here there is a brief survey of major developments.

FINANCIAL AFFAIRS

The overall financial record of an organization provides the most general summary of its activities, but for nationalized industries it is not a very revealing one. At one time the sole purpose of industrial activity was considered to be profit, and though now most enterprises acknowledge a multiplicity of objectives, financial viability is a prerequisite for achieving them. For public corporations there are special rules about financial behaviour.

The nationalization Acts all stipulated that the public corporations were to cover costs taking one year with another – though there is no bankruptcy or other necessary consequence if they fail to do so. The normal consequence of losses is that increased borrowing by the corporation becomes necessary. The standard was thought of mainly as a means of avoiding large profits or subsidies: since the corporations had considerable monopolistic advantages, it was hardly doubted that the standard could be maintained. In fact, many of the corporations have made losses from time to time, and some of them have had considerable loss-making periods. The situation in the various industries must therefore be explained.

The National Coal Board made a loss in many of its early years, and these losses were particularly large in 1947, 1955 and 1959–61. In 1965 a capital reconstruction which involved writing off £400 million of the accumulated losses helped to provide a more realistic basis for the Board's finances.[1]

The early problems of the N.C.B. illustrated the situation in which nationalized concern could find itself. The orthodox response of a trading concern to losses is to adjust either its selling prices or its costs and output, in order to remove them. There have been times when rising costs required a rise in prices, but this has been delayed or limited, for national economic reasons, and deficits thereby incurred. Up to about 1956, prices could probably been raised, and revenue increased. After that, competition and market conditions made this impossible, and there was a period when costs were raised both by the building up of large stocks of small coal and because the Board had to meet the same 'standing charges' (the general overheads of the industry) from a smaller volume of sales. The position was rectified by the capital reconstruction, and improved productivity brought a degree of improvement. A system of Government support to ease the social stresses brought about by the rundown of the industry is now provided. For most of the 1960s the N.C.B. managed to achieve small surpluses, but there were deficits in 1966 and 1969. A crisis developed in the early 1970s which was brought to a head by the dispute over the mineworkers' wage-claim in the winter of 1972, the subsequent strike, and the settlement which left the Board with a large potential deficit.

Without doubt the most serious financial problem of nationalization is that of the railways. For its first three years the British Transport Commission made considerable losses; from 1951 to 1953 there were surpluses, which then turned again to large losses. In 1956 the financial crisis had to be met by legislation. The Transport (Railway Finances) Act authorized advances by the Government up to a limit of £250 million to enable the B.T.C. to meet its deficits. At the same time a modernization plan, described later in this chapter, was put in hand in order to make the railways – the principal cause of the Commission's difficulties – an up-to-date and profitable concern. Nevertheless, by 1960 the British Transport Commission was losing £100 million a year, of which £60 million was lost on the railways' running costs alone. In 1961 the reorganization of nationalized transport embodied a drastic financial reconstruction: £400 million of debt were written off, £800 million put in 'suspense account', and the Treasury took responsibility for British Transport stock. These measures were accompanied by the plan of Dr Richard Beeching for reshaping the railway system, and for a time there was a check to the rate of loss. However, serious deficits continued through the 1960s.

The financial difficulties of the railways are of a long-standing nature. Most of the main-line railway companies failed to make profits and pay dividends in many years between the wars. Until changes were made in 1956 and 1961, they operated under many restrictions devised when they had a monopoly of speedy transport: their charges had to be submitted to a statutory tribunal, which habitually made cuts in their proposals without giving reasons; they had to publish their scales of charges and thus could not discriminate between customers; and as a 'common carrier' they were obliged to transport all goods whether convenient to them or not. In short, they were expected to provide a public service. The financial circumstances of the railways in the 1950s made it finally clear that they could no longer provide a service on such a scale without major revisions of policy, and the controversies of the 1960s were directed towards shaping these new policies. After the Transport Act of 1968 and the consequent provision of direct support for certain passenger services (amounting to £62 million in 1970) British Railways was able to make a small surplus for several years, but the price restraints of 1971–2 meant that special Government grants became necessary. The National Bus Company and the Scottish Transport Group began in surplus, but were forced into deficit by industrial disputes in 1970. Other transport bodies – British Waterways and the National Freight Corporation – kept in surplus with Government grants.

In general the gas and electricity industries have not been in serious trouble. There was a loss on electricity generation before 1950, but not afterwards; and, taken together, the Area Boards concerned with distribution made a loss in 1951–2. The deficit in 1970–1 of £56 million was the first overall loss since nationalization. The Gas Boards together did not make a loss after 1950, though some did so in particular years, until 1967–8. Thereafter somewhat uneasy surpluses were obtained.

The nationalized airlines were in deficit and had to be subsidized during their early years, as foreseen when they were set up. B.O.A.C. made surpluses in the middle 1950s, but serious losses returned in 1957 and persisted until 1963. B.E.A. has occasionally made small losses but has not been in trouble, taking one year with another. The British Airports Authority has so far maintained a surplus.

When the Post Office became a public corporation it began with losses on postal services and was brought into surplus by the telecommunications side of its activities. The newly nationalized steel industry, however, has found itself with some severe economic problems and these have been reflected in financial troubles. Its first two years brought deficits, and a surplus is not expected before 1973–4.

An obvious factor affecting the finances of a corporation is its price policy. There are many facets to this topic, some of which will be discussed in Chapters 6 and 7. But in very few cases have public corporations been able to charge what they would do on commercial grounds. The statutory obligation to break even does not forbid profits, but it clearly does not envisage them on any large scale, and it has discouraged some industries from exploiting monopoly advantages when they could do so; there has been Government pressure to keep down prices to check inflation; there was the Transport Tribunal; and there is the international agreement on air fares. The upshot of these restrictions – certainly up to the 1960s – was that industries which got into difficulties found it very difficult to get out of them.

Comparisons of actual price movements between industries are extremely difficult to make and rarely have any validity. Since prices rise in steps, the period chosen for comparison may be crucial – a period starting just after a large rise and ending just before another one will show an extremely flattering result for a particular industry. There are usually many complicating factors, such as changes in tariff structure, as in electricity, or changes in the quality and nature of the product – coal now has to be obtained from deeper mines, and is more extensively processed to meet modern requirements. Most important, prices reflect not only costs and efficiency, but also changes in policies about industrial finance. It is often pointed out that loss-making by a nationalized industry means that it has, in a sense, to be supported by the taxpayer. While this is so, it should also be stressed that the losses are evidence that the consumer, directly or indirectly, has been getting the benefit of below-cost prices.

It will be noted from the foregoing that after a widespread improvement in nationalized industry finances in the 1960s, there was a serious check in many cases in the early 1970s. This was associated with the Government's anti-inflationary policies, designed to restrain price increases. In particular, in the summer of 1971 the Confederation of British Industry took an initiative whereby many of their member-firms undertook to limit price increases to five per cent per annum. The nationalized industries joined in this restraint, but for many of them it brought the financial problems described above.

When the surpluses or losses of nationalized industries are considered, the method of calculation should be borne in mind. Most of the industries' capital requirements are financed by fixed-interest loans, including the original compensation stocks. The effect of this type of finance is that the interest paid is reckoned as part of costs, and what appears in the accounts is the surplus *after* this interest has been paid. The payments are not unreasonable, of course, for all industries must pay for their capital in some way. However, though practice in private-enterprise firms varies somewhat, usually only a part of capital is obtained by loans, sometimes a small part; most is remunerated through dividends on equity shares, out of profits. The concept of public-enterprise surplus differs, therefore, from that of private-enterprise profit, because of different ways of paying for capital. The logic of the method of presentation is plain in either case, but the differences should not be ignored.

The financial record of nationalized industries, by itself, does not provide a criterion of success or efficiency or competence. Three reasons may be adduced: (1) frequent modification of policy by the Government to protect the national economic interest; (2) the way surplus is calculated; (3) the fact that, since 1961 at least, somewhat different criteria – targets or guidelines – have been laid down.

INVESTMENT

One of the main factors in the financial position of a nationalized industry is the size of its investment programme.

At the time of nationalization many of the industries were in a backward condition, either generally or in part. The need to revive them was one of the main arguments for Government action, and it made nationalization acceptable to many non-socialists.

The scale of finance necessary for investment was, and still is, very large. At first it was thought that money could be raised by borrowing in the usual way, at least for some industries. The Government and other public authorities habitually borrow very large amounts 'through the market', by issuing stock and otherwise. Since the purchase of this type of security carries no voting rights, lenders to a nationalized industry are not in the position of shareholders, and the principle of public ownership is unimpaired. Early public corporations, including the Central Electricity Board and the London Passenger Transport Board, raised capital in this way, under Government supervision.

In the post-1945 corporations two Government controls on investment were prescribed by statute. First, major investment plans must have Government approval, on their economic merits. Second, borrowing to finance investment must have Government consent. The Acts permit varying ways of raising loans for the industries, but the Government is always involved. There is also a statutory limit to the total amount that each corporation may borrow. When this limit is reached, legislation to raise it is necessary, thus providing Parliament with an opportunity for debate and control.

With the exception of the National Coal Board, the post-1945 corporations began by borrowing from the market with the support of a Treasury guarantee. The N.C.B. received investment funds through the Ministry of Fuel and Power. For the others, the existence of the Treasury guarantee ensured that if private subscription to their issues of stock fell short, then the Exchequer would support them. The large sums needed during the 1950s made this the case on many occasions.

In 1956 the Chancellor of the Exchequer, Mr Harold Macmillan, decided to simplify the system by providing for all borrowing by the nationalized industries to be done through the Exchequer. This enables the Treasury to take a considered view of the borrowing situation, and to avoid having to meet sudden situations by inconvenient means that interfere with its other money-market operations. It borrows on its own credit, that is to say, in convenient ways and at convenient times, and then in turn meets the needs of the nationalized corporations. Though this system was introduced as a temporary measure, the size of the requirements is so large that reversion to market-borrowing by the corporations has proved impracticable, and this will probably remain the situation.

In 1965 the Air Corporations Act provided that part of the Government loan to B.O.A.C. would earn, not fixed interest, but a sum varying with the surplus – in other words, a payment akin to dividends on shares. In 1969 a similar arrangement for public-dividend capital was made in the British Steel Corporation.[2]

It should be stressed, however, that there is now another major source of funds. Many private-enterprise firms retain a high proportion of their profits, so that they can finance much of their own investment and do not have to appeal to the public for funds. Since 1961 it has been recognized that nationalized industries might do the same. They now adjust their price and sales policies so that a part of their investment can be paid for from their own reserves. The amount that can be financed in this way varies from industry to industry, and the need for Exchequer finance on a large scale will continue for many years.

Investment, whatever its source, is expected to yield a return. The size of this return has been made explicit since 1961 for most of the corporations: it varies from industry to industry, usually in the region of six to eight per cent on the value of their net assets in a period of five years.

It has been a general practice of the nationalized industries to try to organize their investment on the basis of long-term plans, though this intention has been hampered, if not frustrated, in some cases by the need to fit in with changing Government economic programmes. The first of these to appear was the National Coal Board's *Plan for Coal* of 1950. This was succeeded in 1956 by *Investing in Coal*, and in 1959 the *Revised Plan for Coal* was issued. Plans of a similar nature were issued in other industries – in gas, *Fuel for the Nation* in 1954 and *Gas Looks Ahead* in 1958; and in electricity, *Power and Prosperity* in 1955 and *Power for the Future* in 1958. The railways' first response to its critics in 1955 was set out in the *Modernization and Re-equipment Plan*.

Since the 1950s, however, investment planning in the national-ized industries has been involved in attempts at wider national economic planning, and contributions from the nationalized industries can be found in the N.E.D.C. programme, *Growth of the U.K. Economy to 1966* (1963), in the *National Plan* (Cmnd.

2764) issued by the Department of Economic Affairs in 1965, and in the same Department's green paper, *The Task Ahead*, in 1969.

By far the largest capital investment programmes among the nationalized industries are those for electricity and the Post Office. The constant challenge of rising demand has faced electricity since nationalization, and maximum winter demand is now expected to rise by about five and a half per cent a year. New power stations, modernization of equipment and the building up of transmission systems are all costly forms of capital. Annual expenditure in Great Britain has been at over £500 million in recent years, and is forecast to remain at least at that level. Post Office capital investment is largely concerned with telecommunications, and it has risen rapidly in recent years, and will continue to do so – from £460 millions in 1970–71 to nearly £600 millions in the mid-1970s. New technical developments in telex, data terminals and subscriber trunk dialling have accompanied rising demand. Mechanization of postal sorting will also need capital equipment.

The gas industry is also concerned with a change of technology, which has meant expenditure on new transmission and conversion of appliances for natural gas. The rise in investment which this necessitated is now believed to have passed a peak of about £200 millions in 1970–71, and it is expected to decline somewhat. In the other fuel industry, coal, there has been a programme of modernization and development to improve efficiency in a time of falling demand. Investment is expected to vary between £60 millions and £100 millions a year.

Investment in the surface-transport industries is expected to be fairly constant in the period to 1975, at around £150 millions a year. About £90 millions of this is the British Railways programme, in the aftermath of the modernization of the 1950s and the reshaping of the 1960s, and is directed to track and signalling improvements and some further electrification. The National Freight Corporation has a programme of about £25 millions per annum, largely devoted to new vehicles, and the National Bus Company and the Scottish Transport Group also devote most of their investment to new and better buses.

The investment of the airlines is being taken over by the new British Airways Board. The programme fluctuates considerably around £100 million a year, and is of course largely concerned with the acquisition of new aircraft – Tridents and Boeing 747s – and includes provision for Concorde. Eventually a big investment of the British Airports Authority in the third London Airport at Foulness will become necessary, and its present level of about £9 million a year will grow to £30 million in 1975-6 and much more after that.

The greatest problem, perhaps, about the level investment in nationalized industries is with steel. In 1972 a long-term review was being carried out. A major project is in hand at Scunthorpe, but later stages of the industry's plans are in doubt; provisionally, expectations are for a rise from about £150 millions to about £250 millions a year. In May 1972 it was announced that the investment programme for 1973-4 would be £200 millions.

Altogether, then, the capital investment on the nationalized industries was under £1,700 millions in 1970-71. This was about 18 per cent of total capital formation in the United Kingdom. Comparisons over time are difficult because of the changing scope of nationalization, and the experience of different industries varies a great deal. Nevertheless, total nationalized industry investment, as a proportion of national investment, seems to have declined from a peak around 1960, bearing in mind the inclusion of steel and the Post Office at the end of the decade.

An influential school of thought on national economic management holds that to vary public investment with the state of the economy is an essential part of full employment and of anti-inflationary policies. During the 1950s, therefore, the nationalized industries were subjected to several cuts, at short notice, in their capital programmes; at other times they were encouraged to speed up such work. The resulting dislocation proved technically damaging and economically expensive. A slow-down can mean that important projects are not ready in time; and a speed-up can encourage projects that do not in the event yield an adequate return.

CAPITAL EXPENDITURE IN NATIONALIZED INDUSTRIES
1970–71

	Expenditure on fixed assets £ million	Percentage of national capital formation
National Coal Board	77·0	0·8
Electricity Council and Boards	427·0	4·4
North Scotland H.–E. Board	13·6	0·1
South Scotland Electricity Board	70·1	0·7
Gas Council and Boards	205·1	2·1
British Steel Corporation	152·0	1·6
Post Office	463·8	4·8
British Overseas Airways Corporation	84·1	0·9
British European Airways	38·7	0·4
British Airports Authority	8·9	0·1
British Railways Board	97·5	1·0
British Transport Docks Board	10·8	0·1
British Waterways Board	0·7	–
National Freight Corporation	25·4	0·3
National Bus Company	13·6	0·1
Scottish Transport Group	3·4	–
TOTAL, nationalized industries	1,691·7	17·4
TOTAL, public sector 1971*	4,461	45·9
Gross domestic fixed capital formation, 1971	9,719	100

* Includes Government departments, armed forces, local authorities and other public bodies.

Source: Mainly White Paper, *Public Expenditure to 1975–76* (Cmnd. 4829, November 1971)

The planning of public-enterprise investment has been affected by the developments of the 1960s in economic planning and in the control of public expenditure. Information about capital programmes for the nationalized industries for five years ahead can be found in the annual White Paper on *Public Expenditure*,[3] published each autumn. At about the time of Budget in the spring, the Government publishes a White Paper on *Loans from the National Loans Fund*[4] which explains how the capital requirements of the nationalized industries are being financed.

These reforms help to show how investment in nationalized industries fits in with national economic planning. Since they do not compete in the market for new capital, the amount of capital to be provided for each industry has to be determined by other means. An estimate of the future situation of each industry has to be agreed, therefore, with the central Government, taking into account the probable growth of the economy as a whole and the fact that the various industries are to some extent in competition with one another and with other suppliers.

In making such calculations, the Government's planning authorities must have some idea of the role they expect nationalized industries to play in the economy and in society. As indicated, the financial objectives of the industries have been clarified in recent years, and the success of the corporations in meeting these targets will presumably help to decide their scale of operations – and hence their share of national investment in the future. Nevertheless, the Government has acknowledged the 'public utility' character of many of the concerns: they are not expected to secure high profits, and their primary function is to meet the basic economic requirements of the nation. In Chapter 7 this question of the aims of nationalization is discussed at length.

EFFICIENCY AND TECHNICAL PROGRESS

The object of modernization and development in industry is to improve the productive process – to make it in some sense more efficient. The investment just described should result in higher productivity and should involve innovation of a technical as well as an organizational nature.

It is not easy to define 'efficiency', let alone measure it: indeed, it means different things to different people and in different contexts. There is some information about productivity, however, which is generally relevant.

In the coalmining industry, productivity is usually measured in output per man-shift. At the time of nationalization, just over one ton per shift was produced for every man in the industry, or 2·9 tons per shift for each worker at the coalface. For a time improvement was slow, and in the middle 1950s it came virtually to a standstill – the attempt to secure maximum production meant keeping inefficient high-cost pits in use. But in the 'sixties investment has borne fruit and progress at times has been rapid: in 1971 about 2·4 tons per man-shift was produced, or 7·1 tons per man-shift for faceworkers. This of course does not compare with the situation in the United States, where conditions are much easier, but it is much the same as in Western Europe.

Productivity in the generation of electricity has been aided by technical improvement and by larger generators. In 1948 the thermal efficiency of steam-generating stations was 21 per cent; by 1971 it was over 28 per cent. In terms of output per employee, productivity has increased considerably: in 1948 a capacity of 10,263 megawatts was met with 151,000 employees, and for the 1971 capacity of 49,281 megawatts, only 188,000 employees were necessary. In the gas industry the sharp technological discontinuities has made direct comparisons difficult. Their effect may be seen, however, in that in 1964–5 the amount of gas sold was 3,189 million therms, requiring 121,288 employees; in 1970–71 the expansion of the market for North Sea gas meant that 6,167 therms were sold, needing 115,845 employees in the industry altogether.

The productivity of surface transport is also difficult to assess, owing to changes in organization as well as in measuring output. Much operational improvement has taken place: the first ten years of railway nationalization, before the radical modernization and reshaping programmes, brought an increase in 'net tonmiles per engine-hour' from 520 to 638. Calculations for a more recent period show an improvement in labour productivity from 1958 to 1968 of 50 per cent. A programme of work-study and method-study has brought much improvement.

Ways of measuring the efficiency of airlines include the number of 'passenger miles' flown per employee. By international standards B.O.A.C. has done very well in this matter, and B.E.A. rather badly. However, this seems to be connected with the fact that B.O.A.C. is a long-distance airline and B.E.A. flies exclusively on shorter routes. Nevertheless, if one takes the two airlines to-gether, the British record for improving productivity in this way still compares favourably with most foreign airlines.[5]

These measures of productivity are not the only possible ones, and there is room for argument about their value as tests of effi-ciency. Some improvement is to be expected from investments and technical progress; the question is whether the degree of improvement reflects adequately the resources that have been put in. For this reason the return on capital that is being used offers a more general measure of the efficiency of the industries, and this is usually the form in which the Government's financial objectives for them have been cast. Again, the place of this type of objective among the aims of nationalization is further considered in Chap-ter 7.

Improvement in efficiency does not happen merely through pouring in money. It is dependent in the long run on technical innovation, and this in turn is sustained by research. All the major nationalized industries have research programmes and research organizations.

The National Coal Board has maintained a wide-ranging re-search effort. The Coal Research Establishment at Stoke Orchard, near Cheltenham, deals with the fuel itself and its by-products; it spent many years in developing the smokeless fuel, 'Homefire'. At Bretby there is the Mining Research and Development Estab-lishment, which is concerned with engineering and mining tech-niques. The Coal Board does not itself manufacture mining machinery, but works in close collaboration with firms which do so. There are also numbers of other research activities connected with the industry, including the Coal Survey (absorbed in the Board's general scientific organization in 1961), which explores the country's reserves of coal and helps to plan their exploitation.

Similarly, the other nationalized corporations have research institutions of their own. Among the most notable is the British Rail Technical Centre at Derby, probably the largest of its kind in Europe and much concerned with the development of the Advanced Passenger Train. Steel, when renationalized, inherited an organization, and there is now an organization BISRA/IGL formed from the former British Iron and Steel Research Association and various inter-group laboratories. Besides central institutions, such as these, the industries sponsor other projects either at smaller stations or attached to the operations of the industry. They are also important supporters of research associations – the Coal Utilization Research Association and the British Electrical and Allied Industries Research Association, for example. They may also be interested in (and subscribe to) the work of bodies such as the Medical Research Council, and they finance particular research projects in the universities.

It is impossible to assess by means of a general survey the effectiveness of research. It is of the greatest importance that the investigations should be related to the actual problems of the industry; it is equally vital that management should have the scientific understanding necessary to grasp the significance of what has been done and what could be done. Only with this mutual comprehension will research be seen as part of the essential progress of the industries, and not merely as a marginal good cause. The promotion of research is thus only partly a matter of finance and manpower: it also depends on good organization and communication.

The research position in British industry was considered to be generally weak in the 1950s and has since been strengthened. It was heavily concentrated in the aircraft-construction and electrical industries. The nationalized industries reflect these variations. The airlines rely largely on other bodies – the constructors and the Aeronautical Research Council. The Coal Board has built up its activities from scratch; others have had to expand existing arrangements as well as they could. A difficulty for some – coal, gas, the railways – was the unglamorous image of their industry: they were unable to attract brilliant minds in the way that electronics and atomic energy could.

The Atomic Energy Authority in fact provides a striking illustration of the opposite problem. It is an example of the 'science-based' industry, where the difficulty lies in building effective production out of creative discovery, rather than in applying scientific research to established and often conservative industries.

In practical terms the years of nationalization have brought great technical changes to the industries. Coal-cutting by machinery has long become normal, and over 90 per cent of coal is power-loaded. The average size of power stations on nationalization was under 50 megawatts; the standard capacity of new stations built in the 1960s was 500 megawatts. Gas has undergone two technological revolutions in the last decade – the change-over to imported methane and oil-based production, and then to natural resources from the North Sea. By 1971, 69 per cent of gas available was some form of natural gas. The railways have abandoned steam for electrical and diesel traction. Airlines now fly jet liners, whereas routes had to be pioneered with converted troop transports. The Post Office is in the middle of a technological transformation in telecommunications, and is beginning one in postal sorting. Such rapid changes are characteristic of the twentieth-century: they provide the material with which systems of management, including nationalized systems, must cope.

LABOUR RELATIONS

For many advocates of public ownership the improvement – indeed, the transformation – of labour relations was the main object of the change. Under capitalism, it was thought, workers could not be treated fairly, because all other interests had to be sacrificed to the need to make as much profit as possible. A publicly owned enterprise would be under no such compulsion and therefore could be expected to treat its employees honestly and decently. When this became recognized, the bitterness would disappear from industrial negotiations and an atmosphere of understanding, and eventually of co-operation, would be achieved. These expectations were strongest, of course, among those for whom socialism was a moral crusade: if the causes of social injustice were removed, then greater harmony might reasonably be hoped for.

The form chosen to implement public ownership was, however, the managerial public corporation. No fundamental change was made in the status of the workers, who remained employees with no direct voice in the control of their enterprises. The Acts merely made negotiating machinery and joint consultation compulsory.

The trade unions remained independent and necessary organizations, bargaining with employers about wages and conditions as before. In these circumstances the improvement of labour relations became a matter of patient, step-by-step amelioration, of the gradual breaking down of traditional attitudes. Progress was slow and halting, constantly bedevilled by economic stringencies and social frustrations.

Events in this field have caused disappointment in some quarters and allegations of failure from others. The truth is that much disillusion was inevitable, because hopes were pitched far too high, and because they rested on a mistaken diagnosis of the causes of industrial conflict. Moreover, there are strong political arguments for the trade unions maintaining an independent position and not taking any share in or responsibility for management decisions. For if they do become thus involved, the workers will find themselves once again individuals and subordinates in a hierarchical system, without the protection for their rights or influence for their desires which independent collective organization brings.

Though nationalization cannot claim to be the solution to industrial conflict, the principle it embodies does have some relevance to the problem. Public corporations have an explicit responsibility to the nation, enforced by a deliberate system of accountability and control. Their policies are therefore tied to public opinion – at any rate, in so far as this is manifested through the machinery of political democracy. And if this conception involves the provision of services, or the setting of prices, or the acceptance of fair standards that might appear uneconomic or unnecessary to a private business, then the public corporation must acknowledge its wider responsibilities. 'Having willed the end, the Nation must will the means,' said a court of inquiry in a wage dispute. In other words, labour relations in nationalized industries are affected by the fact that public employers have a duty to serve the national interest, not vaguely and indirectly, but in a precise way that can be determined by the Government.

Nationalization has given further impetus to the tendency to centralize wage bargaining. In nationalized industries the main wage and salary settlements are made between the boards and large unions, and are negotiated at national level. National wage agreements, at least on basic scales, are insisted on by most trade unions, and they embody the belief that people doing the same work should get the same pay. But the creation of national public corporations as employers has increased the unions' determination to present a strong and, if possible, united front in negotiation with them. There may be deeper social forces at work in some cases: for example, decentralization of the coal industry was resisted by the National Union of Mineworkers in case it should 'set coalfield against coalfield'.

It has sometimes been alleged that in the 1950s publicly owned industries took the lead in granting wage increases to their employees, and that this initiated inflationary wage-rounds throughout industry. In retrospect, however, there seems little evidence that nationalized industries were often in the lead with concessions. On the contrary, many of the critical disputes – on the railways, for example – arose because wage standards had fallen below those in other occupations. The truth of the matter seems to be that certain occupations apparently take the lead in raising wage rates, but these are in industries where there is little or no payment above the standard rates. Raising wage rates in these occupations is often necessary to catch up with *earnings* that have already risen above standard rates elsewhere. Such occupations include work in electricity supply and on the London buses, but they also include private employments like multiple grocery stores and agriculture.

On the whole, since the arrival of full employment in Britain, nation-wide official strikes have become less common. Many strikes occur in particular places, over local disputes, and are unofficial. In the 'sixties, however, the shape of industrial relations became a political issue, partly because of the alleged prevalence

of unofficial strikes, and also because the need for counter-in-
flationary incomes policy brought conflict with workers in major
industries.

The employees in nationalized industries found themselves at
the centre of these problems. Whatever benefits or good relations
better management might have brought, the general economic
and political pressures were there. The National Board for Prices
and Incomes (1965–71) was set up by the Labour Government to
help the consideration and resolution of issues in these matters,
and many of its reports concerned incomes in the nationalized
industries. These included the pay of pilots employed by B.O.A.C.
(in October 1968 and October 1969), pay and bonuses in electricity supply (October 1965, September 1967 and July 1968),
railway pay and conditions (January 1966), pay of staff in the gas
industry (October 1968) and productivity agreements in the bus
industry (December 1967).

There were some strikes that were more than local, of course,
in the 'fifties and 'sixties – a strike of footplatemen on the railways in 1955, London busmen in 1958 and airline pilots in 1968,
for example. But versions of pay restraint or incomes policy which
rely in some special way on the public sector are obviously critical
for the nationalized industries. It may be that a Government sees
the importance of this sector as large, and basic to other parts of
the economy; or it may look to it merely for an example. In the
early 1970s the Conservative Government abolished the National
Board for Prices and Incomes, and adopted an attitude to pay increases which led to some sustained industrial disputes. These included a work-to-rule by power-station workers in autumn 1970,
a strike of postal workers in the early part of 1971, and the first
major national strike in the coal industry, lasting six weeks, at the
beginning of 1972.[6] In the spring of 1972 a work-to-rule brought
a long and complex crisis on the railways, involving both the
'cooling-off' and the strike ballot procedures of the Industrial
Relations Act 1971. These were the biggest series of strikes ever
experienced by the nationalized industries.

For several reasons, therefore, the Government seems likely to
play a controversial part in wage negotiations. (This is discussed as

a form of ministerial control in Chapter 6.) The industries are economically important and therefore attract the concern of the Government from the economic point of view. At the same time, their 'public sector' status, and sometimes their financial situation, makes them susceptible to control.

There have undoubtedly been positive achievements in labour relations in the nationalized industries. It can be argued that the advantage of a broad national viewpoint and the necessity of looking at problems in their long-term aspects, which are general features of the situation of national concerns, are particularly relevant to personnel matters. The efforts of the National Coal Board, by consultation and by arrangements for transfer and redundancy pay, to soften the hardships brought about by its continued and severe contraction are surely worthy of commendation. In the same industry long negotiations resulted in a national power-loading agreement with the National Union of Mineworkers in June 1966. This established a day-wage system over the major part of the industry, in place of traditional local piecework systems. This was a considerable advance, though not without hazards: it reduced points of friction and hence the number of local disputes, but it made the national wage-scale even more critical, as was apparent in the big winter strike in early 1972.

The electricity industry pioneered another advance. In 1962–5 a series of changes established a Status Agreement, which embodied a deliberate attempt to raise the social status of the work-force and to establish relationships of confidence, by substituting annual salaries for time rates of pay for industrial staff, and consequently abandoning overtime pay. Such a change must involve maintenance of expected earnings by the workers concerned, and the need to do so was an issue in the power-station dispute of autumn 1970.

Training and consultation

In two directions, however, the nationalized industries can claim to have made considerable improvements in labour matters. First, they have developed training programmes and promotion schemes. Second, they have given much attention to the processes of joint consultation.

Every major nationalized industry has set up a scheme whereby workers in the industry can progress, by internal training and experience, to better jobs and to higher levels of skill and authority. One of the best known is the 'ladder plan' of the National Coal Board. This provides a series of schemes for young men entering the industry, by which they can become tradesmen, deputies or technicians, or they can enter managerial grades. Day-release and even full-time courses are made available to assist the progress of employees. The N.C.B. also has management-development schemes – providing university scholarships, directed practical training, and experience for non-technical administrators. The other public corporations have similar schemes, adapted to their own structures and requirements.

The boards have a statutory obligation to submit education and training plans to the appropriate Minister for his approval, and this may have compelled them to give special attention to the matter. But in fact, the position of the boards as managers of whole industries gives them both the incentive and the ability to develop technical and managerial skills. To do so is just as important for their future as to invest in new capital. Their resources and influence enable them to make sure that the necessary facilities are available. Moreover, it is clearly their business to do so, for they cannot hope to recruit people to their specific requirements from anywhere else. Large organizations are in general well placed to offer varied and extensive career opportunities, and it is vital for morale that the nationalized industries should exploit this advantage to the full.

The Industrial Training Act of 1964 established a system of training boards in many industries. These are tripartite bodies in which employers, trade unions and educational and training institutions all share. They are empowered to raise levies on firms for training purposes; but firms which carry out training receive payments for so doing, and can hence recoup the cost. Many of the nationalized corporations are involved in these arrangements.

The concept of the managerial public corporation debars employees and their unions from any direct responsibility for running the industries. Nevertheless, machinery for regular consultation between management at all levels and organized labour has been set up. This does not detract from the powers of management to take decisions; but it is designed to ensure that both sides are aware of the facts, and of the views and motives of each other. Where it works effectively, joint consultation makes an outstanding contribution to mutual understanding and to the problem of industrial 'communications'.

There are difficulties, however, in many cases. Foremen and supervisors are apt to resent being by-passed when workers on consultative committees have access to higher levels of management than they do. Some managers regard the system as an unpleasant duty to be carried through as quickly as possible. Workers' representatives sometimes show little interest in matters beyond their immediate conditions of employment. In short, joint consultation cannot be made effective by mere establishment of the machinery of committees. It requires patience and, in view of the wide scope of potential subject matter, a great amount of study and thought by all participants.

The British Steel Corporation has gone a step beyond consultation. After an agreement in 1967 with the Trades Union Congress and the steel unions, sixteen workers chosen from lists suggested by the unions served as part-time members of Divisional Boards (originally Group Boards). They retain their position as workers and spend 60–70 per cent of their time at their ordinary jobs. They remain trade union members, but resign their current offices in the unions; and they are paid an additional salary for their work on the Boards. These arrangements are experimental, and fall short of providing members of the Governing Board of the Corporation itself. Nevertheless when the practice is evaluated it must have significance for the future constitution of all public corporations.

Some advocates of nationalization hoped that, if it did not change the form of labour relations, it would at least create a new professional spirit among its administrators and imbue its workers with the idea of public service. A new type of manager, who would combine the high responsibility and dedication of the civil servant with the drive and initiative of the businessman, was foreseen. Since these changes were not expected overnight but might take a generation to emerge, it is still premature to assess results. The training schemes and plans for management development should help progress in this direction. Yet in matters of morale and social values the influence of leadership is all-important. Conservative ministers have accepted nationalization, but they have not felt able to extol its virtues. Nor have Board members (with some exceptions, usually at the Coal Board) gone out of their way to emphasize the merits of public enterprise as such – no doubt some of them, being ex-businessmen, have doubted the existence of merits. In these circumstances pride in achievement and in technical progress is possible; but while the need to emulate business success is stressed at the top, it is not likely that any very distinctive outlook will flourish in the service of the corporations.

As stated at the outset of this chapter, the record of the nationalized industries does not enable judgments to be made about their success. There has been undoubted progress and achievement: but how can their adequacy be reckoned? There have been weaknesses and commercial troubles: are the explanations of these satisfactory?

In sum, though the financial record of nationalized industries has been chequered, only one major industry, the railways, has been in deep long-run trouble. At one time losses were a main target for nationalization's critics. The investment programmes have been large – some critics in the past suggested over-large.

The criticism of the nationalized industries most frequently heard among economists is that their prices ought to be higher because their return on capital is too low. But among the general public the criticism is almost exactly the reverse: the prices of the nationalized industries have increased, are increasing and ought to be diminished. At the same time the public also blames the nationalized industries when, sometimes in the interests of price stability, they make losses.[7]

The industries have shown much energy in pursuing technical progress, so far as capital has been available. Beyond this, questions of commercial policy and harmonization with the national interest have complicated the simple issues of efficiency and profitability. Improvements have been made in labour relations, but disputes sometimes of major proportions occur. In brief, the facts about nationalization in practice only lead to further problems and controversies. Many of these are discussed in the following chapters.

5 Problems of Organization

CONTROVERSY about nationalization, even heated controversy, has not been confined to the principle itself. The methods, supervision and objectives of the nationalized industries have been subjected to vigorous criticism.

In this chapter and the two that follow, some of the main areas of controversy will be explored. So far this book has been concerned with the facts, historical and structural, of nationalization as it exists. It will continue to set out the essentials of what has been done, but more and more it will be necessary to consider views expressed about these actions, and to try to form an assessment of their merits.

The first set of problems to be examined are organizational. These are practical matters, on which the lines of dispute are not often partisan in the political sense – although the opinions expressed are not less vehement for that reason.

The principle of nationalization, as distinct from municipalization or selective public ownership, has carried with it the notion of unification on a country-wide scale. There have been modifications in the 1960s, but usually a single general organization has been set up for each industry. Since the industries are major ones, the size of each organization tends to be very large.

When considering problems of organization it is probably best to measure size in terms of employment. The largest of the nationalized undertakings in this sense is the most recent, the Post Office, which employed about 415,000 people in 1971. The National Coal Board had 356,000 employees and British Railways 273,000; both were declining but still very large. At its peak, in the early 1950s, the British Transport Commission had nearly one million employees. Industrial undertakings of this size are comparable with the largest in the world. In 1964, General Motors and its subsidiaries had a world-wide employment of 660,000, but few of the great private enterprises reach this scale.

Other nationalized industries are also very large, by any standard. The electricity industry is in fact the largest in terms of capital, and it had 206,000 employees in 1971; gas employed 116,000 and British Steel 252,000. Large operational units included the Central Electricity Generating Board, with 70,000; the London Electricity Board, with nearly 14,000; and the North Thames Gas Board, with over 18,000. In transport, besides the railways, the National Freight Corporation had 63,000 and the National Bus Company 84,000 employees. Measured by employment, the airlines are among the lesser of the nationalized industries. Yet in 1971 the British Overseas Airways Corporation employed 24,000 and British European Airways 25,000. In Britain there are a few private-enterprise firms with over 100,000 workers (examples include Imperial Chemical Industries Ltd, who employ about 175,000, and Courtaulds Ltd with 125,000); but the 'biggest hundred' private firms usually have payrolls somewhere between 10,000 and 100,000. Most nationalized concerns are clearly in comparable circumstances.

Two channels of intellectual inquiry are available for examining the problems of organization in nationalized industries: the study of public administration and that of industrial management. These have traditionally been kept apart, and it cannot be said that anything approaching unification has been achieved in face of common problems. Clearly each approach has valuable contributions to make. In the study of public administration some understanding of the concepts of responsibility, accountability and political policy-making had been achieved by 1945; from industrial management, ideas about the authority of boards, decentralization and standard tests of performance were obtained.

It was generally agreed that the process of take-over and transition to public ownership was smoothly and efficiently accomplished, in spite of many difficulties. But serious organizational issues soon arose, and some account of them must now be given.

GOVERNING BOARDS

It is implicit in the concept of the public corporation that there should be a board or council of some sort in charge of affairs. Within the organization this body has full authority, and its composition is clearly crucial for the success of the whole enterprise.

The rejection of the representative board has been described in Chapter 2. The Port of London Authority had such a board, but the public corporations set up between the wars consisted of independent managers without outside connections or responsibilities. In the case of the London Passenger Transport Board, members were appointed by a special group of appointing trustees indicated in the statute.[1] But in other cases appointment by the Minister was the rule; and even where the Crown made the appointments, it was in fact done on the advice of the Government. In short, the board all derived their positions from the same source and were expected to work as a team.

The post-war public corporations are very similar to one another in their practices concerning the governing boards, partly as a result of earlier experience, and partly because they were originally constituted within a few years of each other by the same Government. It is therefore possible to consider a body of standard practices, with only a few variations, and criticisms of these practices. These practices have survived into the 1960s and 1970s.

The name of the governing board varies – Board, Commission, Council, Authority – but these differences appear to have no practical consequences. There is also some variation in the size of the boards, upper and lower limits being fixed by each statute. Among the largest are the Electricity Council and the pre-1972 Gas Council, with twenty-one and seventeen members respectively, but both these consist largely of the chairmen of Area Boards. The Central Electricity Generating Board has nine members, the National Coal Board has nine and the British Railways Board eleven, and this appears to be the usual range for effective working. Among the new corporations, the Post Office board has nine members and the British Steel Corporation eleven.

The main standard practices may now be indicated. The first, as stated, is appointment by the Minister or the Crown on the advice of the Government. This at once shows the political foundations of the boards' authority, and provides a major means of governmental control. The chairmen and deputy-chairmen are designated as such – that is to say, they are chosen by the Minister and not by their fellow-members on the boards.

Secondly, there are some statutory qualifications for membership. Normally these are very wide. The Minister may appoint to the National Coal Board 'persons appearing to him to be qualified as having had experience of, and having shown capacity in, industrial, commercial or financial matters, applied science, administration or the organization of workers'.

With some modifications, formulae like this are applied to the other nationalized industries. The phrase 'organization of workers' emphasizes the right of trade unionists as such to serve on the boards. There are also some disqualifications: membership of the House of Commons, engaging in trade or business, or becoming of unsound mind are frequent bars to continuing service. Membership of the House of Lords is not a disqualification, and in fact several notable leaders of the industries have been peers. Nor are there any specific political qualifications or disqualifications. Lord Robens was a member of the Opposition front bench when appointed by the Conservative Government, to the National Coal Board. In 1971 Mr Richard Marsh, who had not long before been Labour's Minister of Transport, was appointed by the Conservatives to the chairmanship of British Rail. Other persons with well-known Conservative or Labour sympathies have served on the boards.

Thirdly, there are no formal nominations for places on the boards. Unions, stockholders or customers have no right to have particular persons put on the boards. Nevertheless, it is prudent and desirable for a minister to take soundings before making appointments. These no doubt include civil servants in the Ministry, Government and Party colleagues, trade unions and perhaps existing members of the boards, including part-time members. All these consultations are private, however, and do not bind a

Minister, though he would scarcely make an important appointment without the concurrence of the Prime Minister.

Fourthly, appointments are made for a limited period, most commonly five years. These may be renewed, and appointments are staggered so that whole boards are not changed at the same time. Board membership is not necessarily affected by changes of government, even when there is a change of party control. Members of boards may of course resign at any time; and, more significantly, they may be dismissed by the Minister. This he may do for reasons of alleged incapacity, neglect or inefficiency; and it is clear that he can at least force resignation in cases of severe policy disagreement.

Fifthly, the rules about qualifications and consultation make it possible for members to come from outside the industries concerned. In fact, most of the appointments are promotions of successful managers from inside the corporations; but there continues to be a significant group who did not rise in this way. For example, Lord Robens, Lord Beeching and Sir Ronald Edwards – who held probably the three senior positions in the nationalized industries in 1964 – were all brought in from other employment. Lord Melchett and Mr Marsh provide more recent examples. Furthermore, the practice of appointing trade unionists has not meant that the individuals concerned were from the unions in the industry. Thus in 1971 the Railways Board had Mr Hayday from the General and Municipal Workers' Union, and Mr Ron Smith, from the Post Office Union, was on the British Steel Corporation.

It is now the custom to appoint some part-time members to the boards. Sometimes these constitute a majority. The National Bus Company and the Scottish Transport Group each has only one full-time member; all the rest serve part time. On the Coal Board, the Railways Board and the Electricity Generating Board, however, there is a comparatively small group of part-timers supplementing a majority of full-time members. The function of this latter type of member is to bring wider experience into the industries, to provide knowledge of practices of other bodies for comparative purposes and to give regular contact with people who are not constantly occupied with the details of the industry. It is hoped, that is to say, that this element in the boards will help them to see the wood as well as the trees.

Some criticisms of these standard practices may now be considered.

It has been suggested by left-wing critics that the result of the system has been a preponderance of businessmen on the boards, and that these may be assumed to be hostile to nationalization in principle and unenthusiastic about it in particular cases. Mr Clive Jenkins has shown that, in 1956, out of 272 members of boards of public corporations (including Area Boards), 106 were also directors of private-enterprise concerns.[2]

Most of these appointments are of part-time members, however, and the influence of such members rarely predominates whatever their numerical strength. Moreover, in a community where most of industry is privately owned, it is natural that the greatest supply of managerial talent is to be found there. If outside people are to be brought in (and where industries are being reconstructed the case for doing so is overwhelming), then many must come from private enterprise. This is to say not that morale and confidence in nationalization are irrelevant, but that they depend on political encouragement and a few key appointments rather than numerical balance.

At one time there was also criticism of the amateurism of the boards, and of the appointment of 'retired generals, admirals, etc.' Much of this was misconceived, for the soldiers and sailors were service engineers, transport experts and so on; and in the post-war period there was a supply of ex-service talent available which it would have been pointless to neglect. The practice of making such appointments, and hence the criticism, seems to have diminished in recent years.

It will be convenient in assessing the composition of the boards to consider possible alternatives. A radical revision of the practices that had grown up was proposed by Lord Simon of Wythenshawe in 1957.[3] These proposals serve, incidentally, to highlight the present political situation of board members. Lord Simon contrasted practices in public corporations with those in large private firms, particularly Imperial Chemical Industries Ltd. He argued that board members should normally be appointed from within the industry, on the recommendation of the existing board, and should serve until retirement. To this end, management-development programmes in the industries should be improved, and should lead up to the boards themselves. Ministerial control and accountability to Parliament should not interfere with the effective power of the board.

This plan would change radically the position of the boards, by increasing their security and independent authority. In spirit it involves a reversion to pre-war practice, when there was minimal political control. The ability of Ministers to assert their authority – although legally present – would become in practice very difficult. In fact, there is wide assent to most of Lord Simon's sentiments, certainly to the proposition that eventually board members should be recruited from within the corporations. But even this is not regarded as applicable in a rigid way, and at present the need for rehabilitation of some industries is held to emphasize the need to bring in proved talent with new ideas from outside. In any case, whatever may become normal practice, the right of the Minister to apply or vary the practice is a crucial political responsibility which is unlikely to be forgone.

The question of security of tenure for board members up to retiring age is more controversial.[4] Again, Ministers are willing in most cases to reappoint ordinary board members for successive terms. But there is no guarantee that this will happen, and a board member – particularly a chairman – must feel that disagreement with ministerial ideas will reduce the chance of his continuance in office. The prospect of this insecurity may deter some from accepting board posts. The issue is fundamentally one of the degree of independence that a public corporation can enjoy: whether it may expect to develop a general outlook entirely of its own, or whether it should take its broad philosophy from the elected Government. (This question is the theme of Chapter 6.) However, the possibility of a Government's allowing independence depends in turn on public opinion; if blame is ascribed to Ministers for the state of an industry, then they may be expected to exert maximum powers of control, in order to satisfy themselves that things are going as well as they can make them.

The question of the proper salaries for board members has been one of great difficulty. It arises primarily because of the double aspect of the corporations – as both public services and industrial concerns – and from the fact that there is customarily considerable disparity of payment between these activities.

Since the late 1960s top salaries in the nationalized industries have been divided into three groups. Group A includes the biggest corporations: the Coal Board, British Rail, the Electricity Council and Generating Board, Gas, the Post Office and British Airways Board. Group B comprises the other national corporations: airlines, the buses and freight. In Group C are various area boards and Scottish electricity.

The salaries paid to these various categories since January 1972 have been as follows:

	Group A (£ thousand)	Group B (£ thousand)	Group C (£ thousand)
Chairman	22·5	19·0	12·0–17·0
Deputy Chairman	18·5	15·5	9·0–11·0
Members	12·0–17·0	9·5–13·5	7·25–9·5

These salaries are for full-time members; for part-time members a payment of £1,000 a year is customary. There have been exceptions to the above rates, usually brought about by the recruitment to a board of a businessman receiving high pay elsewhere. The best-known case was that of Lord Beeching, the chairman of British Railways from 1961 to 1965, who received £24,000 when the current standard for chairmen was about £12,000. A premium salary was also paid to Sir Giles Guthrie, chairman and managing director of B.O.A.C. from 1964 to 1968. Lord Melchett, the chairman of the British Steel Corporation, is paid £27,500 a year, the deputy chairmen of the B.S.C. between £22,000 and £25,000 and board members between £16,000 and £21,000. These developments in steel are the only example of higher salaries paid to a whole board, and are explained by the history and special circumstances of the industry.

Many critics, including Lord Simon, have held that the salaries (and allowances, pensions, etc.) should be at least as great as those in leading private-enterprise firms. The Labour Party, in a pamphlet issued in 1957, stated that 'the salaries paid should not be markedly less than those for similar jobs in private business.'[5]

They are clearly not of this order at present. The grounds for paying Lord Beeching £24,000 were that this amount was paid to him as an ordinary director of I.C.I. Ltd; and similar explanations are given for other premium salaries. Moreover, the accounts of other companies show very large sums paid to their boards of directors, so that each member must get more than the standard indicated for public boards. Of course, tax deductions are considerable at this level. Nevertheless, there is a contrast between business and public-service payments – even after changes in the early 1970s, the Prime Minister is paid £20,000 per annum, ordinary departmental ministers £13,000, the chief civil servant of a department £15,750 and Members of Parliament £4,500.

There are thus two main arguments for high salaries – possibly higher than at present – for members of the boards of public corporations. The first is the need to keep and sometimes to recruit high-quality people, in the face of the attractions of private industry. The second is the need for adequate differentials between management levels, so that promotion brings appreciable material rewards – and board salaries determine the ceiling under which other scales must be arranged. On the other hand, there is no case for paying more than is reasonable in the circumstances, or for chasing what many consider to be inflated and socially undesirable levels of remuneration, if it can be avoided. The ideas of public service and of national status may have some influence: circuit judges, at £9,750 a year, are paid less than some successful barristers. Nevertheless, it is not at present practicable, in a mixed economy, to use the public corporations to set the standards for the general range of remuneration in society; and this being so, substantial salaries, influenced by competition from private industry, must be paid for high industrial posts.

In 1968 the question of top salaries was referred to the National Board for Prices and Incomes, and in March 1969 it published its report on *Top Salaries in the Private Sector and Nationalized Industries* (Cmnd. 3970). Though exact comparisons of size and responsibilities were impossible, it showed that there could be no doubt that lower rates of salary (often about half) were paid to top executives and board members in nationalized concerns. The provision of fringe benefits was also less. The report also contained a striking demonstration that, though at the lower managerial levels the steps in pay corresponded to increases in the 'size' of the jobs, at higher levels this was not so. After a point the salary differentials between different levels became very compressed. There were even one or two cases where board members had lower salaries than senior executives. While not suggesting that pay in the public sector should entirely match that in the private sector, the report nevertheless made proposals designed to provide 'headroom', so that the structure beneath the boards could be reformed.

Since the abolition of the National Board for Prices and Incomes in 1971, the question of top salaries for nationalized industries has been the concern of the Top Salaries Review Body, in common with those in other types of public service. Changes were brought about in stages, following the N.B.P.I. report, and these have been followed again by increases – made necessary by the inflationary conditions of the early 1970s – recommended by the T.S.R.B., under the chairmanship of Lord Boyle, in a report published in June 1972. These are the salaries, backdated, set out above.

The role of the boards

Though all public corporations must have a board of some sort at the head of their affairs, the purpose of this body and the manner in which it exercises its powers have been the subject of extensive dispute.

The controversy lies mainly between supporters of the *functional board*, sometimes called the executive or managerial board, and those who advocate the *policy board*, or one with mainly supervisory duties. The functional board takes direct control of the affairs of the corporation, each member (apart from the chairman and perhaps deputy-chairman) exercising control over a particular aspect of the industry, through a department of the headquarters' organization. In the policy board the members have only general responsibilities, and the actual running of the industry is carried on by senior executives appointed by the board. Thus the board discusses and determines the policy to be pursued in any field of activity, but it leaves its execution to others.

The most striking example of the supervisory board comes from a public corporation outside the main industrial complex, the British Broadcasting Corporation. This has a board of governors of seven part-time members, whose duties are broadly supervisory. In fact the B.B.C. has always been run by its Director-General, in whom full executive authority is vested, including control over programmes. This distribution of power was established in the time of Lord Reith, the first Director-General, a man of strong will and determination, and has been little modified since. In this case it seems that the Director-General must not only exercise administrative power, but must also have great influence on policy. When the post-war corporations were set up, most national boards had a functional or executive nature, though the Gas Council and the original British Transport Commission were mainly concerned with co-ordination.

The arguments for the functional board turn on the need for realism and effective authority. Only if board members are in day-to-day touch with problems and if they must personally carry out what has to be done, it is said, will they fully appreciate the necessities of a situation. If they can proceed by passing orders to others, they will become remote and perhaps perfectionist; and they may develop ideas at variance with those of their senior executives, causing disharmony and inefficiency. The functional board fixes responsibility: the members themselves decide what is to be done and do it, and there is no room for misunderstanding or shifting the blame.

For the policy board it is said that it gives its members time to think about major policy and to reflect on future development. They do not become absorbed in detail, and they can stand aloof from disagreements and minor problems. They can, moreover, be mindful of the corporation's responsibilities to the public and its attitude to Government policy. This system permits devolution of responsibility and thus gives scope for initiative and decentralized authority.

The views of the Fleck and Herbert committees were at variance on this as on other matters. The Fleck report provided for each board member's having specific responsibilities, and it recommended that 'the board should insist on their policies being properly carried out by the subordinate formations and should ensure that discipline obtains.' The Herbert committee, on the other hand, saw the board as 'a group of men ... ready to help, to co-ordinate and to stimulate, and relying on direction only where persuasion fails'.[6]

In the industrial public corporations, variations in arrangements continue, though some similarities have emerged. The Electricity Council is clearly a policy board, but then it is stronger than the B.B.C. governors, and those members drawn from Area Electricity Boards have functional responsibilities. In other boards the usual practice is for the board to regard itself primarily as a policy board, but for the full-time members to take a particular interest in one or more aspects of the corporation's work, and to work closely with the headquarters' executives in these fields. The chairman, deputy-chairman and part-time members ensure that a board's business is carried on major issues, and that it does not become so preoccupied with internal harmony as to neglect its wider responsibilities.

These arrangements seem to be working fairly well in most cases. It is possible that the need for a functional board or a policy board varies not only with the structure of the various industries, but also from time to time in each industry as its main problems change. One factor that must be borne in mind is the position of the Minister. If he and his department, wisely or unwisely, exercise a close supervisory interest, or if the Government has itself prescribed particular policies for an industry, then the need for a policy board declines. This raises, of course, the problem of ministerial control discussed in Chapter 6. The creation of the British Airways Board in 1972 to deal with broad policy clearly affected the role that the boards of B.O.A.C. and B.E.A. could be expected to play.

In any case, the proper role of the board depends to some extent on the nature of the structure beneath it. The degree of centralization and decentralization in nationalized organizations must therefore be discussed.

CENTRALIZATION AND DECENTRALIZATION

The main practical problem of organization for a public corporation lies in the extent to which its operations shall be controlled by central authority, or shall be devolved to lesser bodies. This is regularly a matter of hot contention, on which there is not infrequently more than a whiff of dogma on either side.

For each corporation the basic situation is prescribed by statute. As explained in Chapter 3, the original statutes tended to give more detail, and to impose more decentralization, as the process of nationalization progressed between 1946 and 1949. By statute, therefore, the National Coal Board is not decentralized, and the Gas Council was, before 1972.

A distinction may be drawn between geographical and functional decentralization. In many corporations there are subordinate authorities in different parts of the country – divisions, areas or regions. There is also separation, however, between different processes and stages of production – in electricity, for example, between generation and distribution.

Although no subordinate formations were prescribed in the Nationalization Act of 1946, the National Coal Board set up a structure which broadly survived until the end of 1965. There were nine Divisions in the main coalfields, each of which controlled a number of Areas. The Areas became the main operational units of the industry, each running many pits. The Divisions had a divisional board in control, appointed by the National Coal Board. Areas were controlled by area general managers (called Directors after 1965), always appointed by the national board, not the divisional one. Before 1965 there were usually Groups within the Areas. The collieries themselves are controlled by managers, who are mining engineers. This is essentially a production organization;

there is in addition a system of Regions, concerned with general distribution and covering the whole country, not merely the coalfields.

In the original Acts both the electricity and gas industries were provided with Area organizations, controlled by boards appointed by the Minister himself. In electricity these are concerned with distribution to the consumer; in gas they were responsible for both manufacture and distribution. The original British Electricity Authority of 1947 was both a generating and a supervisory body; and the Area Boards were represented on it by four of their number in rotation. The Gas Council was largely a federal body: apart from chairman and deputy-chairman, it consisted entirely of the chairmen of Area Boards. Thus, in contrast to some of the other industries, the main focus of operations in gas and electricity distribution is the Area: the national bodies have co-ordinating and general-policy functions. The establishment of the British Gas Corporation in 1972 meant that the Areas became subordinate formations, subject to reshaping in the future by the Corporation itself.

The British Transport Commission of 1947 was a body designed to co-ordinate a number of functional Executives. Some of these had their own schemes of devolution, and to some extent a regional system persisted in the railways, based largely on the old main-line companies. The two nationalized airlines have no subsidiary authorities, though considerable autonomy must be given to officials operating abroad.

The arguments about decentralization that took place in the 1950s must now be examined. They were particularly concerned with the coal and electricity industries. Important developments in the organization of other industries have also taken place in recent years.

The creation of the National Coal Board as a large unified organization was a complete transformation for the coal industry, which had previously consisted, in the main, of relatively small firms. The new structure was soon subjected to attack. The early resignation from the Coal Board of Sir Charles Reid was followed by articles in *The Times* in which he set out a new structure for the industry, abolishing Divisions and giving great autonomy to twenty-six 'corporations'. Further criticisms followed, notably from Conservative Party sources.[7] The N.C.B. therefore asked one of its members, Sir Robert Burrows, to conduct an inquiry into the organization of the industry.

Sir Robert's report was made in 1948 and is summarized in the Coal Board's annual report for that year.[8] Besides changes in the constitution of the national board, it suggested further decentralizing moves – executive power should pass from Divisions to Areas, and the position of colliery managers should be strengthened. The national board should leave executive action to its officials. Some proposals of the Burrows report were put into effect with the aid of the Coal Industry Act of 1949.

Demands for the radical decentralization of various nationalized industries continued. The Acton Society Trust in 1951 produced reports on the *Extent of Decentralization* and *Patterns of Organization*, criticizing the size and centralization of the corporations. The most drastic plans were set out in 1953 by Professor T. E. Chester and Mr Hugh Clegg in *The Future of Nationalization*. This book condemned the creation of unified national bodies to run whole industries, since this almost inevitably led to over-centralization. In the first place, the very existence of a central authority with full powers meant that grievances and disputes were normally pursued to that level, and the taking of most decisions at headquarters became habitual. Secondly, it made a hierarchy of control necessary, and in a large organization this meant a tall 'pyramid' with inevitable remoteness at the top. They recommended that the actual ownership should be held by production units more of the size of large firms, while over them regional and national organizations with functions limited by statute would meet the need for some general co-ordination. Chester and Clegg described how such a structure might be devised, not only for coal, but for the other nationalized concerns as well.

The National Coal Board continued with its basic structure unaltered, but it was influenced by the general climate favouring decentralization. In October 1953 the board issued a general directive on organization which stated, among other things, that

'Divisional Boards are bound to consider but not necessarily to accept the advice or suggestions of Headquarters' Departments', and in general it emphasized that various levels of authority had advisory or service functions in relation to one another. Shortly after the circulation of this directive, the N.C.B. appointed a special committee of outside experts to carry out a full review of its organization. The committee, under the leadership of Dr Alexander Fleck, the chairman of Imperial Chemical Industries Ltd, reported in February 1955.[9] It reversed the whole trend of criticism and development of the previous eight years, and its assessment is worthy of careful examination. Among its findings were:

(a) The basic structure of the board's organization was sound and should not be altered. It was correctly based on the principle of 'line and staff'. This means that there is a direct line of command from national board to coalface, and that the authorities on it (divisional board, area general manager, colliery manager, etc.) have the power and the duty to impose broad policy. To each level is attached specialist staff, and these communicate with corresponding specialists by 'functional' channels without necessarily involving 'line' authorities. Nevertheless, the committee insisted that the views of specialists at superior levels should normally prevail, and should not be considered merely advisory.

(b) The N.C.B. had mistaken the meaning of decentralization. 'The board appear to have assumed that decentralization means that they should not, or need not, impose their will on Divisions and Areas. We do not agree with this policy.' Properly understood, decentralization means that each level specifies the powers to be exercised by the level below, and leaves it free to exercise them; it does not mean that superior-level policies can be ignored.

(c) Control should be exercised, not by interference, but by modern techniques of approved programmes, periodical reviews and inspections. It was right for the board's headquarters to scrutinize major capital projects very carefully; the right of area general managers to authorize projects should be reduced from £100,000 to £50,000. Attention should be given to devising adequate performance standards for collieries, as distinct from fore-casts. A scheme for control of operational expenditure by standard costs should be imposed without delay.

(d) Divisions should be retained, and divisional headquarters organized on a common pattern. Areas should also continue, the area general manager in control to have an assistant. The manager need not be a mining engineer.

(e) Colliery managers, who had 'been taught to mine but not how to manage', should have assistance and attend special training courses.

(f) The general directive of October 1953 should be withdrawn and replaced by a more forceful document.

The Fleck report ended the period of hesitant decentralization in the National Coal Board, and most of its recommendations were carried out swiftly and effectively under a new chairman, Sir James Bowman. A new general directive was issued in July 1955.

In the electricity industry, events took a very different turn in the mid-1950s. The Government appointed a committee under the chairmanship of Sir Edwin Herbert 'to inquire into the organiza-tion and efficiency of the electricity supply industry'. From these wide terms of reference a number of important conclusions emerged. The principal ones concerning organization were:

(a) The separation of generation from distribution was sound, but there should be a further separation of generation from general supervision and policy-making. A new generating board should therefore be set up.

(b) More freedom should be given to Area Boards in a number of respects, and in general control should be 'judicious and stim-ulating'. The headquarters staff of the corporation was too large, and both the Area Boards and subordinate officials on the generat-ing side complained of too much interference. This led to con-fusion of responsibility, and over-occupation with detail at the top.

(c) The central headquarters took too long to approve and took too close an interest in the design and planning of generating stations.

(d) Area Boards should allow district managers to run their own shows and to exercise discretion in dealing with labour and the public.

The Government accepted the main principles of these recommendations, and by the Electricity Act of 1957 a new structure broadly in line with the proposals was set up. Sir Ronald Edwards (a member of the Herbert committee) eventually became chairman of the new supervisory Electricity Council.

There is a clear contrast of general philosophy on organizationa matters between the Fleck and Herbert reports, and almost direct contradiction on particular topics. To some extent this may be due to differences between the industries, and differences between the condition of the industries at the time. It is clear, however, that when lower-level officials complained to the Herbert committee of frustration, they were listened to sympathetically. The Fleck committee was less well disposed to these complaints, and perhaps judged harshly the quality of these personnel. They thought that it was prudent in the circumstances for higher-level (and more capable) officials to be able to impose their expertise. Again this may reflect genuine differences: the shortage of specialist skills in the coal industry meant that talent was most economically used if located with relatively high-level authorities.

It is now many years since the Fleck and Herbert reports were published, and the organizational problems of the industries are not what they were. In coal, several developments present a need for organizational change: the physical concentration of the industry into fewer and larger pits; the growing number of qualified men; the completion of the building up of strong central services, and the growth of competition from other fuels. There has been some cautious functional decentralization, and independent executives for brickmaking, coal products and opencast working have been set up. In December 1965 a more drastic reorganization was announced, to be carried out between 1966 and 1970. Divisions and

Groups were to be eliminated, and Areas reduced in number. The main problem for the N.C.B., however, is to devise adequate techniques of accountability for their Areas, so that, with checks on their efficiency, they can be given greater autonomy. There has also been some decentralization in electricity generation, with project groups and regions now responsible for most operations. The Fleck and Herbert reports seem destined to become classics of their kind, however, each persuasive in itself, and yet disturbing in that they present an unresolved clash of organizational philosophy, not fully explained by industrial circumstances.[10]

OTHER DEVELOPMENTS

There are not always documents like the Fleck and Herbert reports to guide understanding in other industries, but in recent years rather more published information about organizational matters has become available. There is a long story in transport.

The structure prescribed by the 1947 Transport Act was criticized on several grounds. First, the Transport Commission was too weak and too remote to be able to impose integration on the operating Executives. Secondly, these Executives were each concerned with a particular type of transport, and so were not conducive to integration in their day-to-day working. In the event, the Conservatives' 1953 Act (which abolished the Railway and other Executives) was intended to promote competition rather than improve co-ordination, and for this decentralization was considered a necessary approach. In 1954 a 'Railways Reorganization Scheme' was published.[11] It left the London Transport region undisturbed, but set up six Areas in the rest of the country. These were supervised by Area Boards (appointed by the Commission) with executive control in the hands of a chief regional manager. Thus both the Transport Commission and the Area Boards were concerned with policy and supervision, actual management at each level being left to senior officials. In effect, the functions of the old Railways Executive were divided between the Transport Commission itself and the new Area Boards. Other transport activities were devolved to separate managements, though ownership still rested with the Commission.

This structure proved to be temporary. Further reconstruction was brought about in the 1960s by the financial troubles of the railways. The Transport Commission was broken up, the non-railway activities passing to completely independent bodies. The Area Boards of 1954 were renamed Regional Railway Boards, their part-time chairmen to be appointed by the Minister of Transport. They were to have full managerial powers, and the regional general manager was to be a member. Separate regional trading accounts were to provide a basis for testing efficiency. The new Railways Board under Dr Richard Beeching was to 'perform only those central functions which are essential to the running of the railways as a single entity'.

The general argument behind this progressive break-up was that there was no advantage in bringing together functions that are disparate in character and require special handling. The need of the railways was for a policy board that would be able to give attention to commercial viability, as distinct from operating efficiency, and to the future size and shape of the system. This attention could only be given if irrelevant administrative duties were shed. The virtues of regional autonomy were that it fostered rivalry and emulation (though hardly competition in the economic sense) and that it made possible some comparative calculation of efficiency.

The drastic revisions of these policies brought about by the Transport Act of 1968 have been described in Chapter 3. The main structural change for the railways was the transfer of their responsibilities for some freight – sundries and container traffic – to the National Freight Corporation. The Act obliged the British Railways Board, however, to make a report on organization, which it did in December 1969. The preparation of the report was assisted by the work of McKinsey and Company Inc., management consultants, and its proposals were largely put into effect in 1970.

The report saw the new framework as having two essential components. First, management organization and responsibilities should be clearly defined, so that each manager could be made fully accountable. Secondly, in order for performance to be monitored against a plan, there should be a systematic planning and control process. From these principles, the major organizational proposals were:

(a) 'The British Railways Board should assume a mainly non-executive role, and give greater emphasis to corporate planning, policy-making and longer-term direction ...'

(b) 'The Board should delegate responsibility for the management of British Rail and each of its other businesses to a chief executive for each business ...'

(c) 'The organization for British Rail should be restructured under the Chief Executive (Railways) ...'[12]

The report went on to detail the collective responsibilities of the Board, and of the chairman, deputy chairman, chief executive, full-time members and part-time members. The Chief Executive (Railways) should be responsible for developing and managing the railway business, within board policies: in particular, he should set out five-year railway objectives and strategies, and develop five-year plans; and ensure the effectiveness of railway organization as a whole. Railway headquarters departmental duties were set out. Regional Boards, which had been abolished as statutory bodies, were to continue in an advisory capacity.

The Railways Board published a second report on organization in April 1972.[13] This declared in favour of a 'territorial' main principle of organization, in preference to a functional or a business division of work, because this principle could integrate functions at an intermediate level and minimize decisions to be taken at headquarters. The eight Territories, which replaced Regions and Divisions, were designed to maximize self-contained freight flows; and apart from London major conurbations were not split. The new arrangements substituted two tiers for three, and meant that between 4,500 and 6,500 fewer posts were needed in the organization. The headquarters' role in planning and control of inter-territory services, however, was strengthened, and it also maintained its unified control of main lines and freight trunk routes. Local management was organized by function, the Area Managers themselves concentrating on operations, customer service and man management.

The National Freight Corporation was also required, in the Transport Act of 1968, to report on its organization, which it did in December 1969.[14] The Corporation, notwithstanding its task of integration, is in fact several businesses; and in many of its operations small-scale operation is customary. The Corporation has therefore tried to keep a simple organization. It consists essentially of a general-policy board, with headquarters administration; and a number of operating units (which are organized as companies) to manage and sell the Corporation's services. Regrouping of these takes place as necessary, but fundamentally the structure remains. A body known as the National Freight Federation provides common services for the operating units. These fall into four main groups – parcels and small lots, general haulage and container traffics, special traffics and shipping. Well-known names, such as National Carriers Ltd, Pickfords Ltd, British Road Services Ltd and Freightliners Ltd, in fact designate units within one or other of these groups.

The story of British Steel Corporation organization is complex but well-documented.[15] The Iron and Steel Act of 1967 required a review of organization, and a first report was in fact prepared by a preliminary organizing committee and presented just after vesting day in July 1967. Circumstances necessitated early changes, however, and two other organization reports appeared in 1969.

The first report contained a useful review of the situation of the industry on nationalization. It went on to devise an organization that would not disturb existing efficiency but would give scope for economics of scale. To this end, it proposed the creation of four Groups (Midland, Northern and Tubes, Scottish and Northwest, and South Wales) based on existing companies, and grouped partly on geographical and partly on product considerations. It was hoped that there would be strong rivalry and non-price competition between the Groups. The second report, based on eighteen months' experience, announced the reform and abandonment of company identity within the structure, and it stated that the multi-product Groups set up on nationalization would be unsatisfactory in the long run, and that a new system based on products should replace it. The third report described this new structure of product Divisions. The four Divisions are: General Steels (plate, heavy and light sections, billets, rods and bars and wire); Special Steels (alloy, stainless, forgings, castings and special engineering products); Strip Mills (strip, sheet and tinplate); and Tubes (tubes and pipes). Each steel works is allocated to a particular Division, and there is hence some overlap where a works produces more than one product. The interests of the Corporation in chemicals and in constructional engineering were also organized in separate Divisions. Each Division operates as a profit centre, but in order to enable the Corporation to function effectively as a unit, certain matters are reserved for central decision: finance, development planning, policy for raw materials and the general determination of social policy, commercial policy and regional policy. The report also detailed some management responsibilities; for a time the chairman also acted as chief executive, but this was abandoned in 1971. The conclusion of the report suggested that, after the radical changes of the first years of nationalization, a period of consolidation would be desirable.

The structure of the nationalized gas industry was decentralized from the beginning, and for a long time was not greatly changed. The development of production on a national scale in the 1960s, however, brought change into sight. It was argued that the import of methane, the construction of a grid, underground storage and new methods of manufacture would be better carried out by a new central board analogous to the generating board in electricity. In 1964, however, the Government decided that these functions would continue to be developed by the Gas Council (which was controlled by the chairmen of the Area Gas Boards), and the Gas Act of 1965 merely strengthened the powers of the Council. Really drastic change was eventually brought about by the addition of natural gas from the North Sea to sources of supply, and in 1972 the Council and Area Boards were replaced by a unified British Gas Corporation, as described in Chapter 3.

Post Office organization is marked by the very deep separation of the postal from the telecommunications operation, sometimes prompting suggestions that there should be two independent corporations.

The restructuring of the airline nationalization has been noted in Chapter 3. Here it can perhaps be noted that British European Airways had, by 1971, fully applied the 'profit centre' concept in its organization, and it now comprises ten distinct units for which separate accounts, managerial responsibilities and profit targets are stipulated.

GENERAL TRENDS

The discussions about centralization and decentralization have usually been couched in practical administrative terms, but it has not been difficult to detect more fundamental attitudes at work. For some the very idea of large unified organizations on a national scale implies bureaucracy and remoteness, and their preference for decentralization is a protest against bigness in itself. On the other hand, centralization seems to others to ensure equal treatment for all, including workers and consumers. The trade unions in particular have traditionally favoured basic national rates of pay, so that those who do the same work receive roughly the same reward.

At the outset nationalization was intended, among other things, to bring order and system into confused and diverse industries. For this purpose, and for the change of ownership itself, strong central authority was essential. Moreover, there was at the beginning a considerable shortage of managerial talent and specialist skill, in coalmining especially but in other industries too. Central power was needed to make use of such knowledge as was available, and to see that these qualities were deployed efficiently throughout the industry.

The trend towards large-scale operation, and towards the formation of business units comprising many separate undertakings, has proceeded independently of public ownership, and seems to show that in some fields at least there are advantages in central management. In these large private businesses, similar questions of decentralization arise, and again are met by varying solutions. Of course, some public corporations are larger than any private business, but even so, centralized control may still have advantages.

The general administrative factors favouring centralization in industrial concerns are the need to make careful use of scarce resources – of skill or capital; the need to bring about rapid adaptation to new techniques or new habits of thought; the need to keep some general policy to the forefront; and the desire to maintain national standards and uniformities in some respect, often for the sake of economy. In general terms the things that decentralization fosters are the development of initiative and the taking of responsibility by many individuals, especially young ones; the opportunity for experiment and new ideas; the closer adaptation of practice to local or special circumstances, and the reduction of interference, reporting, regulation and the like to a minimum.

There are also some economic factors in the discussion. Centralization, by imposing standardization and by unifying purchasing and sales practices, enables maximum advantage to be taken of the monopoly power of organizations; and it is argued that this is an advantage yielding material benefits which ought not to be forgone. On the other hand, decentralization can offer some of the advantages of competition, and even where full competition in the economist's sense does not occur, some rivalry and emulation may be possible.

Two political factors that affect nationalized industries may be added. First, the public corporation is a responsible and accountable body. It has to answer for its actions to the Minister, to Parliament and to the public; its problems in doing so are discussed in Chapter 6. But the existence of such a system means that the central authority – which in the main has to speak for the corporation – must have means of communication with and control over all parts of the industry. Without them it is not in a position to answer, and it cannot make sure that the views it expresses correspond with what is being done in all branches of its organization. Those who favour decentralization, therefore, have tended to distrust public accountability; the Herbert committee, for example, stated that 'if the public insist on having an answer on every point ... they must put up with the inevitable bureaucracy and rigidity they themselves bring into being.'[16] Wisdom and moderation in these matters may achieve – and have achieved – sensible practices; but the duties of the central boards to the nation must impose some limits on the degree of devolution they permit.

Second, national spirit in Scotland and Wales, and to some extent nationalist politics, make it desirable to set up separate units for those countries if possible. In Scotland the coal industry, railways, electricity and gas all have independent or autonomous organizations. In Wales not so much has been possible. In the past, divisions of the National Coal Board and regions of British Railways extended beyond Wales; and though smaller units (areas and territories) now operate in these industries, they reflect functional needs rather than a national principle. In electricity there is a South Wales Area Board and one (MANWEB) for Merseyside and North Wales; in gas, however, there was, until 1972, one Area Board for all Wales. The reasons for these arrangements are technical and geographic (and hence economic), but the treatment of Wales in particular gives rise to some national feeling. Nor does the notion that they are being treated very similarly, in the matter of autonomy, to mere English *regions* arouse much enthusiasm in Celtic hearts.

It is perhaps opportune to make some remarks about the trends of the last few years in the organization of nationalized industries. The first decade or so was marked by some dogmatic controversies, described above in the context of the Fleck and Herbert reports. In recent developments there has been a move towards greater flexibility – that is, statutes give less detail, and provide greater scope for the recasting of structures by boards and Ministers. The regional structures of railways and gas, for example, once statutory, can now be changed by the Boards. Accompanying this greater freedom of manœuvre has been a welcome move towards greater information. The reports on steel, railways and freight described above were statutorily necessary, and help to explain a great deal. The new British Gas Corporation will be required to review its organization from time to time and to lay reports about it before Parliament. Political pressure, probably towards decentralization, can thus be exerted on these matters without imposing rigidity.

It is arguable that there has been an appreciable degree of centralization in the industries in recent years. Certainly in some cases this has been so. But there has also been a widespread adoption of the principles of accountable management, and of the definition of objectives and responsibilities which this entails. 'Profit centres' are being established, and distinct activities of the corporations are marked out, often by creating subsidiary companies for each type or area of operation. There has been a noticeable tendency to employ professional management consultants even for tasks at the most general organizational level, and the philosophy of McKinsey and Company Inc. has influenced several corporations. The devolution brought about by developments of this type is defined and limited; it certainly gives decision-making power to managers in various sub-units, and so helps to diffuse responsibility. However, there must be strong central authority in the first place to set up the arrangements, and this can be used to revise the structure drastically, as the coal and steel examples show.

In spite of the emotions sometimes engendered by different schools of thought, problems of organization should be capable of settlement on practical grounds. Some advances have been made in recent years in the theoretical study of organization, and what was once the realm of folklore may eventually be understood in a more scientific way. But it seems prudent to remember that organizations should change: that absence of alteration is likely to mean that there is little dynamism in the industry itself.

6   Control and Accountability

THE EFFECT of nationalization in practice is to break up the traditional set of ownership rights – rights of use, of access, of disposal, of benefit. Some of these rights have passed to the governing boards of the corporations; others are exercised through the agencies of Government and Parliament.

It is fundamental to the idea of the public corporation that there should be some ministerial control and some public accountability – but not too much and not of the wrong kind. Not surprisingly, it has proved difficult to get these matters arranged to the general satisfaction.

There is, of course, a link between control by the Government and accountability to the public. Nevertheless, there is in principle a distinction between the two processes. Control is a purposeful and positive activity, by which definite lines of action are determined. Accountability is an acknowledgment of responsibility, involving the giving of information and explanations about past and current activities. It implies a position of stewardship or of trusteeship on the part of the managers of the undertakings.

MINISTERIAL CONTROL

Each public corporation is controlled by a particular Minister, and it is through his department that the corporation conducts nearly all its relations with the Government. In most cases now – coal, gas, electricity, steel, airlines – it is one or other branch of the Department of Trade and Industry that is responsible. This large Department now includes the work of the former Ministries of Power, Technology and Aviation. The nationalized transport industries – railways, freight, waterways, buses – are the concern of the Department of the Environment, which took over the former Ministry of Transport; there is a Minister of Transport Industries within this Department.

As with organization, the nationalization Acts give some preliminary indication of the situation. The Minister appoints and can in practice remove the members of the boards. Open and persistent defiance of a Minister may be ruled out, therefore, to begin with. The statutes also provide for a Minister to give 'directions of a general character ... in relation to matters appearing to the Minister to affect the national interest'.[1] Such directions can be issued only after the Minister has consulted with the board.

These powers – of appointment, removal and direction – provide a Minister's basic political strength. They are supplemented by statutory provision on particular topics. The corporations (excluding the airlines) must submit schemes of reorganization, substantial capital development, training, education and research for the Minister's approval. They must also provide him with such information as he requires.

Additional matters subject to Government control include the management of reserve funds or surpluses, and, in electricity, the definition of Areas.

It should be noted that, besides the relevant Minister, the Treasury sometimes has the right to be consulted – on the disposal of reserves and surpluses, on the salaries of board members, on stock issues and on the form of the corporations' accounts. The functions of the Treasury since the war have been such as to make it also a department with a great deal to say about the investment plans of the industries and other economic aspects of their activities.

The statutes provide at most a skeleton on which flesh and blood relationships can develop. The main power of general direction has been little used, and then in exceptional circumstances – to check further progress into steel nationalization when the Conservatives came to power in 1951, for example, or to limit rises in passenger fares on the railways in 1952. Even with the subjects of the specific legal powers listed above, experience now provides a much better guide to the realities of the relationship than does the text of the Acts.

Do these legal stipulations express the full intentions of the nationalizers? It may be suspected that two factors were at work in the late 1940s. First, there was a clear desire that an elected Government should be allowed to have its way: the public corporations were not to be allowed to become independent powers in the country, able to ignore the political will of the electors, as formulated by the Government of the day. This was almost the sole motive in nationalizing the Bank of England, and its effect on the other corporations lay in the provisions for definite political supremacy. There is no indication, however, of any clear ideas about how often such political intervention would be needed, or how close an interest a Minister would take in the affairs of a corporation. The experience of pre-war public corporations seemed to indicate that what might be needed was an occasional veto, or the setting of a new policy line now and again. Nevertheless, the deep political interest in the affairs of the newly nationalized industries could have suggested that such a degree of abstention would not be practicable.

A second factor was the type of Government policy necessary to maintain full employment. This had its statutory expression in the rule about approval of investment plans. It was widely believed, moreover, that the public sector of the economy, if large enough, could be used to maintain a high rate of activity. The industrial public corporations were expected to play a key part in this, and hence a Government's economic planners would need control more intimate than that which had existed before the war.

At all events, a system of regular contacts between the heads of the nationalized industries and Ministers soon grew up. There were from the beginning urgent national problems – of fuel shortage, for example – which made close co-operation desirable, and Ministers found that they needed to be well informed to cope with public criticism. Constant involvement in practice meant high-level, if informal, policy discussions. Mr G. R. Strauss has explained that, when Minister of Supply, he had weekly talks with the chairman and deputy-chairman of the Iron and Steel Corporation, and they discussed 'every single problem, not only of national interest but on every conceivable detail concerning that Corporation. There was not a subject with which I was not concerned.'² This is not to say, of course, that a Minister uses the meetings to impose his views: there is no doubt a process of mutual influence and consultation. Nor need the process be as frequent or as detailed for other industries as in the example given by Mr Strauss. There is no doubt, however, that procedures of the same type existed, and continue to exist, for all the main industrial public corporations.

The contacts between Government and public corporations are not confined to the top level. Civil servants keep in touch with the staff of the corporations on many matters, routine and occasional. Government departments are expected to accumulate their own knowledge and understanding of particular industries, in order to form disinterested judgments about industrial problems. But though their views may eventually differ from those held inside the corporations, the building up of information and comprehension can be done only by co-operation with those working directly on the affairs of the industry.

It must be accepted, therefore, that there is an elaborate system of consultation between the Government and the nationalized industries. With what subject is this most concerned? Four categories may be indicated:

(a) The general forward planning of the industry is clearly one such matter. The statutory powers of the Minister in relation to investment, finance, research and training are all focused in this direction, and, even if they did not exist, any Government that had to take responsibility for economic prosperity would want to assure itself about the prospects for the basic industries. In addition to Government departments, the National Economic Development Council has, since 1962, been concerned with economic growth and future prosperity. The chairmen of the National Coal Board and the Electricity Council are members of the N.E.D.C., and the staff of its office consult directly with all the corporations as they prepare their prognostications.

The financial troubles in which many of the newly nationalized industries found themselves made further consultations necessary. The deficits incurred made the financing of investment programmes exceptionally difficult, and again the statutory requirements were reinforced by practical necessities, obliging all concerned to co-ordinate their activities.

(b) The central financial aspect of a corporation's business is the price at which it sells its products. (The proper criteria for fixing prices are discussed in Chapter 7.) It must be emphasized, however, that at all times appreciable changes in price levels in the national-ized industries have been, in one way or another, the concern of the Government. It is acknowledged that a 'gentleman's agreement' – dating from wartime conditions in the coal industry – always ensured that boards submitted proposed prices for the Minister's information or even approval. The responsibility for the changes, including their form, extent and consequences, must in normal circumstances remain with the corporations. In cases where the Government has intervened, therefore, the industries have been anxious to find a way of ensuring that the Government has also accepted public responsibility, and the usual techniques of private consultation have not provided any guarantee of this.

Some examples have come to light in the past. For example, in 1955 the prospect of mounting losses caused the National Coal Board to propose a substantial rise in the price of coal. The rise was delayed for four months by the Minister of Power, and though an even larger rise was then made, the N.C.B. incurred a heavy loss that year.[3] In 1956 the Minister of Transport revised, and effec-tively reduced, rises in charges proposed by the British Transport Commission, even after they had been approved by the Transport Tribunal – again with serious effects on the industry's financial position.[4] Comments on the situation have led to some changes over the years, as stated in the White Papers of 1961 and 1967, discussed in the next chapter. In 1965 the Labour Government set up the National Board for Prices and Incomes, and many price problems were referred to it; indeed, in September 1967 it was announced that all major increases in the nationalized industries would be its concern. The N.B.P.I. was abolished by the Con-servative Government, but prices are still the concern of relevant

E

Government departments. In April 1971 a proposed increase of 14 per cent in the price of steel was reduced to seven per cent by Governmental order, showing present practice – Government action openly declared in specific cases.

(c) Wage negotiation is another subject of major Government interest; and here the extent of intervention is at its most obscure and controversial. Negotiations take place between the corporations, as employers, and the trade unions representing the employees, and formally the Government takes no part. Yet in fact there is no doubt that the views of the Government are made known to the corporations, and their negotiators can hardly fail to take these into account. If the corporation is in a weak financial condition, it will be in no position to ignore such pressure. If a rise in labour costs cannot be absorbed, then prices will have to be raised, which, under the 'gentleman's agreement', will require Government approval. Further, in cases such as the railways, where higher charges might not bring in greater revenue, then a subsidy may be necessary. In such a situation the Government's part is indispensable, and more open.

Usually, however, the Government stays in the background, and much resentment is expressed by trade unionists at this situation. They complain that they are negotiating only with shadows, and that the true 'paymasters' do not come forward. However, it cannot be denied that the corporations are the employers and must take a large part in wage settlements. On at least one occasion they have acted contrary to Government advice, for the Electricity Council was publicly rebuked by the Prime Minister in November 1961 for granting an increase in excess of what the Government thought justifiable.[5]

Nevertheless, the general position of the Government in wage negotiations is ambiguous. Clearly it expects to have its views respected, and hitherto it has seemed to assume that its rights inside the 'public sector' are greater than outside it. If a Government wants *special* influence over these settlements, however, then there is surely a case for its being openly represented in negotiations, and for making its attitude clear at the outset.

(*d*) These three broad categories of Government influence should not obscure the wide range of topics actually discussed. In addition to plans, prices and wage settlements, a miscellany of particular topics is considered – the siting of power stations, land for opencast mining, air-charter policy and so on. The Government is also known to exert influence in order to maintain various uneconomic activities. A classic case is the air service in the Highlands and Islands of Scotland provided by British European Airways, which always makes a loss, borne by the corporation. Or again, the industries may be obliged to co-operate in general policy changes. The Government's decision in 1970 that a private-enterprise 'second force' airline should be sustained meant that B.O.A.C. had to yield important routes, including West African operations, and that B.E.A. had to give up some regular flights between London and Paris.

On two occasions, April 1961 and November 1967, the Government has published White Papers setting new general policies for the nationalized industries. These documents contain several propositions discussed in this chapter and the next. Here it is relevant to note that the White Papers set new standards and new principles merely by the executive action of the Government itself. There was no legislation. The White Papers were drawn up by the Government, in consultation with the corporations in the usual manner. Their effectiveness as a determinant of the general framework of policy illustrates the power of the system of ministerial control that has grown up.

In sum, on a great range of problems there is discussion between the Government and the public corporations. Apart from generalities, decisions on the problems rest with the boards of the corporations. The regular contacts mean, however, that the boards are open to much persuasion: they may be subject to influence; they may be vulnerable to pressure, and they can be threatened with direction – though the actual use of powers of direction remains highly exceptional.

Too much control?

For long it was thought that, in the nationalized industries the influence of the Ministers had increased and was increasing. Ought it to be diminished?

It should be emphasized that the influence is not necessarily one-way. Indeed, if the object of informing the Minister is to help him meet criticisms in Parliament, or in his own department, then the balance of advantage may be with the corporations. On most specialized topics the expertise available in the industries should be sufficient for their actions to be defended successfully. As a matter of personality, too, a determined board chairman may find it possible to persuade an average Minister even more often than he is persuaded by him. In day-to-day terms there is undoubtedly a two-way process of influence. Nevertheless, the ultimate, legal, powers lie with the Government, and their presence cannot fail to sway many situations.

It should be remembered that private industry also has close relations with Government departments, either through trade associations or directly. Here again there is a process of mutual persuasion. The oil companies are believed to inform the Ministry of Power about prospective price changes; and if they do, the Minister can easily put considerations before the companies about these changes. But this is an exceptional, and in any case a voluntary, arrangement. In principle the powers and responsibilities of Ministers vis-à-vis private firms are very different, and so the means of influencing them must also be very different.

On occasions the relationship between Minister and public corporation has been described in doubtful terms. A well-known example is the statement made in March 1953 by Lord Swinton in the House of Lords, to the effect that 'the Minister's day-to-day contact with the chairman of a nationalized board is very like one's relationship with one's own officials in one's department.'[6] Again, in the White Paper on the *Reorganization of National Transport Undertakings* of 1960, a chart shows the Minister of Transport at the head of a new structure, with responsibilities for overall co-ordination and general efficiency.[7]

These formulations, literally interpreted, are a travesty of the original conception of the public corporation. The Minister has certain very strong powers in relation to a public corporation, but he was not intended to control it in the way he controls his own department. Moreover, his functions relate to policy rather than efficiency. A public corporation cannot be expected to operate properly where these misunderstandings of its status prevail.

The general motives that impel Governments to take such a close interest in the affairs of corporations should be remembered in this context. The supervision of plans, about which there is little controversy, is at the heart of the matter: and the need for it arises from the Government's responsibilities – unavoidable in the twentieth century – for national economic well-being. This responsibility for the national economy also explains the Government's interest in prices and wage settlements. The miscellaneous matters are supervised for more political motives – the need of the Government to meet questions and criticisms about the general activities of the corporations. Thus it is usually its care for the economy that has led the Government to threaten the independence of the corporations; and in particular the notion of the 'public sector' as a sphere in which the Government had direct powers of control has meant drastic limitations on the corporations' autonomy. In the 1960s an attempt was made to build a system of economic planning on a wider basis, and if this had succeeded, then special control over the investment, prices and wages of the nationalized industries may no longer have been necessary. Even so, the nationalized industries are mainly basic industries on which the rest of the economy depends. As such they are naturally subject to close Government attention, whatever their formal status.

If these are the Government's motives, then what accounts for the acceptance of the situation by the public corporations? In the background, of course, are the formidable legal powers of the Minister, and the urgencies of past crises have bred habits that have persisted. Public corporations are obliged to give information, and it is therefore difficult to refuse to discuss problems arising from the facts. If there is man-to-man discussion, then compromises, accommodations and mutual understandings arise naturally. More-over, large numbers of published directives might give outsiders the impression that boards were being judged incapable of managing their affairs properly.

The causes of ministerial intervention have been explained. There does not seem to be any prospect of the general causes diminishing in importance – the Government will still be con-cerned with national prosperity and with meeting criticisms. If the corporations are free from financial difficulties there may be oppor-tunity for relaxation of pressure. However, the absence of difficul-ties depends in large measure on Government policy about public-enterprise prices. From 1961 to 1970 there was some effort either to allow the industries to establish a financially viable level for prices, or, at least, to accommodate the system of control to general arrangements for price restraint. The fact is that Government policies about prices, in the national interest and under pressure from public opinion, can put the corporations in the position of unpopular supplicants; and this constitutes an inherent weakness in their bargaining position.

At various levels, then, and on a variety of topics there are contacts between corporations and ministries, many of them entirely informal and in the normal day's work. The key relation-ship must lie between the Minister and the board chairman. Strictly speaking, the dealings may be personal and confidential with no actual decisions reached. Of course, the Minister is but one member of the Government, and the chairman must carry the support of his board. Nevertheless, there is here more than a channel of communication: there is a policy-making nexus of some sort.

In the past, a good deal of criticism has been directed at this process. Not all of this has been well directed. The informality, for example, may be exaggerated. In 1968 Lord Robens said of his meetings with Ministers: 'I believe in a straight business agenda so that we put down on paper on an agenda the things I want to discuss and the things the Minister wants to discuss, have a very good discussion about them, and then come to conclusions be-tween us.'[8] It should also be emphasized that confidential discussions are a common necessity of twentieth-century government. Ministers are constantly meeting representatives of trade associations, trade unions, local authorities and other bodies in the ordinary way of business. There is nothing exceptional about the public corporation which gives rise to 'informality' of this type; and there does not seem to be much possibility of its elimination.

There is, certainly, a school of thought that calls for its drastic reduction. It has been urged that industrial public corporations should largely be controlled by means of the 'general directive'.[9] Similarly, there is a call for the development of an 'arms-length' relationship between Ministers and corporations. The meetings are said to result in 'lunchtime directives' – that is to say, the Minister's wishes expressed privately and informally are nevertheless accepted by the boards' chairmen. In fact it is hard to see what can be done to alter the situation. There is indeed positive value in personal contacts that promote a 'meeting of minds' and better understanding. It is surely better to acknowledge the legitimacy of the process than to engage in a futile attempt to prevent it. The procedures give opportunity for mutual influence; the eventual outcome will depend partly on the personalities concerned and partly on the basic powers of the participating institutions.

The S.C.N.I. report of 1968

It is necessary therefore to look not so much at the style of contact as at the underlying position. The Select Committee on Nationalized Industries in various reports expressed its concern, and in 1968 it published a long report directly on the subject of ministerial control. This contains a great deal of useful and relevant material, worth study for its own sake, and there is much of value in its evidence and appendices. Here its actual proposals must be considered.

Clearly one of its major premises was that ministerial control had been unsatisfactory, confused and in some way excessive. 'Running through much of the evidence has been a sense of confusion, a general lack of clarity about purposes, policies, methods and responsibilities.'[10] At one stage the reported formulated ten guiding principles: (1) there should be ministerial concern with the public interest; (2) Ministers should exercise a broad oversight;

(3) industries should otherwise be left free; (4) there should be clear demarcation of responsibilities; (5) control should be strategic rather than tactical; (6) control need not be wholly formal; (7) Ministers and industries should be publicly accountable; (8) the measure of management is not pure commercial or social achievements, but carrying out duties given to them; (9) improvement of management should be the first objective, but ultimate sanction may be dismissal; (10) proper exercise of control depends on the attitudes of Ministers and board members.[11] These propositions, couched in administrative terms, preceded a long examination of the economic and financial framework and of the operation of ministerial control in various areas – appointments, policies, prices, investment, borrowing, staff matters, social obligations and other topics. Eventually the report came to 'the heart of the matter' and asked 'What has gone wrong?'

It found chief fault with the sponsoring departments; and its diagnosis of the causes of the trouble centred on the distinction between the Government's responsibilities, in the public interest, for *policies* for the industries and its concern with ensuring their *efficiency*. These, it maintained, had been confused; and its remedy lay in their separation within the machinery of government.

Hence the committee's striking proposal for a new Ministry of Nationalized Industries. This would have several duties (listed in twelve items), including the making of appointments; however, its chief purpose would be to supervise efficiency, by concerning itself with pricing and investment policies, financial objectives, the review of investment programmes and the furthering of co-ordination. The advantages claimed for such a Ministry were that it would develop expertise in dealing with nationalization problems as such, and show a more consistent attitude to the various industries. The creation of the new Ministry would involve the drastic reconstruction of existing departments. The duties of the Government in policy-making were to be divided among other departments.

The report rejected suggestions for an independent efficiency audit, and for the creation of a holding company intermediate between the Government and the operating corporations.

The outcome of the report

Though the report was often admired for much of its analysis and content, the proposals set out above did not find much favour. Critics did not accept that the proposed Ministry would achieve its objectives – to lessen confusion and reduce intervention. The Government's verdict was also unfavourable. In a White Paper it acknowledged that a conceptual distinction could be made between the Government's responsibility for efficiency and its responsibility for the wider public interest; but it denied 'that the two responsibilities give rise to separable and distinct functions which would be best exercised by different departments'. Separation would complicate rather than simplify decision-making; sector responsibilities (including for example the oil industry) could not easily be detached from efficiency-responsibility; two departments would mean more staff; and the concentration of one department on efficiency would lead to greater intervention rather than less.

It may be added that the S.C.N.I. proposals also fail to provide at all effectively for public-interest policy-making, which was to be scattered among diverse ministries. Energy policy and transport policy could scarcely be developed in this way. In the event the machinery of government was reconstructed in 1969–70, but in a contrary direction, and the great Departments – of Trade and Industry and of the Environment – were built on functional lines.[12] The idea of a Ministry based on the status (i.e. nationalized) of its client industries was clearly incompatible with this principle.

For a time, then, the great researches of the Select Committee in 1966–8 ended in anti-climax, for its remedy was rejected and not widely supported anyway.

Economic marching orders

These controversies should not obscure the emergence, in the last fifteen years or so, of an orthodox view of how the nationalized industries should be controlled. Professor A. H. Hanson once stated: 'Ministers should give the industries their marching orders, appoint the right people to run them, and then leave them to get on with the job.'[13] The orthodoxy is a form of this 'marching orders' theory. It is that *control is essentially a matter of prescribing rational economic instructions*. Hence the close connection of control with the aims of the industries, discussed in the next chapter. Some supervision and some checking of results may be needed: but the rationality of the instructions should ensure conformity with the national interest, and so other intervention can be largely relaxed. This is of course not completely achieved in practice, but it seems to be very widely held now that proper relationships can be achieved on these lines.

To say that this view has emerged as an orthodoxy is not to endorse its adequacy. It may be suggested that preoccupation with economic rationality has not helped to provide a satisfactory set of relationships because the concepts of that science do not provide for such things: the objectives may be right, but the means of monitoring or control are not yet well arranged. At all events there seems to have been an over-optimistic view about the possibility of a reduction in Government concern by means of the 'marching-orders' concept: the industries are rarely 'left to get on with the job'. Nor, it may be remarked, would revision of Governmental machinery have such an effect, for the causes have deeper political roots – in modern public expectations of the efficacy of Governmental action and in the omnicompetence of political means to secure remedies for industrial (or other) failings. For the time being, a sound strategy on intervention might lie in reduction by simplification; thus proper techniques of investment appraisal reduce the burden of the vetting of particular projects. The various institutions concerned each have their roles to play. As Mr Jack Diamond, then Chief Secretary to the Treasury, put it: '… it is the responsibility of the industry to make sure it is efficiently run; it is the responsibility of the sponsoring department to make sure that the industry has "taken pains" before concluding that it is efficient; and it is the responsibility of the Treasury not to provide large sums of money until it is satisfied that it will not be wasted.'[14]

The development of thought about ministerial control may be summed up thus.

At first, reliance was placed on the distinction between general policy matters, the concern of the Government, and 'day-to-day' management, left to the boards. This provided inadequate guidance. The phrase 'day to day' is totally unrealistic as a description of the management responsibilities of a high-powered board of a public corporation, which must and will concern itself with policy at a high level.

Secondly, following the Herbert report of 1956, there was an attempt to drive a distinction between commercial or 'purely economic' matters, to be left entirely to the boards, and national interests, on which the Government might from time to time intervene.

Thirdly, the White Paper of 1961 insists that nationalized industries have wider obligations than firms in the private sector, and it implicitly rejects the idea that they can be left to their own economic devices. The financial targets are imposed by the Government, not internally generated by the enterprises themselves. The same is true of the guidelines of 1967. Thus the 'economic marching orders' orthodoxy has become established. It has not led, so far, to any noticeable decrease in Government intervention.

ACCOUNTABILITY TO PARLIAMENT

If the pre-war public corporations were subject to little control by ministers, their accountability to Parliament was virtually non-existent. The strengthening of Government control over the post-war corporations was expected to carry with it closer parliamentary interest. This interest was thought to be catered for automatically under the conventions of ministerial responsibility. The theory of the public corporations' accountability to Parliament was simple and logical. The Minister had certain powers over the corporations. For the exercise of these powers he was answerable to Parliament, just as he was answerable for all his other powers. On those matters where the Minister exercised no powers, there was no accountability. This would correspond with the extent of the corporations' managerial independence. In so far as the post-war corporations were under greater ministerial control, so parliamentary discussion could be greater too; but all depended on the Minister, and the possibility of accountability depended essentially on him. In practice this was expected to mean that Parliament could discuss 'broad policy' but not 'day-to-day management'.

This technique of accountability did not weather parliamentary storms very well, and modifications have now been introduced. Their nature can best be understood if the means of information and debate available to Parliament are reviewed.

Three different methods may be distinguished: debates, questions and select committees.

Debates on the affairs of nationalized industries may arise in several different ways. Sometimes there is important legislation concerning an industry, perhaps revising its whole structure – the Electricity Act of 1957, for example. The passing of such measures obviously gives rise to extensive discussion; and though for any particular industry they may occur rarely, in fact there is some legislation concerning the public corporations almost every year. Secondly, the annual reports and accounts of each industry are presented to Parliament by the Minister responsible; the reports of the Select Committee described below are available as subjects of debate. Not every industry is properly debated every year, but two or three are chosen annually for full discussion. Thirdly, other opportunities may be taken to start debates: the Opposition may find time, on one of the days when it has choice of subject; or private members may use their special opportunities; and the debate at the beginning of each session when there is a general review of Government policy may contain reflections on these industries.[15] The Government itself may find it opportune to move a motion concerning a nationalized industry. Economic and financial matters provide other opportunities: there is an annual debate on public expenditure, the White Paper on *Loans from the National Loans Fund* may be debated and from time to time public corporations wish to raise the statutory limit on their borrowing powers, which can only be done by legislation.

This may seem a formidable list. But in fact, debates on the annual reports are the only regular general discussions; and some industries may pass several years without being examined in this way. In any case, only limited aspects of the work of the corporations are likely to be raised, often those which have caught the popular notice. On the floor of the House of Commons, too, partisan attitudes are at the fore, and little light may emerge even from lengthy exchanges. In debates the nationalized industries cannot be directly represented, but in a sense Ministers speak on their behalf. Since public corporations are not the same as departments, this is not entirely satisfactory. What Ministers defend is the Government's attitude to the nationalized industries, and this may not be quite the same thing as defending the nationalized industries.

Debates may also take place in the House of Lords, where procedure is flexible and general motions on the industries can be discussed. Legislation, of course, must go through the usual stages in the Lords.

The story of parliamentary questions on the nationalized industries shows most clearly the difficulties of maintaining the original theory of accountability. At first, indeed, nationalization had the unexpected effect of removing some matters from parliamentary scrutiny. The railways, for example, had been taken over by the Government during the war, and Ministers had answered questions – on points of some detail – about their running. Transference to a public corporation, therefore, took them out of the Minister's emergency control, and, in accordance with the theory of managerial independence, questions on details were refused an answer.

In spite of this embarrassment, Ministers set out to maintain a fairly strict rule about questions. Questions were allowed only on matters that were the Minister's responsibility, and it was primarily for him to acknowledge what was his responsibility and what was not. When he had indicated subjects he considered to be outside his responsibilities, officials of the House of Commons then refused to accept further questions on those subjects. One modification only has been made to this rule. In 1948 the Minister of Fuel and Power refused to answer questions about electricity load-shedding, as this was for the Electricity Authority to deal with, not a matter of general policy. Officials of the House of Commons noted this refusal, and accepted no more questions. But the electricity situation worsened, load-shedding became frequent and obviously a

matter of national importance. It was impossible to keep the subject out of parliamentary discussion. In June 1948, therefore, the
Speaker announced that subjects on which answers had been refused could nevertheless be raised, by question, if he considered
them of sufficient public importance. Since 1948 the rule has been
maintained virtually without change. In spite of their early criticisms, the Conservatives made no substantial alteration when they
came to power in 1951. Later statements of the rule are merely
reformulations and make no difference.

Two practical developments, however, have made the operation
of the rule less onerous than it might seem. At a very early stage
Ministers found it possible to give information while not accepting
(or even explicitly denying) any responsibility, by prefacing their
answers with, 'I am informed by the board that ...', or some such
formula. This creates a degree of flexibility for the Ministers,
though it does not mean that they are bound to provide information on any topic. Secondly, Members of Parliament have developed techniques for avoiding the rule. Questions may be asked
about a Minister's responsibilities, not merely his positive actions.
It is therefore possible to ask why he has *not* taken action on a
particular matter. To make certain, a Member may ask why the
Minister has not issued a general direction on the point: and clearly
this is a question relating to the Minister's powers, which must be
answered. By this and similar methods a considerable range of
questions can be asked, and once the topic is aired, further implications may be drawn out by means of supplementary questions.

There is thus a gap between the rigid principle and the actual
working of parliamentary questioning. What is in fact possible may
be indicated by examples from the session 1970–71 when questions
were asked about the conversion of appliances to natural gas; the
development of the advanced passenger-train; a possible review of
the financial target of the Generating Board; the investment of
pension funds in the electricity industry; the disposal of unused
railway land; and rural bus services in Wales. By asking for a
'general direction', the possible exemption of pensioners from
minimum electricity charges and the supply of ducted air-venting
by gas boards were raised. Factual information was often supplied

by written answers. A question asked in May 1971 illustrates a common technique. Dr John Gilbert, M.P. for Dudley, asked the Minister of Posts and Telecommunications 'if he would give a general direction to the Post Office that they seek to install public telephones on all station platforms'. The Minister, Mr Christopher Chataway, replied predictably: 'No, sir. This would not be a suitable subject for a general direction.' The Member, however, was able to ventilate the subject in his supplementary question: '... As the Minister will not do anything to try to get us telephones on trains, will he get them on railway station platforms where we are equally prisoners of British Rail? There are no telephones on the platforms at Euston. At Birmingham they are on the right side of the ticket collector, but a long way from the platforms. At many stations they are even outside the premises.' Again, the Minister replied: 'I am sorry to cause disappointment to the hon. Gentleman, but I should be abusing my powers under the 1969 Act if I were to issue general directions on the subject.'[16]

The case for more questions is simply that the corporations are public bodies, and public bodies should be open to scrutiny whatever their strict constitutional position. Members of Parliament with constituencies in which the nationalized industries operate are particularly anxious to raise local grievances. The case against detailed questioning depends partly on constitutional principle and partly on the needs of industrial management. The right to question should be, constitutionally, conterminous with the responsibilities of the Minister – to widen the scope of questions would widen his responsibilities and automatically destroy the independence of the public corporations. It would make the corporations operate like the Civil Service, and would be inimical to efficiency. It would lead to over-centralization, too much record-keeping, and excessive caution – in short, the need to have an answer to all possible questions would inhibit initiative and risk-taking.

The outcome of these conflicting considerations is a situation of some confusion. It is difficult to see how the rule could be altered, assuming that the corporations have managerial autonomy. Yet ways are found in practice of avoiding it, and it is hard to believe that it provides an easy guide for a Minister who has to decide whether a question should be answered or not. It is interesting to note that there is no rule which limits the scope of questions about concerns in which there is Government shareholding (such as Short Brothers and Harland, of Belfast).[17] In these cases any topic may be raised. Attempts to secure greater rights for Members of Parliament recur, but parliamentary scrutiny has concentrated in recent years on a more powerful and searching instrument than the question: the select committee.

A select committee of the House of Commons is a group of Members, usually small, appointed by the House to carry out reviews and investigations on general aspects of Government activity. Its membership reflects the party balance in the House of Commons itself. It has power to call for written evidence and to question witnesses; but its duty is merely to report to the House – it has no independent authority. The select committees regularly appointed by the House include one on delegated legislation and two on Government finance, the Expenditure Committee and the Public Accounts Committee. Reforms in the 1960s led to the creation of several more such committees, and new committees on Scottish Affairs, Science and Technology, Race Relations and other matters are now regularly appointed.

The Public Accounts Committee has the function of examining the accounts of Government departments and other public bodies, to ensure that money is being properly and economically spent. The accounts of the public corporations fall within its terms of reference, and for some years there were tentative examinations of these accounts. At first it took evidence mainly from civil servants whose duties included contact with the nationalized industries. In 1951–2 it took evidence from the auditors of the accounts of the British Transport Commission, two eminent commercial accountants. The work of the committee, however, was hesitant and not very searching. It was hampered by lack of expert guidance, and the committee was reluctant to spare the time from its already full programme that a really thorough examination would require.

In fact, it was doubtful if the Public Accounts Committee was an appropriate body for such inquiries. If the work was to be done properly, then a special body concerned with the nationalized industries as such was required. Such a body was early proposed by a Labour M.P., Mr J. Baird, and was extensively canvassed by a Conservative Member, Mr Hugh Molson (now Lord Molson). But before the Select Committee on Nationalized Industries was successfully launched, there were many doubts and difficulties and one false start.

The nature of the doubts has already been indicated: they centred on the undesirability of subjecting the 'business' or 'commercial' style of management, appropriate to the nationalized industries, to constant probing and detailed criticism. Many evils were alleged to arise from such investigation – bureaucracy, centralization and lack of enterprise being the most frequently cited. The statement of Lord Heyworth, the chairman of Unilever Ltd, expressed the situation of the industrial manager very forcefully, and indeed has become something of a classic.

> I look upon myself as someone who is perpetually in a fog ... If people came to look at everything I did in a year after the events, the shareholders would be horrified because they would see that some of my decisions were quite wrong. The more I felt that someone was looking over my shoulder all the time and was going to examine these things at any time later, the less I would be inclined to take a decision, the less decisive I would become, and pretty well certainly the less good would be the results.[18]

This view from a successful private businessman was reinforced by similar fears expressed by the existing chairmen of nationalized industries. Nevertheless, one chairman, Lord Hurcomb of the Transport Commission, thought that some sort of parliamentary committee might be useful, and in 1953 a committee of the House of Commons reported in favour of establishing a committee to examine the nationalized industries, with the object of ' ... informing Parliament about the aims, activities and problems of the Corporations and not of controlling their work'.[19]

The first Select Committee on Nationalized Industries, set up in 1955, was abortive. In its terms of reference precise limits were set to what it could do, and it was prohibited from examining anything that was a ministerial responsibility, anything to do with collective bargaining, or anything that was a matter of day-to-day management. Nevertheless, it was to consider the *current* activities of the corporations. After a few months of trying to find something useful to do, the committee reported that nothing worth while could be done within its terms of reference.

In May 1956 the Government agreed to set up a new committee; at the end of November a motion to set it up was moved by Mr R. A. Butler. The Labour Party opposed the motion, Mr James Callaghan arguing that such a committee would blur the chain of responsibility from the boards to Ministers. The motion was carried, the committee was appointed in December and began work in February 1957.

The Select Committeee on Nationalized Industries (Reports and Accounts) has the following terms of reference:

> ... to examine the Reports and Accounts of the Nationalized Industries established by Statute whose controlling Boards are appointed by Ministers of the Crown and whose annual receipts are not wholly or mainly derived from moneys provided by Parliament or advanced from the Exchequer.

There are thus no restrictive limitations on its work: it is left to the committee itself to chose its subjects of inquiry and to conduct its investigations in a reasonable manner. The corporations subject to its surveillance are the trading bodies: thus the B.B.C. and the Atomic Energy Authority are excluded. In the 1960s, however, the Select Committee initiated efforts to get its own order of reference extended to cover other bodies, and published a special report on the subject.[20] This report provides a useful source of information about Government business concerns beyond the public corporations. Its effect was to secure an extension of the reference of the S.C.N.I. To the original words quoted above are now added: ' ... and of the Independent Television Authority, Cable and Wireless Ltd, and the Horserace Totalizator Board, and to examine such activities of the Bank of England as are not ... ' And here the reference goes on to list some excluded matters, such as monetary and financial policy and the private banking activities of the Bank.

There are thirteen or fourteen members of the committee, and in spite of the initial forebodings it has conducted its affairs in an entirely non-partisan manner, votes being very rare. It calls for and examines written memoranda, and questions witnesses orally – civil servants, members of the boards, senior staff of the corporations and independent experts.

The S.C.N.I.'s main method of investigation is to examine in detail the work of each corporation. It has varied this procedure, however, on several occasions to consider general questions affecting all the industries, such as *Ministerial Control* (1967–8) and *Relations with the Public* (1970–71). On other occasions only part of the work of a corporation may be investigated, such as the *Exploitation of North Sea Gas* (1967–8). Reports on the *Bank of England* (1969–70) and on the *Independent Broadcasting Authority* (1971–2) reflect the widening scope of the committee. From 1966 to 1969 it divided into sub-committees, and was able to engage in two major investigations concurrently.[21] This practice was resumed in 1971. A list of major reports is provided in Appendix A.

The S.C.N.I. is generally considered to be a very successful body. The nationalized industries have accepted it with good grace and regard it as a very useful link with Parliament and with the informed public, though from time to time they complain about the burden of work brought about by the need to prepare evidence. There is little doubt that the general understanding of Members has been improved by its reports, and that their debates are more enlightened as a result of the committee's influence. The atmosphere of discussion on nationalization is, between election campaigns, more moderate, constructive and well informed. Their reports and proceedings constitute first-class material for the research worker. In some degree this acceptance is due to the political restraint of the committee. It concentrates on the evidence put before it and the inferences to be drawn from it. Conservative members of the committee do not condemn weaknesses as inherent in the principle of nationalization, nor do Labour members try to extol its successes as springing from that very principle. Their reports, therefore, light no fires of party controversy.

These are considerable achievements; yet their extent and their nature should be noted. Sir Toby Low (now Lord Aldington), a former chairman, has pointed out that the S.C.N.I. 'has but to unravel the facts and point the moral. Others take the action.'[22] The morals pointed by the committee have sometimes been the guide for action; but often they have not. The Government continues to appoint special committees to advise it – the Stedeford committee on the railways and the Edwards report on the airlines were more powerful instigators of policy than any S.C.N.I. report.

It must also be remembered that the S.C.N.I. is very lightly staffed. During the discussions before it was set up, there were suggestions that it should have expert help, and an official similar to the Comptroller and Auditor General was proposed.[23] But in fact no office of comparable skill and power has been set up. When the S.C.N.I. began, it was arranged for it to have the assistance of senior Treasury Civil servants who were concerned with aspects of the nationalized industries in their normal work. This was not very successful, and most of the work of the committee has been done with the assistance of one or two clerks – that is to say, officials of the House of Commons, including eventually a statistician. In July 1959 the committee produced a special report in which they asked for the services of an accountant and an economist, and the staff of the committee was augmented as a result.[24] A later step was the granting of the right to engage the services of independent experts as advisers; and Professor Maurice Peston and Professor A. H. Hanson served the committee in this capacity. The committee does not provide a rigorous examination of the efficiency of all parts of the industries: ' … it was not our duty to go into their day-to-day activities; it was not our duty to make an efficiency or financial audit; neither was it our duty to check in detail the rightness or wrongness of technical decisions and so on.'[25]

The success of the S.C.N.I. does not refute the arguments of those who feared detailed examination of day-to-day management; on the contrary, its achievements have been made possible by its restraint and its refusal to pursue minor points. Its function, usually, is to provide a clear explanation, in non-technical language, of the problems of the industries, accompanied by shrewd comments and criticisms. It is arguable that when it has attempted more, as with the *Ministerial Control* report, it has not done so well.

Further accountability

Should something more be done? The assistance provided for the S.C.N.I. is modest, and raises the question of whether more formidable investigations should take place.

The efficiency audit is a widely canvassed proposal of this nature. There are several versions, but in all there is essentially a body of expert assessors – cost accountants, management consultants, production engineers, and the like – who would carry out thorough examinations of aspects of the work of the industries. In early proposals, Professor W. A. Robson would have this done by an 'audit commission', with its reports available to the S.C.N.I.; Professor Sargant Florence and Mr Henry Maddick connect it with the work of consumer councils; Lord Morrison suggested that the public corporations themselves should control such a unit. In any case it would provide more than general comments on policies: it would provide specialist scrutiny, and measurement where possible, of the actual operations of the industries, in whole or in part. If constituted as a permanent body, it would acquire a knowledge and understanding of public enterprise which could lend great authority to its views.

The latest proposals of this kind were put before the S.C.N.I. in its *Ministerial Control* investigation by Professor Robson, Professor Hanson and Mr W. Thornhill. Attention was particularly drawn to the work of the Commission de Vérification des Comptes des Entreprises Publiques in France.[26]

This proposal has been strongly resisted by the boards, who regard the measurement of efficiency in this way as a function of management, not of external accountability. An audit unit, they believe, would become a fault-finding and perfectionist body in order to justify its own existence, and it would undermine the morale of management if outsiders professing superior skill were imposed upon them for the purpose of publishing criticisms.

There is no doubt some psychological truth in this attitude. But the assessment of efficiency could make a vital contribution to public accountability, and if the boards insist on its being an internal function, then the reports and surveys that emerge should be available at least to the Select Committee on Nationalized Industries.

Another scheme of public accountability, which was canvassed in the 1950s, was the periodic committee of inquiry. This was the method approved by the Labour Party. At first, intervals of seven years between inquiries for each industry were proposed, but in the policy document *Public Enterprise* of 1957, this was lengthened to ten years. The investigations would be conducted by Government committees constituted in the normal way: that is, varied and balanced sets of individuals chosen by a Minister, fresh for each inquiry. This is the system by which the broadcasting authorities, the B.B.C. and the I.B.A., are examined. It has not been applied methodically to industrial undertakings, though some inquiries have taken place which follow the principle roughly – the Chambers committee on London Transport (1955), the Herbert committee on electricity (1956), the Mackenzie committee on Scottish electricity (1962) and the Edwards committee on British air transport (1969). There have also been unpublished reports. The nationalized industries were not enamoured of this proposal either, especially if the inquiries were to take place at short intervals without any clear purpose, since such investigations take up a great deal of the boards' time and trouble. The successful establishment of the S.C.N.I. does not rule out these special inquiries, but it probably ensures that they will take place only when the Government has some definite purpose in mind, beyond general review.

All accountability is based on the presentation of information. It should not be forgotten that the public corporations are obliged by statute to publish extensive reports and accounts annually. These take the form of documents submitted to the relevant Minister, and are in turn presented by him to Parliament. Their scope and contents form the starting point of the inquiries of the S.C.N.I. The real strength of the system lies, however, in the fact that reports and accounts are published: and so a great amount of information, statistical and descriptive, is made available to all.

The report reviews the general financial and economic positions of the industry, including its sales and marketing problems; describes its production, its productivity and its technical advance during the year; gives an account of labour relations and personnel matters, and discusses research and training progress. Some are embellished with photographs. The accounts not only cover financial matters but also include non-monetary statistics of production, manpower, technical efficiency, and so on. Apart from the usual balance sheet and some other financial accounts, most information is presented in tabular form rather than as two-sided accounts. The first object of the accounts is to give a general view of the state of the industry; and notes on the accounts explain the methods used (e.g. for valuing stocks) to arrive at the figures. Special accounts for particular activities and sub-units are given, and tables are provided showing developments in production, profits or losses, and so on, over ten-year or similar periods. Annual reports of the main nationalized industries are usually documents of some forty to eighty pages, and the accounts are of similar length.

In finding out about the nationalized industries, perhaps the critics neglect the most obvious way. This is to communicate directly: to write a letter, or even to arrange an interview. No doubt there is a limit to the trouble staff can be expected to take, and some information which for commercial reasons they will not divulge. But in general, requests for information receive helpful replies. Nothing is more annoying to the public corporations in discussions of accountability than the assumption that, without parliamentary questions or statutory compulsions, no information would be available. There is, of course, more to accountability than information. Where facts are needed, however, the simplest course for Members of Parliament and private citizens alike is to write directly to the board's headquarters. A considerable correspondence is in practice dealt with throughout the year, and when parliamentary debates are in prospect many M.P.s are supplied with information, on the Opposition as well as the Government side. No official doctrine about the relations between a public corporation and the Opposition in Parliament has yet been formulated, but it has generally been assumed that greater freedom is possible than for civil servants. However, in July 1971 the Secretary of State for

Trade and Industry, Mr John Davies, suggested in a written answer in Parliament[27] that the time had come for the development of a code of practice in this matter. Most employees of nationalized concerns should be as free as those in other industries,

> It is, however, desirable that the senior staff of the corporations should establish a tradition of public service irrespective of party allegiances, and it follows that they must exercise a measure of discretion in political matters which will prevent them from engaging in the more controversial forms of political activity.

All the main nationalized industries have public relations and Press departments through which they try to spread understanding of their activities and build up the public reputation of their own industry. Some of the industries, such as coal and the railways, have large labour forces which are liable to be influenced by the image presented by the mass media. It is important, therefore, for the self-confidence of the industries as well as for their external standing, that the impact of publicity be favourable. Most industries advertise for sales and recruitment purposes as well as prestige. London Transport acquired an early reputation for the high quality of its posters and publicity material, and in recent years advertising-slogans like 'A living fire', 'High-Speed Gas' and 'It's quicker by Rail' have become as familiar as their private-enterprise counterparts.

Whatever its merits, publicity is not accountability, and a special aspect of the responsibility of the corporations remains to be covered.

CONSUMERS' REPRESENTATION

Though the Labour Government of 1945–51 accepted the theory of the managerial public corporation, it was sensitive to the interests which had been baulked of representation on the boards. It therefore provided in the statutes for compulsory collective bargaining and joint consultation with the workers in the industries.

It also set up machinery for the representation of consumers' interests.

At one time it was thought that the Government itself, being democratically elected, was an appropriate spokesman for the consumer. The pressures on Government action, and the motives behind it, however, are many, and in practice the interests of producers and its own political concerns have usually been to the fore. Since consumers are numerous, it is reasonable to regard relations with them as an aspect of accountability to the public: but since as consumers their interests are of a specific type, it is right that special machinery should be available to express their views. For the main nationalized industries, with the exception of the air corporations, consumers' councils or consultative councils were established. In the coal industry there are two: the Industrial Coal Consumers' Council and the Domestic Coal Consumers' Council. In electricity there is a consultative council in each Area, fourteen in all. There are also twelve gas consultative councils in the Areas, and since 1972 – when new arrangements were made – a central council as well. In transport there is a Central Transport Consultative Committee, as well as Transport Users' Consultative Committees for Scotland, Wales and nine English Areas. New councils have been set up for steel and the Post Office.

The number of members of each committee is about twenty, and they are all appointed by the relevant Minister. Otherwise there are considerable variations in administrative practice. The coal councils are financed by the Department of Trade and Industry, which provides administrative staff; in other cases expenses and staff are provided by the corporations. Frequency of meetings varies between eight a year for some gas or electricity councils, and sometimes only four for the transport committees. On the coal councils there are at least two representatives of the National Coal Board; in electricity the chairman of the consultative council is ex officio a member of the Area Board. Since 1962 the transport consultative committees, however, have had no representatives of the public corporations as members.

The selection of members by the Minister to represent the consuming public has given rise to some problems. A high proportion is drawn from local authorities, and hence from local political parties. For the rest, the usual method is to ask organized interest groups to suggest names, from which the Minister chooses individuals. However, some interests are not conveniently organized (domestic coal consumers, railways passengers), and there must be resort to women's organizations and other general bodies. These can suggest public-spirited individuals, but there is no guarantee that they have any particular background knowledge of the market or of consumers' affairs.

The purpose of these councils and committees is to make recommendations to the boards about consumers' needs, and to develop mutual understanding between suppliers and customers. Their field of interest lies between that of broad policy and that of petty grievances. When they were first established, they tended to discourage individual complaints; the general practice now is to insist that customers with grievances should first approach the management of the boards directly, but after continued dissatisfaction the councils are prepared to take up issues. The councils do not want to become general complaints bureaux, but they are open as channels of appeal, and it is obviously desirable that they should deal with the serious grievances of consumers. In fact the various councils now take up some thousands of complaints annually. Again, there is no point in spending time voicing obvious truisms, such as that consumers want lower prices. The reasons for increases, however, are explained to councils, and the structure of tariffs is discussed. Inefficiencies and waste which come to the notice of consumers can be brought to the attention of the boards. Standards and methods of service are, after prices, the main topic of interest. One of the difficulties of the Domestic Coal Consumers' Council is that the National Coal Board is normally not in direct touch with domestic consumers. There are some coal merchants on the council, but they are not in a position to redress complaints about other firms. Moreover, in these circumstances it is not easy to be sure in a particular matter how far the Coal Board may be at fault and how far the merchant.

The most significant work of the transport committees has been concerned with railway closures. It has been the practice for each proposed closure to be considered by the appropriate Transport Users' Consultative Committee. Objectors may appear before the committee, and the committee reports to the Minister of Transport, who makes the final decision. In these cases the committees are acting more in the role of public inquiries than as normal councils. In 1962 their structure was modified (the representatives of the railways being omitted), and a definite procedure for the cases was laid down. The duties of the committees are confined to reporting on hardship – how much would arise from a closure and how it might be alleviated. They do not go into the financial background, which is the prerogative of the railway management.

The impact of consumers' representation on the community has not been exciting. Many criticisms have been made of the system. First, it has been said that the relations between the corporations and the consumers' councils have been too close and too good. It should not be the function of a transport users' committee to assess fairly the arguments about branch-line closures – the committee should be the body that marshals the consumers' case before some other authority. The presence of board representatives on some councils has been particularly criticized; their expertise gives them a great advantage in discussion, and in any case their presence makes the councils moderate and impartial bodies instead of partisans of the consumers.

Secondly, the very existence of the councils is not widely known, and their complex structure makes it difficult for a consumer to understand them. A survey carried out in 1966[28] showed that though there were some areas where as many as 20 per cent of people interviewed were aware of the existence of a particular consultative council, in general lower percentages were found – much lower in the case of Transport Users' Consultative Committees. There has been discussion from time to time of ways of improving the position, and steps have been taken to this end, but no very drastic transformation has so far been achieved.

Thirdly, it is argued that the councils have too little money, too few staff and too little knowledge. They are in no position to challenge the boards' experts; they can only present a layman's view. It is important, of course, that the councils should retain a consumer outlook, and examine problems strictly from this point of view, limited in some respects as it may be. It is not part of the duty of consumers' representatives to set up as rival authorities on management. But nevertheless wide information, including comparative information, is necessary: and this type of expertise needs to be built up. It has been proposed that a central servicing unit for the various consumer councils should be set up, which would facilitate 'monitoring' of aspects of the work of the industries where there is close consumer contact, such as timekeeping by trains or speed of telephone connections.[29] Other proposals have looked to unification of the councils, or to the creation of a consumers' ombudsman. In recent years some of the councils – such as that for the Post Office – have widened their activities by employing the services of consultants.

The fundamental problem for consumer councils, however, lies in their relationship with their clientele, the consumers. The members owe their positions to appointment by the Minister, and the councils have had to cultivate relations with the public. There was no great popular demand for them at their inception, and at their worst they seemed like heads without bodies, looking after the interests of people who were unaware of this protection. In the 1960s, however, a widely based movement for consumer protection gathered strength, and resulted in greater public interest in consumer matters. These developments may provide what the machinery for consumers' representation in nationalized industry most needs – popular backing and pressure. They are then likely to obtain the resources of staff and expertise they require, because the need for them will be manifest. Certainly contacts with other consumer bodies (instead of the corporations themselves) would help to create a better consumer ambience for their work.

Some other bodies concerned with the regulation of public enterprise may be mentioned here for the sake of completeness. The Transport Act of 1947 established the Transport Tribunal (in succession to a Railway Rates Tribunal). This consisted of three members appointed by the Minister of Transport, and its authorization was necessary for schemes of charges in nationalized transport. Under the 1953 Act, schemes setting out only maximum charges were authorized, and such a scheme came into operation in 1957 on the railways. Traders could be charged less if the transport authorities wished. When increases were proposed, the Tribunal held hearings at which objections were raised from a miscellany of sources. It then issued its decision, which commonly made cuts in the proposals without giving reasons. The justification of this system lay in the monopoly power once held by transport services, particularly railways. In fact the railways have had to meet strong challenges in recent years from road services, whose charges were unregulated. Between 1948 and 1962 the Tribunal and other controls served to hamper competition in transport. The work of the Transport Tribunal has therefore been drastically reduced; after 1962 it dealt only with charges for passenger transport in London, and dock charges; and in 1969 it was deprived of its duties towards London passengers.

Another regulatory agency with special relevance to nationalized industries is the Civil Aviation Authority which since April 1972 has taken over (among other duties) the work of the Air Registration Board and the Air Transport Licensing Board. It thus tests the airworthiness of new aircraft and the skill of maintenance engineers, and also grants licences for regular services and controls charges on internal routes. It is advised by an Airworthiness Requirements Board on some matters. The Mining Qualifications Board determines the technical competence of mine managers, and the relevant ministries, not the corporations, control the Mines Inspectorate and the Railways Inspectorate, both concerned with safety questions.

Since December 1970 the activities of the nationalized industries have been subject to the investigations of the Monopolies Commission; and a report concerned with electricity and gas connection charges was made by that body in July 1972. As a result, a standard set of charges was accepted by the electricity boards.

These bodies are outside the main stream of accountability and control. An attempt must now be made to put the general position in perspective.

THEORY AND PRACTICE

Habitually, the problems of accountability and ministerial control have been discussed in terms of too much or too little. The dangers of too much supervision have been emphasized by the 'business efficiency' school of thought; the scandals of too little have been pointed out by those who stressed the need for the application of constitutional and democratic principles. In fact, the issue of 'more' or 'less' supervision has been misleading. The real need is to devise satisfactory *methods* of control and accountability, for there is general agreement that detailed administration should be left alone and that the boards should be answerable somehow for major policy. The main method of accountability (the S.C.N.I.) has come near to a solution of its side of the problem; the main method of ministerial control (informal consultation) is less widely accepted.

One of the perennial fears of the boards is that they will be expected to cope with restrictions and behavioural standards appropriate to a public institution, while at the same time their performance is assessed according to the standards used for business enterprise. The sort of achievement that should be aimed at is discussed in the next chapter. But it is relevant here to point out that accountability for private industry is a very limited affair indeed. The theory of the joint-stock public company is that its directors are responsible to the shareholders, and answerable to them at annual and other general meetings. In practice this procedure is almost always a formality, and there exists great managerial freedom, highly prized by leading businessmen. It is, of course, only the boards of directors themselves who are so unhampered by supervision: within the structure of large business organizations, systems of review and control operate of necessity. But not having to explain past actions became a custom of industrial management at the top, and this habitual freedom has made businessmen wary of different situations.

There is a sense in which private-enterprise companies may be held to be publicly accountable as well as accountable to their shareholders. They are required to publish certain information, and under certain circumstances the Secretary of State for Trade and Industry can order an inquiry into a company's affairs. These arrangements are almost entirely concerned with the protection of investors and prospective investors. The conception of industrial management as a form of trusteeship, with responsibilities to employees, consumers and the community, is widely held among businessmen today. But it has not been given any institutional form, and the public accountability of private enterprise remains rudimentary.

The question arises, of course, whether all techniques of accountability are as frustrating to initiative as businessmen usually have supposed. The notion of public accountability has normally been associated only with public ownership; but it is not, in the case of the nationalized industries, dependent on the spending of public money. If the principle is rather that of a fundamental responsibility to the community, then methods of accountability for large privately owned industrial concerns may be sought for.[30]

At all events, the disparity in public accountability has involved a disparity in public knowledge. If this leads to sounder public understanding, then it is to the advantage of the nationalized concerns; but if it leads to denigration and stress on their failings, then the absence of comparable sources of information about private industry can cause widespread resentment.

This chapter has shown how the two principles of Government control and public accountability have grown apart. The duty of public accountability, in the sense of giving explanations of how responsibilities are being carried out, does not necessarily imply control or further intervention. Only if it demonstrates serious deficiencies does it do that. It does provide a background of informed opinion, however, against which active control must operate.

It may be argued that the most serious result of the separation of accountability from control is constitutional. The influence of the Ministers on the industries is now much greater than they need acknowledge in the House of Commons, for they cannot readily be made responsible for private discussions. If a deficiency in public accountability remains, it is less with the industries themselves than with the Minister's power over the industries. However, Ministers hold private discussions with trade associations and many other bodies, as all students of interest-group activities know, and it would be absurd to expect different arrangements with public corporations.

These developments – in accountability and in strong government influence – have led some critics to doubt the permanence of the public corporation as an independent institution. Professor A. H. Hanson, for example, states that '... one could write a history of public enterprise in this country since 1946 under the title of "The Decline and Fall of the Autonomous Public Corporation". Although its final chapters are still on the stocks, the general trend is unmistakable.'[31] Professor Hanson goes on to argue that similar trends exist in other countries, and that the need for the public corporation arose from misunderstandings about business efficiency. He suggests that it might be possible 'to preserve the form and something of the spirit of the public corporation and yet hold the nationalized industry entirely responsible to its Minister'.[32]

In fact, the 'decline' of the public corporation has not been a decline in the corporate form for public trading activities: it has only been a decline in the autonomy of such bodies. The distinct Government agency for business-type activities continues in most countries, and its widespread adoption in different parts of the world is one of the greatest tributes to its viability. In Britain atomic energy has been transferred from a Government department to an independent agency. The Post Office has moved since 1933 in the direction of greater commercial independence, and in 1969 it became a public corporation. Thus the detachment of public industrial enterprise from the main structure of the Civil Service is hardly in question: separate staffing, the corporate form and commercial accounting procedures have come to be practical necessities. The industrial undertakings are not comparable with governmental bodies trading in a marginal way. Their conduct cannot be left to routine: it constantly needs policy decisions of an entrepreneurial character. Following the Fulton report on the Civil

Service in 1968, there have been efforts to discover means of 'hiving off' further activities from the central government departments.

What is at stake, in fact, is not the public corporation *form* at all, but the degree of control and the nature of accountability.

It should be remembered that, as stated in Chapter 2, the detachment of the public corporation is only one feature of a much wider movement this century towards administrative independence. The causes of this are various, but they include the need for functional efficiency and the need to concentrate the attention of Parliament and Ministers on major issues. At all events, the general pressures for institutional variety in public bodies do not seem to have abated, and the position of the industrial public corporations cannot now be considered unusual or anomalous or experimental – there are too many institutions in similar circumstances.

There are some grounds for supposing that the idea of the public corporation, therefore, still has validity. It is certainly true that ministerial control in some cases is very close. But this varies, as indeed the Ministers' concern with the private sector varies from industry to industry and from time to time. At least the public corporation offers scope for the relaxation and reimposition of Government control and parliamentary attention. It is not dead yet.

7 The Aims of Nationalization

THE MERE fact of ending private ownership in some of Britain's basic industries was undoubtedly a major political transformation. The new public corporations have had to cope with problems of organization and control, reviewed in previous chapters. The fundamental issues now to be examined concern the objectives of public enterprise once it is securely established.

It was once a commonplace with both admirers and critics of capitalism that the object of private enterprises was to make as much profit as possible for their owners. In fact, the motives and behaviour of the controllers of private business are (and probably always were) more subtle and complex than this crude generalization implies. Nevertheless, profit-seeking still provides a rationale for such concerns when they are in doubt about policy decisions; and it was on this assumption that ideas of competition in industry and the economists' theory of the firm were built.

No such simple rule exists for public enterprises, and the principles on which they are to be run are matters of deep controversy. The question that has to be answered, indeed, is that of the ultimate purpose of the activities of the nationalized industries: what, in the end, are their objectives?

The objects of private firms are decided by their directors and owners: whether they are wholly self-regarding, or whether they acknowledge a variety of responsibilities, is for them to decide, according to their lights. For nationalized concerns the issue runs deeper. It is a matter of public policy; of how the community as a whole should best be served. It is thus a matter of social or political philosophy. In the discussion that follows in this chapter much of the terminology is economic, but this should not disguise the fact that value judgments are necessary, and that very general assumptions about the nature of society underlie many of the issues in dispute. The way in which such considerations force themselves into the discussion – which arises from the needs of practical administrators in search of guidance – makes the topic almost as crucial for the political theorist as the question of public ownership itself.

The assumptions of the nationalizers

A beginning may be made by recalling the hopes and beliefs of those who were moved to end private ownership in these industries. What were their expectations?

They did not profess to have answers to all future problems, and they did not foresee many of them. Mostly they were persuaded that the weaknesses of the old system were so manifest that its replacement was the great issue. Other bridges – administrative, technical – might be crossed when they were reached. They had, however, a general background of economic ideas that were relevant.

First, the public enterprises would be non-profit-making. There would be no shareholders demanding satisfaction, and therefore the controllers of the concerns would not have to serve their interests. Nor were the industries to make profit for the purposes of the State. In the hands of a radical reformer like Joseph Chamberlain, municipal enterprise was used for revenue purposes, to reduce the rates. The break-even principle embodied in the nationalization Acts eschewed any such purposes.

Secondly, the nationalizers thought poorly of competition, certainly in the industries concerned. They recast the industries under unified management with monopolistic powers. The new corporations were regarded as vehicles for the administration of entire industries, rather than as enlarged firms.

Thirdly, the industries were enjoined to serve 'the public interest' in some sense. The full implications of this phrase were not clear, but it emphasized the rejection of private or sectional interests; and thus embodied one of the main political values of the development.

Fourthly, the industries would be subordinate to the Government and would be expected to co-operate fully with the Government's plans. In part, these plans would be prompted by Keynesian desires to maintain economic activity in the face of weak demand, but they would also be expected to help the location of industry and other political aims.

In the event, these views could serve only as the merest skeleton for policy guidance. At first there were urgent tasks to perform – reorganizing industries, rehabilitating equipment after years of neglect, and overcoming serious shortages as peacetime demands asserted themselves. In these circumstances the question of the ideal policy seemed, to practical minds, academic and abstract.

Nevertheless, practical administrators were soon in need of guidance: about investment, about pricing, and about various priorities. Even before the post-war emergencies were over, it became necessary to form some ideas about the future development of nationalization, and for this purpose it was clear that the motives (and prejudices) of the original nationalizers provided no adequate basis. Moreover, the Labour Government was replaced by a Conservative one in 1951, after only three or four years of nationalization, and even where it did not denationalize, the new Government felt able to search for new styles of conduct.

The statutes

To some extent the views of the Labour Government that carried through the nationalization process have been perpetuated because they were embodied in the statutes. They included rules about ministerial control, and they prescribed general duties relating to the public interest. The National Coal Board, for example, is charged with: '. . . making supplies of coal available, of such qualities and sizes, in such quantities and at such prices, as may seem to them best calculated to further the public interest in all respects, including the avoidance of any undue or unreasonable preference or advantage'.[1] Other nationalization Acts have similar passages. They also prescribe the break-even rule for finance – that revenue shall not be less than outgoings, taking one year with another – and so give some sketchy guidance for pricing policy.

The Transport Act of 1947 had prescribed a 'properly integrated' system as the goal of transport policy, but this was repealed by the Conservatives, just as they revised the structure of the electricity industry by legislation.

PRICING POLICY

The goods and services produced by nationalized industries are sold, in more or less free markets, to other industrial concerns or to final consumers. Prices are therefore subject to the forces of supply and demand, and the effects of variations in charges depend on conditions in the markets for the products. In Chapter 6 the great influence exercised by the Government on the prices charged by the public corporations was discussed. But how should these prices be decided?

In order to cover their costs as prescribed (and without aiming to maximize their profits), most of the nationalized industries began by basing their prices on the average of their costs. Critics, mainly economists, objected to this practice, and a long controversy about the merits of rival pricing rules took place. The argument of the critics favoured 'marginal costs' as the basis of prices, instead of average cost, and the controversy centred mainly on the coal industry. It is more costly to produce coal from some pits than others, and it was suggested that coal prices should be raised to the level of high-cost production (i.e. costs at the margin). This would encourage the efficient use of coal. It would also lead to a more accurate picture of the coal industry's claims to further development, since its higher prices would reflect the cost of producing additional coal. This case should be distinguished from another case for raising coal prices, which was based on the desirability of financing investment as far as possible from the Board's own resources.

The arguments about marginal- versus average-cost pricing flourished in academic as well as practical circles.[2] At first it was clear that marginal-cost prices would be substantially higher prices, and coal-consuming industries were reluctant to appreciate theoretical arguments leading to higher fuel costs. Moreover, the Government was engaged, in the 1950s as in later years, in a long struggle to hold down the general price level. In the Coal Board the concept of marginal cost seemed to have little relevance: in an extractive industry, additional production 'at the margin' was not available. Enlargement of output, then being attempted, depended on a long-term programme of new investment. Again, the effects of marginal-cost pricing on coal industry finances would be extremely dramatic. Before 1957 there was a coal shortage, and marginal cost was well above average cost; this would have ensured large surpluses. The situation changed, and marginal cost became much lower than average cost. Prices at this level would have involved very great losses.

The pricing policies of nationalized industries were also criticized for excessive uniformity. There was a tendency to charge flat rates for the whole country, irrespective of cost differences. Thus the Coal Board quoted prices for coal for domestic purposes delivered (to the merchants), and not pit-head prices – transport costs being averaged over the whole supply of this type of coal. The railways charged the same rate per mile for passengers at all times, though the rush-hour travellers made necessary much equipment that would not otherwise be required. Similarly, electricity consumed at peak hours – for which extra capacity is needed – was priced at the standard rate.

Over the years there have been considerable modifications to this practice. Differential tariffs have been introduced in the electricity industry; there is differential pricing in gas between districts; since 1956 railway charges for freight have taken account of commercial considerations and in later years a variety of cheap passenger fares have been introduced; in 1961 the price of industrial coal produced in Scotland and the north-west (where costs are generally high) was raised above the standard level. Nevertheless, there is still some averaging in the nationalized industries. One reason for retaining it is administrative convenience, and another consumers' preference for seemingly equal treatment. But there are also possible grounds of public policy, and further consideration is given to the question later in the chapter.

What is the significance of these controversies for the aims of nationalization? Broadly, those who advocated marginal-cost pricing and discrimination between consumers did so on economic grounds. They conceived the nationalized industries as very large firms, and expected them to be concerned with the maximization of economic advantage for the community, through the proper allocation of resources. Some thought that imposing these principles on the public corporations was making the best of a bad job; others thought nationalization could have positive advantages for the achievement of economic rationality. 'Nationalization undoubtedly provides the ideal framework within which a proper integration of costs and prices could easily be arranged . . . But the framework has not been used in this way.'[3]

In any case, the object of marginal pricing was to make the position of the nationalized industries dependent on consumers' preferences as these operated through the price mechanism. In Britain, democratic socialists and planners had always assumed that the freedom of the consumer would remain. Marginal-cost pricing would ensure, it was claimed, that consumers' choices were reflected in the relative prosperity (and future-output decisions) of industries. In principle the nationalized industries should be treated no differently from other industries, and their behaviour should be that which is expected, ideally, from competitive firms. The interests of the nation were best expressed through the market – a reformed market if necessary – and to allow nationalization to distort market forces was to betray economic rationality.

The advocates of average-cost prices were not flatly opposed to these arguments: typically, they doubted only their practicability. But there was more than a hint of a different attitude to nationalization in the remarks of some members of the Ridley committee:

> . . . in their opinion the overriding principle is that coal is so important to the economy that it should be sold at the lowest price which is consistent with the National Coal Board's covering its costs. Indeed they assume that one advantage of the nationalization of coal is to realize this principle . . .[4]

In other words, a nationalized corporation should follow different principles from a privately owned one.

The disagreement about pricing policy was in fact the forerunner of a wider controversy about the behaviour appropriate to a nationalized industry.

THE HERBERT REPORT AND THE COMMERCIAL SOLUTION

Various implications of the report of the Herbert committee on electricity supply, published in 1956, have been discussed in previous chapters. Its most important contribution, however, lay in its thoroughgoing commendation of commercial principles: 'We state our view without any qualification that the governing factor in the minds of those running the Boards should be that it is their duty to run them as economic concerns and to make them pay.'[5]

The report carried the discussion well beyond the issue of pricing policy. It considered the role of the industry as a trading body, and declared at the outset that its efficiency was to be measured in strictly economic terms: success depended on meeting wants at the lowest possible cost. The committee dealt with all non-economic considerations that might affect policy by saying that they should be left to the decision of the Government.

In the report there was no shrinking from the consequences of its declared principles. The price of electricity was to be related as closely as possible to its costs, and those customers who caused the cost to rise should meet the increase: 'The first principle of tariff-making should be to secure that charges reflect the costs of supply.' Capital for the nationalized industries, said the report, would best be raised on the open market, without any special guarantees by the Government – though this should not apply to electricity if it did not also apply to the other nationalized industries.

Three examples of the committee's approach in more specific matters may be given. In its purchases of heavy electrical plant, the Central Authority had given precedence to British manufacturers, and had not sought tenders from abroad. The Herbert committee condemned this, and recommended that 'the Electricity Boards should seek the best and cheapest plant . . . irrespective of origin.' Again, owing to the distances involved, the costs of connecting new customers in rural areas are greater than in towns. The boards should charge the customers for this, and the rate of progress in making connections should be decided by the normal economic and commercial tests. The retail trading of the boards through their showrooms should be as vigorous and commercially progressive as that of other concerns, and in hire purchase, for instance, they should charge whatever rate the market would bear, despite their ability to finance hire-purchase cheaply.[6]

The general philosophy of the Herbert report may be summed up thus. The decisive criteria for judging an industry are economic; other matters are peripheral. The nationalized industries should be directed exclusively towards satisfying these economic standards; other considerations should be imposed, if necessary, by the Government. The committee scarcely concealed its view that there would be few occasions on which such interference was desirable; nor did it conceal that private industry provided the model and exemplar of what it proposed.

> We attach great importance therefore to the industry being run on business lines. It should have one duty and one duty alone: to supply electricity to those who will meet the costs of it and to do so at the lowest possible expenditure of resources consistent with the maintenance of employment standards at the level of the best private firms. Any deviation from this task should be undertaken only on precise instructions.[7]

The merits and the practicability of these unambiguous principles must now be examined.

Difficulties of commercial principles

In Chapter 6 it was explained that Government control over the nationalized industries had been greater than anticipated at the outset. This in itself indicates that the freedom of action associated with commercial principles has not been forthcoming. In spite of the appeal that such principles had for Conservative politicians, it was not found possible to apply very readily the doctrines of the Herbert report to all the nationalized industries. The Government's attitude was declared in a White Paper in 1961; but before this is described, the difficulties need to be explained.

(1) *Social costs*. Production always entails costs; in other words, some resources are used when goods or services are provided. For the use of resources – for labour, for capital or for raw material – the producing organization normally pays, and so meets its costs of production.

In practice, however, not all costs are charged to the producing organization. Undesired effects of productive activity constitute costs, but sometimes the incidence of these effects is so widespread and indeterminate that no effective method of payment can be contrived. In other cases services are provided for the community at large, and producers do not pay for the use they make of them, except as general taxpayers. Examples of indeterminate incidence include pollution of the air by smoke and fumes, and inconvenience brought about by the operations of industry and transport – aircraft noise, for example. The provision of roads is an obvious example of a community service used by producers. The principle of both types is the same – costs of production are borne in some way by the community in general, not by the enterprise itself.

When an enterprise behaves solely in its own interest, it does not bother about these sorts of costs, because it does not have to pay for them directly. They are met in some way or other by the community as a whole, either by tax-financed provision or by leaving the general public to bear the losses they bring about. They are therefore part of 'social costs' (that is, the costs to society as a whole), but not of private or business costs. The term 'social costs' as normally used by economists means 'total costs to society'; and it includes private costs.

In some cases, of course, better accounting and more ingenious methods of payment might enable some costs, now paid socially, to be brought home to those responsible. In the nature of things, however, full social costs are not easily chargeable.

From the operations of a nationalized industry, unpaid social costs may be incurred on a considerable scale, for they are large industries and often basic to the rest of the economy. What responsibility should the public corporations take for these costs?

The situation may best be explained through leading examples. Aircraft noise has already been mentioned. Do the public airlines have responsibilities in this matter, beyond complying with regulations? Should they sponsor research? Should they operate quieter aircraft, if these are otherwise less efficient? It is clear that something should be done about this matter; what is not so clear is the distribution of responsibilities. Perhaps the Government should enforce stricter regulations. But without research and experience it is hard for them to judge what is practicable. If the corporations fly different aircraft, should they be compensated for any loss of revenue this brings about?

The extension of overhead electricity cables and pylons arouses perennial controversy. It costs ten or more times as much to put lines underground as it does to run them overhead; yet it is generally held that pylons and wires can do great damage to the beauty of landscape. How is this damage to be assessed, and at what point does it become worth while to put them underground? The problem was made particularly severe by the erection of a new 'supergrid' in the 1960s, and by the policy of building large, efficient power stations near the sources of fuel – that is, coalfields and oil refineries. It is cheaper to convey the electricity by cable to the big consuming areas (such as London) than to site the power stations there and transport the fuel. Nevertheless, the pylons bring about a social cost which, if it could be measured, might affect the economics of the situation.

One of the best-known problems of social cost concerns the Scottish coalfield. (Social values and long-term considerations, discussed below, are also involved.) Many of the pits in Scotland operate at relatively high cost, and the National Coal Board is often urged to close them down. If this were done, there would be considerable unemployment and distress in mining towns and villages.[8] Much 'social capital' – housing, public services – would become redundant; and there would possibly arise a need for new social capital in places to which ex-miners moved. Should these costs, which fall on society as a whole, be estimated and taken into account by the Coal Board in deciding the future of the pits? Should the Board consider only the welfare of the industry, and leave social institutions to take care of the social consequences? Or are there other possibilities?

The greatest problems of social cost, however, are probably those concerning the transport system. In the first place, one form of transport (motor) uses facilities (roads) provided by the community. There is therefore a question of whether road users – especially particular types of road users – pay adequately, through taxation, for this provision. If they do not, then they have an artificial advantage over rival forms of transport (rail and air). Secondly, increased traffic on the roads brings about congestion, delay and general loss of amenity for road users – that is, it causes social costs. Thirdly, when the retention of old forms of transport (such as the railway branch lines) or the building of new ones (such as motorways) is considered, the general advantage to a locality of good communications needs to be reckoned – many people benefit who never actually travel. There can be social gains as well as social losses.

It is in the transport field that the most elaborate attempts have been made to incorporate social costs into economic calculations. A technique of 'cost-benefit analysis' has been developed by which the full economic advantages and disadvantages to the community of a transport service can be measured.[9] It sometimes involves fairly bold estimation (e.g. in putting a money value on delays caused by congestion), but nevertheless provides a more reliable guide to the economics of transport services than do commercial accounts. Again, the question is whether nationalized transport itself should be guided by this type of analysis, or whether the analysis should be used by the Government merely to impose restraints.

(2) *Social and political values.* Important as they may be, social costs do not constitute the only 'social' problem for nationalization. The fundamental issue is whether or not industrial policy is to be formulated in purely economic terms, and whether economic criteria alone provide a proper standard of judgment. Social costs are themselves an economic concept, and their consideration in policy-making serves only to establish a wider economic objective instead of a merely commercial one. There are, however,

other matters generally described as 'social' which cannot be dealt with in this way. These are social values such as freedom, equality, social justice and community spirit. We do not normally judge a society merely by its standard of living. We expect a variety of principles to be observed. Moreover, there is often agitation for reform and desire for improvement in directions which cannot be tested against the measuring rod of economic efficiency. Should such matters be taken into account in shaping the aims of national-ized industries?

Some examples may clarify the issue. In both employment and in customer relations there arise opportunities for racial or colour discrimination. Many people would expect the practice of a public corporation in such matters to be determined without reference to economic advantage. Publicly owned buses, for example, and British Railway hotels should not operate a colour bar, whatever effect there might be on their revenue. Again, when the public houses of Carlisle and nearby districts were nationalized, the objectives were not to maximize sales and profits: on the con-trary, caution and restraint in sales were required at the time.

Scotland is a country with its own national identity. In order to sustain this identity within the United Kingdom, there is a need for social and economic standards to be comparable with those in England. If, therefore, the preservation of the quality of Scottish life is considered an end in itself worth pursuing, then industries may have to adapt their policies with this in mind. Similar con-siderations apply to Wales. It is also considered by many people that life in rural England should be sustained for its intrinsic social and aesthetic qualities. Transport and other services, particularly electricity, are therefore urged to make special efforts to meet rural needs.

A final example is provided by the employee's situation in modern industry. In spite of emergency provision through social services, most people are dependent on payment from work for their livelihood. Continuous and secure employment has great im-portance for the maintenance of the tenor of individual and family life, therefore, beyond its economic function as an exchange of purchasing power for current labour services. It may be held, consequently, that employment should be maintained wherever possible, and that individual enterprises have social obligations in this matter, since they are the direct providers of employment and actively demand the services of employees most of the time.

In short, these examples derive from conceptions of 'society' and 'social' as something wider, more comprehensive, and in some ways embodying higher values than 'economy' and 'economic'. In consequence, the economic organization should, it is claimed, adapt the requirements of its own maximum efficiency to meet the greater human needs described as 'social'.

There is also a political order, which in turn has requirements for successful functioning. To meet them, an industrial enterprise might be expected, for example, to accept collective bargaining and joint consultation, and to eschew personal and partisan discrimination, whether or not these were to its commercial advantage. The system of public accountability described in the last chapter can be justified as a contribution to the *political* well-being of the nation, irrespective of its effect on the efficiency of the nationalized industries.

The counter-arguments to these views do not deny that 'social' and 'political' values are often of great importance, though it can be suggested that they are used merely as forms of resistance to change. What is disputed is the responsibility for taking care of such values. All social activity, including economic activity, has side effects and long-run consequences, many of which cannot be foreseen. It is not reasonable, it is argued, to expect industrial managers to make assessments of these matters. Particular institutions should concentrate on doing their own jobs well, and for nationalized industries this means concentrating on economic efficiency. If in some cases there is a pressing need to look to social or political matters, then this should be done by those responsible, presumably the Government itself. Where action is considered necessary, it should be imposed by external authority. This solution – leaving non-commercial matters to the Government – recurs throughout this chapter. Its adoption might mean the clarification of responsibilities, but it is probably too much to hope that there would be any clear distinction between social values and the other factors – social costs, national economy, and the long term – discussed in this section. Yet the existence of this category is perhaps the most fundamental point to grasp about the formulation of policy objectives – because it is the most difficult to assimilate to any formula.

It is sometimes claimed, of course, that the techniques of cost-benefit measurement do yield such a formula; that by this means the best possible assessment of all factors is taken into consideration. Critics nevertheless maintain that this merely provides a particular form of rationality; that quantification based on 'best estimates', which are nevertheless extremely doubtful, is not sensible; and that other frames of reference are possible, and what they show has also rational validity. The controversies about the Roskill report of 1970 on the siting of the third London airport have so far provided the main focus for this issue.[10]

(3) *The national economy.* The nationalized industries are adjured by statute to pay attention to 'the public interest'. This constitutes an obligation to work for something more than the good of themselves or any other limited group or section of the community. When the extent and causes of ministerial intervention were set out in Chapter 6, the key role of ideas about the national interest was apparent, the most important notion being that of central direction of the economy in order to maintain full employment, to check inflation and to promote growth. This implies that the policies of the nationalized industries were to be subordinated to more general ends. The subordination has had two aspects.

In the first place, the formulation of high policy for the industries should take place with the broad economic prospects for the nation in the forefront. In other words, there should be an attempt to foresee a role for the industry in the economy. The success of a particular nationalized industry should be achieved in such a way that it harmonizes with other industrial developments. Ultimately, it is the success of the whole economy that is aimed at, and the success of a nationalized industry is measured by its contribution to the total situation.

Secondly, nationalized industries are expected to co-operate to the full in the current economic policies of the Government of the day. Wages, prices and investment programmes have all had to be adapted to comply with emergency programmes devised by the Government to meet critical economic situations. The story of the attempts by the Government to direct the economy in the 1950s and the means used to promote stability and progress are too complex to rehearse here. The programmes were applied, of course, over the whole economy and not just in the public sector. But the political and administrative power of the Government ensured that such measures were not neglected or evaded by the public corporations; indeed, there was a feeling that unless the nationalized industries provided a good example, other enterprises could scarcely be expected to comply.

An early example of how the policy of a nationalized industry was expected to fit in with national needs was given by Sir James Bowman, chairman of the National Coal Board, in 1957. The prices obtainable for British coal in Europe were much higher than those on the home market, yet only limited exports were allowed by the Government, in view of the need for adequate fuel supplies in Britain.[11] From the point of view of the economy as a whole, this might have been reasonable, but it was clearly not in the interest of the Coal Board's finances.

In the early 1970s this sort of consideration became of dominating importance. The style of national economic management preferred by the Conservative Government meant that nationalized industries had to maintain price restraints (and to attempt resistance to wage claims) that brought their finances into difficulties more widespread than hitherto in their existence.

It must be emphasized that the national interest in these matters is conceived in economic terms. Social and political values are not necessarily at stake here. The difficulty for the 'commercial solution' is, rather, that the nationalized industries have been expected to sacrifice their own immediate financial advantage to *wider* economic objectives. Clearly, non-commercial factors discussed under other headings may also be national in scope.

(4) *The long term.* There is a further type of public interest which has affected nationalization policies but which is difficult to classify. Considerations of this type are not commercial, because they

could not enter into the ordinary calculations or accounts of the corporations. They may, however, be at least partly economic in character, if guesses and hopes about *future* material welfare can be regarded as economic. Since the benefit will mainly accrue, if at all, to later generations, it may perhaps be right to regard attention to them as being fundamentally of a moral or ideological character.

The atomic energy programme for civil purposes is perhaps the most striking example. It is largely a research and development activity, and so far none of the nuclear power stations that have resulted have been able to produce electricity as cheaply as modern conventional stations. Nevertheless, the programme is persisted with. Since 1965 it has been claimed that at last a new type of advanced gas-cooled reactor is being developed that will make nuclear generation economically worth while. 'Fast breeder' reactors may eventually be even more advantageous. There also appears to be in the background a belief in the need to develop nuclear technology in Britain as an essential scientific skill; to neglect it would endanger the country's future intellectual, if not economic, independence. Similar arguments are advanced about the computer industry.

This is, of course, only one aspect of the question of the security of future fuel supplies. The demand for productive energy in the world has been rising rapidly and seems likely to continue to do so. The costs and availability of supplies for Britain from abroad must always be relatively uncertain, in face of this rising world demand, and it is therefore argued that prudence dictates special care of indigenous production, mainly the coal industry. Mining skills, technology and capital equipment are all highly specific; closed pits cannot be reopened like factories; and the development of new mines is expensive and slow. The long-term needs of Britain for secure energy supplies therefore imply some protection for the coal industry against short-run fluctuations in market forces. Arguments of this sort were used in the discussions on national fuel policy in the 1960s. They secured limited acceptance – mainly resulting in support which slowed the run-down of the industry.

The rehabilitation of the railways affords a further example. Market forces allowed to operate commercially would not have sustained the railways as a going concern, let alone provided capital for modernization. Yet future transport needs are likely to be such that an efficient railway system will be essential, and investment now by the Government can be justified by future economic and social requirements.

The situation of the airlines also contains elements that may be regarded as matters of long-term faith, though national prestige is said to be involved as well. At least up to 1964, B.O.A.C. flew certain international routes, subsidized some other connected airlines, and ordered British-made aircraft to an extent which could be regarded as commercially prudent only on the most optimistic calculation of future developments. In July 1964 the Minister of Aviation, Mr Julian Amery, insisted that B.O.A.C. take twenty British VC-10 aircraft, though the chairman, Sir Giles Guthrie, would have preferred to cancel the orders and buy American aircraft instead. This helped the British aircraft construction industry, whose continued survival was thought to be in the long-term national interest.

When the supply of capital is involved in these problems, it may be said that private investors are capable of taking a long-term view, and that their judgments of future national needs (and hence of the future prospects of the industries) are likely to be as reliable as those of the Government. The sums involved are often very large, however; and the long term may be very long indeed. The answer of the capital market, in fact, is not in doubt: the funds would not be available. In these circumstances the Government has to decide for itself whether the future, as it sees it, justifies special treatment for the industries.

Cross-subsidization

These four types of difficulties show that the principle of commercial operation cannot be applied easily and without qualification. Before there can be any general assessment of the argument, however, a further issue must be broached – that of cross-subsidization and subsidies in general. If there are, for argument's sake, to be activities of public corporations that do not pay for themselves, how are they to be sustained? How is the extra finance to be provided?

The essential principle of cross-subsidization may be explained briefly. Production involves costs, and since it is the consumer who gets the benefit of the production, it seems appropriate that the producing organization should look to him to meet the full costs of what he receives. If this does not happen, there is a likelihood of misdirection of production, for strong demand will arise from people who are being undercharged. Moreover, if the demand from consumers is not a fair reflection of their wants, then the controllers of industry will make distorted decisions when planning future production. In any case, the payment of artificially low prices by one set of consumers means that others are paying unnecessarily high prices; that is, a subsidy is being paid. If this process occurs within the range of a single organization, it constitutes a concealed or cross-subsidy.

In a sense, cross-subsidies are unavoidable in business operations. It is impossible to cost every sale; and in any case prices must be announced in advance, before all costs can be known. In practice the problem is concerned with charges made for similar types of products or ranges of goods, or to similar classes of customers. That is to say, should cross-subsidization occur, even though it may be administratively practicable to avoid it?

There are many instances of this problem in the nationalized industries. The Electricity Act of 1947 instructed the new boards to 'promote the simplification and standardization of methods of charge'. This principle invited cross-subsidization, for a simple tariff might not reflect the different costs involved in supplying different types of customer (e.g. industrial, commercial and domestic) at different times of day (peak hours and off-peak). Similarly, on the railways fares are standardized, though costs on different routes, at different seasons and at different times, may vary greatly. The problem appears more acutely where really high-cost supplies are involved, and where easily reckoned losses are incurred. Some of the problems have already been mentioned, such as the high-cost coal mined in Scotland, the expensive rail services on branch lines, some air routes and rural electrification. Normal or 'standard' charges in these cases mean (if there is no external subsidy and the board concerned is not making a loss) that other customers are paying more than they need. Therefore, besides the question of actually maintaining these high-cost services, for social or national reasons, there arises the question of whether the other customers of the boards are the appropriate source of funds for the purpose. This constitutes the essence of the cross-subsidization issue.

Cross-subsidization may take more subtle forms, though the issue is the same in principle. Certain railway or airline routes may pay very well, but no reduction in charge is made, because the corporation wants to build up its profits or its reserves, or check its losses. Revenue from profitable services may in practice enable a corporation to offer keen prices where it faces sharp competition or wishes to make a special effort. The Coal Board, for instance, tries to keep down the price of anthracite, though it is expensive to produce, in order to compete in the market for domestic central heating. A distinction may perhaps be made between cross-subsidization that occurs because the producing organization discriminates in the allocation of overhead costs (some activities not paying their fair share); and cross-subsidization in which some activities do not meet even their direct costs. These latter forms are usually enforced, by moral or administrative pressure, or by legal obligation.

The successful practice of cross-subsidization depends on the strength of the sellers in certain directions, which are used to sustain the weaker lines. Usually a degree of monopoly is necessary. Nationalized industries have statutory rights which give them the necessary monopoly advantages in many fields, and hence a measure of cross-subsidization is available to them.

The need to cross-subsidize can constitute a burden, however. Even the legal monopolies of the public corporations do not protect them against all types of competition: other types of products or forms of services may be substituted for the ones they provide. Hence to compel nationalized industries to pay cross-subsidies may hamper their competitiveness in lines where they should be strongest. If main-line railway transport, for example, has to be profitable enough to carry non-paying lines, then it may itself have unnecessary difficulty in competing with road vehicles or internal airlines. Nor, in such a case, would the fares put on offer before the prospective traveller reflect the true costs of the alternative means of transporting him.

For these reasons cross-subsidies are not particularly popular within the nationalized industries. Nevertheless they continue to exist, and there are reasons that impel the corporations to maintain them.

There is, of course, no case for eliminating cross-subsidies where the accounting or administrative expenses of doing so nullify the gains. This factor can be very important, for the maintenance of public goodwill may be involved. There may be an element of social cost if the methods of charging create time-consuming trouble and expense for the customers.

Cross-subsidies are also maintained for the purpose already reiterated: to meet 'social' needs, and to keep up productive units or markets that may be viable in the future, but which could not easily be restarted if stopped. Among these non-paying activities may also be included 'pioneering' enterprises. New air routes, for example, or new types of fuel on the home market, may not pay at first, especially if heavy capital or development costs are included. If these are regarded as promotional activities, the losses can be treated as capital expenditure. But if the ventures are paid for out of current revenue, this amounts to a cross-subsidy.

Cross-subsidization may exist through the initiative of the public corporation itself, or through its reluctance to remove the more subtle forms of it. It may also exist through the instigation of the Government. The willingness of the Government to encourage cross-subsidization in particular cases may enable the industry to appeal for protection of one sort or another. If cross-subsidization is to succeed, then monopoly advantages elsewhere may be necessary; and if the whole policy is agreed on with the Government, then governmental powers may be used in its support. Thus, if the Government agrees to maintain coal-working

in central Scotland, then some protection to the coal industry may
be appropriate.

The alternative to cross-subsidies is, of course, open subsidies.
The Government may choose to sustain particular activities or a
level of general activities from its own funds, as it has done for the
railways. If capital projects are involved, it may lend money on
favourable terms.

The open subsidy has great advantages. It makes clear to all
concerned what is happening. The finances of the public corporations are not put at a disadvantage. Morally it seems proper that an
activity wanted by the Government (as the agent of the community) should be paid for by the Government (through taxes on
the whole community). Nevertheless, there are also disadvantages.
Methods of calculating appropriate subsidies are not entirely satisfactory. Regular payment of fixed amounts lessens the incentive to
reduce costs, and this lack of cost-consciousness may spread to
other activities of the corporation. The attitude may arise that all
non-paying activities deserve subsidy. Nor may it be easy for a
Government to find the money – there is, after all, strong popular
hostility to taxation. It is possible, for example, for Passenger
Transport Executives, through local authorities, to subsidize
buses and local trains. Yet any further burden on the rates would
be politically difficult and socially unfair.

Cross-subsidization seems likely, with some effort, to be diminished. But it is unlikely to be abolished. It does not discourage cost-
consciousness quite so much as do regular outside subsidies, and it
sometimes provides a means of relatively painless finance for
necessary services.

THE WHITE PAPER OF 1961

In 1961 a first attempt was made by the Government to formulate
official doctrines about some of the questions raised in this chapter.
The drafting of the statement no doubt helped the Government
to clarify its views and in any case the public and the nationalized
industries themselves were entitled to know the Government's
attitude.

This White Paper, *The Financial and Economic Obligations of the*

Nationalized Industries,[12] consisted mainly of a review of the industries in financial terms. It prescribed a new framework in which they were to work:

(*a*) The obligation to meet costs 'taking one year with another' was made more precise – surpluses were to cover deficits over a five-year period, if possible. Moreover, revenue should include provision for replacement of assets as they became worn out or obsolete, and for further capital development. After discussion, each industry would be set a target for the five-year period (subject to review each year), which would indicate how much revenue, beyond its bare running costs, it should try to earn.

(*b*) The existing practices in relation to investment and borrowing were endorsed – that is to say, forward plans would be examined by the Ministries, and special attention would be given to those expected to yield a low return.

(*c*) These proposals meant that the industries would have to try to increase their net revenue. In the past many of them had made losses even over five-year periods; and they had not provided much of their investment funds. The main way to secure the increased revenue would be to reduce costs. But the White Paper recognized that the industries must be given freedom to alter their prices – in practice to raise them – in order to meet the prescribed financial standards.

(*d*) Price rises were one of the matters discussed in Chapter 6; it was noted that Ministers had considerably restricted the industries' freedom of action. The White Paper stated that the arrangements for discussing prices would continue, but that public statements might be made if a board's proposals were altered (see pp. 129–30).

(*e*) The Government accepted the view that commercial performance might be hampered by non-commercial activities. It did not propose that all these should be abandoned. Nor did it propose to provide subsidies from its own finances. The solution announced was to take these non-commercial activities into the reckoning when calculating the five-year target:

> These activities will, so far as practicable, have been taken into account in fixing the financial standard for each undertaking. To the extent that commercially unprofitable activities are subsequently imposed from outside, a Board would be entitled to ask for an adjustment of its financial objectives.[13]

In the next two years, financial objectives were agreed on these lines with the various boards. They vary from industry to industry and are expressed in different ways, but they represent generally a return of between six and eight per cent on the value of their assets (calculated after allowing for depreciation). In calculating the five-year objectives the special character and prospects of each industry are taken into account. The White Paper acknowledges the 'public utility' nature of many of the industries, and does not expect from them the same performance as from other industries. They are different, that is to say, because they are basic industries rather than manufacturing concerns, not because they are nationalized. The railways have special financial arrangements, already described, and are excluded from this framework for the time being.

In a sense, the White Paper was regarded as a step towards commercial standards. Certainly the new five-year formulae are more realistic than the statutory 'one year with another' doctrine; and the greater precision means that both the industries and the Government can manœuvre only within strict limits in their attitude to prices. This pro-commercial tendency of the White Paper is openly declared at the beginning: '. . . They are not . . . to be regarded as social services absolved from economic and commercial justification.'[14] However, in the last paragraph there is a different emphasis:

> The nationalized industries are from their size and nature bound to play a major role in the economic life of the country. They cannot, however, be regarded only as very large commercial concerns which may be judged mainly on their

commercial results: all have, although in varying degrees, wider
obligations than commercial concerns in the private sector.
The object of these proposals is to find for each industry or
Board a reasonable balance between these two concepts.

There is of course no direct contradiction between this passage
and earlier parts of the White Paper. Nevertheless, this is not the
language of the Herbert report. Once 'wider obligations' are
stipulated, the criteria of policy-making must lose their economic
simplicity.

Some comments may be appropriate. It is difficult to see how
the five-year targets can be used as tests of efficiency, even though
the White Paper treats failure to reach the objectives as 'inadequate performance'.[15] The targets are determined by administrators, after negotiation with the boards, and determined in advance.
They are, therefore, in a sense predictions – not predictions
of what will happen, but predictions that the objectives will
be reasonable. As things turn out, the targets may be very difficult or very easy to achieve. A great deal depends on the economic
circumstances of the time, and on the Government's policies in
response to the circumstances. The provision for annual review
seems to recognize this. In any case, the board was appointed by
the Minister, and, even on the narrowest interpretation of his
functions, he must carry responsibility before Parliament for
choosing competent board members.

It has always seemed, therefore, that the five-year targets should
be regarded as essential working rules for the industries, on which
they can base policy decisions, rather than as objective tests for
measuring the quality of their performance.

In sum, the White Paper proposed a new economic self-
reliance for the industries. Their policies on prices, it promised,
were no longer to be subordinated to anti-inflationary needs, to
public pressure or to other non-commercial considerations. The
White Paper stressed that this would end any excess demand
brought about by low prices, or over-investment occasioned by
the excessive demand.

It has been argued, in fact, that the low-price (and loss-making) period in the nationalized industries brought considerable advantages to industrial consumers, who were getting products and services below cost. Between 1949 and 1958, it has been suggested, a 'subsidy' averaging £100 million a year was paid out by the nationalized industries to their customer industries – that is, they were undercharged by that amount.[16] It should also be remembered, however, that the undercharging brought financial weakness which meant that investment funds had to be obtained, through the Government, from the rest of the community. This borrowing process, of course, carried a burden of interest payments not necessary with self-finance.

The White Paper of 1961 attempted to give the nationalized industries a degree of self-reliance. This was never absolute, and in fact the procedures it prescribed were soon part of a wider attempt at economic planning by the Labour Government. It constituted an important step in putting the determination of policy for the industries into the world of economic concepts. Nevertheless, it is important to stress that it did not 'commercialize' the industries – partly because it noted their wider obligations, but also because their *economic* obligations were prescribed by the Government. There is no indication of such a system in the Herbert report, which seems to have assumed that (though other obligations came from the Government) economic objectives were either self-evident, or at least generated within the industries. The 1961 arrangements did *not* confine the Government's role to a few marginal subsidies, as some advocates of commercialization imagine. They gave to the Government responsibility for determining the economic scope of the industries.

THE WHITE PAPER OF 1967

Partly owing to its limitations, but also owing to the stresses brought on by the economic crises of the 1960s, it became necessary to amplify the doctrines of the first White Paper.

In November 1967, therefore, the Labour Government published its White Paper, *Nationalized Industries: a review of economic and financial objectives* (Cmnd. 3437). This discussed generally the problems of investment in the industries, their pricing policies, their cost controls and their financial objectives. On these matters its main proposals were as follows:

(a) Investment programmes are framed in the light of Government policy for the sector, should be based on consistent criteria, and projects should normally show a satisfactory return in commercial terms. The best possible methods of appraisal should be used, and this means discounted cash-flow techniques for all important projects.[17] For the test rate of discount eight per cent was prescribed, a figure broadly consistent in real terms with the average return on low-risk projects in the private sector of industry at that time.

(b) Common pricing policies should also be applied in the industries. Not only should overall costs be covered, but prices should relate to costs of particular products or services, to eliminate undesirable cross-subsidization. Moreover, they should 'be reasonably related to costs at the margin'. Though in some circumstances these would be short-run marginal costs, the main consideration would be the long-run cost of supply on a continuing basis. These long-run marginal costs would include provision for capital replacement.

(c) Continual critical attention should be paid to costs, to make sure satisfactory financial results were not obtained merely by monopoly power. The National Board for Prices and Incomes would make inquiries into cost-control machinery in the industries, and the annual investment review would provide an opportunity to check efficiency.

(d) The system of financial objectives, though not a perfect or sufficient formula, had proved its value. The targets should continue, but be interpreted flexibly. There might be different objectives for different parts of an industry's activities.

The Government declared in the White Paper that if social or wider economic costs meant 'that the industry has to act against its own commercial interests, the Government will accept responsibility'. This acceptance might mean special payments, or adjustment of the financial objective.

In general, the White Paper reserved for the Government a large responsibility for the general lines of economic development in the industries; it noted, for example, that overall cost benefit studies would best be carried out in Government departments and not in the corporations themselves.

In brief, the effect of the 1967 White Paper was to add two policy 'guidelines' – on investment and on prices – to the earlier financial target. Hence the economic instructions required by the theory of ministerial control outlined in the last chapter were threefold: a prescribed discount rate, general rules about pricing, and a financial objective generally expressed in terms of return on capital.

These three items, however, did not complete the picture, for a large measure of 'sector' policy-making was reserved to the Government, and it continued to operate an appraisal procedure for investment projects and for particular price changes. There was nevertheless a more fundamental aim behind the developments: an attempt to set a place for the nationalized industries in the economy that was not only conducive to efficiency, but was also in some sense fair and non-discriminatory. This operated particularly in the matter of prices and incomes policy, where it was 'intended to show clearly that . . . criteria apply equally to price increases in both the public and private sectors'. This could be demonstrated by referring issues to the National Board for Prices and Incomes, an independent body concerned with all parts of the economy. The N.B.P.I. was concerned with many investigations affecting the industries (a list is provided in Appendix B), but after the White Paper it was given the task of checking all major price increases, and it recruited staff to expand its work in this field. It was abolished in 1971.

The application of the White Paper doctrines received some criticism from the Select Committee in its report on *Ministerial Control*. Though it approved the principles as such, it complained that they were not being enforced with sufficient rigour. The financial objective, in the view of the Committee, was merely the residuum of the other two; it should be treated as such, and if necessary should be overridden. The industries' adherence to marginal-cost pricing was suspect, and the Government should enforce it more thoroughly.[18] However, the S.C.N.I. view has in its turn been criticized, as adherence to a dogmatic view which in fact is subject to much economic controversy. 'It is difficult to avoid a suspicion that the members of the Select Committee were taken for an intellectual ride and being on unfamiliar ground they lost their way and were over-ready to accept simple solutions to complex problems.'[19]

MONOPOLIES AND FRONTIERS

A group of issues adjacent to the main lines of discussion must now be described.

There has been a general tradition that publicly owned enterprises are conducted as monopolies. In part this was because it was believed that competition could not work without the profit motive; partly because it was thought that fair competition between privately owned and publicly owned concerns would be difficult to contrive; and partly because the industries concerned were 'natural' monopolies. Indeed, the existence of situations where monopoly was virtually inevitable, such as the supply of gas, provided a strong argument for public ownership in these cases.

When industries were nationalized in 1946–9 the monopoly rights of the public corporations were set out in the Acts, and so made legally enforceable.[20] Not only were existing enterprises taken over, that is to say, but new ventures by private concerns into the industries, as defined, were forbidden. In practice, however, the situation is complicated. There is no doubt that the legal security of the public corporations within defined limits gives them great advantages. The need to meet certain types of competition, however, has been for many of them their most urgent problem. How does this arise?

It is a very common mistake, particularly in relation to public enterprise, to talk about monopoly in terms of the structure of industry. The important arena is the market, and it is the situation among suppliers to the same market (i.e. among those trying to

meet the same sort of demand) that is really significant. Thus the
National Coal Board undoubtedly has a monopoly of coal production (apart from small mines). For many purposes, however,
there are rival fuels to coal: in the markets for domestic heating
and electricity generation, for example, it has to face stiff competition from fuel oil. The legal monopolies of public corporations provide varying degrees of protection, according to the
availability of substitutes. The most effective monopolies at
present among the nationalized industries probably lie with the
use of electricity for lighting purposes,[21] and with the activities
of the Post Office. In heating and other fuel uses there is a strongly
competitive situation, and in most sectors of transport one form
can be substituted for another. A significant private sector remains in the steel industry. There is also the possibility, in principle,
of imports, but there can be little challenge to the present nationalized industries from foreign competitors in exactly the same lines,
again with the exception of steel.

In recent years the Government has refused permission for the
import of coal, though before 1957 the Coal Board itself imported
some from the United States and resold it at British prices – that
is, at a loss. B.O.A.C. must, of course, from the nature of its
routes, meet constant competition from foreign airlines.

In the 1950s the traditional policy of monopoly operation for
public enterprise was considerably modified. The Conservative
Government was at the time pursuing a policy of freedom from
control and the elimination of monopolistic agreements in private
industry. It was natural to accompany this by encouraging competition in public enterprise. Except for the break-up of the
original British Transport Commission, the structure of nationalization was not much changed. By one means or another, however, the various industries were put into positions where they
were more and more dependent on market situations and had to
face competition from a variety of sources. During this period,
too, opinion in the Labour Party became more favourable to
competition, certainly in private industry, and under certain
conditions in public enterprise. The 'competition' that was advocated and that emerged did not of course amount to anything

like full competition in the economist's sense. Sometimes it was little more than a spirit of emulation or rivalry between different Areas or Regions, for example. In other cases it meant that privately owned concerns would be allowed a share of the market, as with independent airlines on internal routes. It was not essential for new private enterprises, or indeed any private enterprise, to be involved. Competition can lie between various public corporations just as it does between private firms. There is no motivation towards profit maximization, but experience shows that administrative and psychological incentives are sufficient to make such competition an effective driving force. There is at present sharp competition in domestic heating between the Coal Board and the electricity and gas authorities (as well as the oil companies); and there is competition between British Railways, the National Bus Company and British European Airways in meeting particular demands.

The question of 'frontiers' is closely associated with that of monopoly. Just as the statutes protect the public corporations from competition within their range of operations, so they often debar the corporations from activities outside that range. In some cases the Acts contain explicit prohibitions of particular activities; in other cases the limitations arise from discouragement by the Government or the restraint of the corporations themselves.

These limits put the corporations at several disadvantages. In the first place, the real limits of an 'industry' must always be vague, and strict rules may prevent natural expansion into ancillary activities. In fact, the public corporations acquired a number of ancillary and miscellaneous businesses in the process of nationalization – such as brickworks, coking plant and farms by the Coal Board, and bus companies and travel agencies by nationalized transport concerns. For many years there were no extensions of this type of activity, but eventually some joint ventures with private enterprise were set up – for instance, B.O.A.C. had a link with Cunard, and the Coal Board has joined with J. H. Sankey & Son, builders' merchants, in marketing solid fuel appliances. Secondly, the establishment of large public corporations is both the effect and cause of the growth of 'countervailing' organizations – large firms, combines and trade associations which bargain with the corporations as suppliers and customers. The strict frontier injects an element of artificiality and rigidity into this process. Neither can advance into the territory of the other; and in particular the public corporations could not, before 1965, undertake manufacturing or distributive activities which they might have found advantageous. Thus the Central Electricity Generating Board does not produce its own generating plant, nor do the Area Boards of gas and electricity manufacture appliances, though they distribute them. The Coal Board does not manufacture mining machinery, and it has not extended its interest in the merchanting of coal to domestic consumers beyond the three per cent of the trade that it inherited on nationalization. The railways, however, have traditionally manufactured much of their own equipment, including rolling stock, in railway workshops. They have also bought similar goods from a sizeable private-enterprise industry. The allocation of orders between the two sources has always been a problem. In 1962 a plan for the rationalization of railway workshops was set up, reducing the number of main works from twenty-eight to sixteen. Moreover, the workshops were to compete with outside firms for construction contracts offered by British Railways themselves. On the other hand, railway workshops did not compete for contracts offered by concerns other than British Railways which they might have secured. In 1964 and 1965 the Labour Government removed the restrictions, and railway workshops were permitted to obtain work from other customers, private and foreign, besides British Railways. It is only in recent years that British Railways have pursued an active policy to make the best and most profitable use (for non-railway purposes) of the many valuable sites that they own. Until 1965, B.O.A.C. was debarred from competing for contracts with the Service ministries for carrying troops to and from overseas stations.

There have been also specific restraints on production for export. Both the 1947 Electricity Act and the 1948 Gas Act prohibited manufacture for export, even in circumstances where production of equipment for use by the boards themselves is allowed.[22]

Finally, there is the question of general diversification. One of

G

the courses open to a private-enterprise concern is to widen its interests, either by setting up new production itself or by combining with an existing firm. Nationalized industries have not been in the habit of developing in this way. For activities closely allied to those of the main enterprise there could be obvious advantages in integration. But also by establishing itself in relatively disparate fields, a business can insure itself against difficulties, both temporary and long-term, in its original line. Such flexibility has not been generally available to the nationalized industries. The 1965 White Paper on *Steel Nationalization*, however, emphasized that the British Steel Corporation would acquire firms with interests in such things as structural engineering, bridge-building and wire manufacture; and moreover, that the Corporation would be able to further diversify its activities when this appeared commercially advantageous.[23]

The existence of the 'frontier' implies a crude balance of disadvantages between the public corporations and private business. The limitation on diversification, however, seemed to give private industry the best of the bargain. Private industry could not enter the cage that protected nationalized concerns, but the public corporations were deprived of the greater scope outside.

It is not difficult to see how these matters affect the aims of nationalized industries. From the point of view of commercial success, the easiest situation is provided by effective monopoly; second best would be complete freedom of manœuvre on the frontier. Few governments are likely to countenance either of these extremes, and the corporations must expect to face some competition and to put up with some limitations on the scope of their activities. Within this range of practical possibility, various controversies proceed, usually on familiar lines.

Thus it may well be argued that competition between public and private enterprise is a good thing. But is the competition fair? Public enterprise may feel that the flexibility of its rivals, and their freedom to neglect social responsibilities, gives them unfair advantages. It is alleged that private firms operating on the fringes of nationalized industries do not undertake costly research or training programmes, and often fail to provide relatively unremunerative

'staple' services, confining their competitive efforts to the more
lucrative parts of the trade. On the other hand, some private firms
might complain that the ancillary and competitive activities of the
public corporations are aided and supported by the statutory-
monopoly activities, which provide technical and management
skills, if not actual cross-subsidies; and, moreover, there is less need
for the public enterprise to make a regular profit.

Another field of controversy concerns competition among the
nationalized industries themselves. There are some who suggest
that the co-ordination and integration natural within each corporation should be extended over the whole of public industry. Wide
co-operation was indeed proposed under the original Transport
Act of 1947. When the Ridley committee reported in 1952 on
national fuel policies, however, it recommended that consumers
should be left to choose between competing services.[24] In 1959
moreover, the Weir committee reported on co-operation between
electricity and gas boards, and found there was no substantial
advantage to be got from their co-operation in meter reading,
collection of accounts, service centres and showrooms, advertising, or the breaking up of streets.[25] In fact the public corporations
have always behaved commercially towards one another, and in
the fuel and power industries there now seems to be wide agreement that this is the right policy. In transport the high social costs
involved suggest that more integration may be possible.

The relevance of these issues to the question of objectives lies
therefore in the environment that monopoly or competition provides. If the corporations are to sustain prescribed standards of performance, then they must be concerned about the circumstances in
which they operate. Social and political obligations are well-
known factors affecting performance. The degree of monopoly
and the room for manœuvre on industrial frontiers are less often
considered, but are no less important.

In recent years, political controversy on these matters has
sharpened. Before 1964, the Conservative policy was to encourage
competition for the industries. The attitudes of the Labour
Government between 1964–70 were favourable to competitive
expansion on the frontiers of the industries, but in practice there

was not very much development in this direction. What has happened is that the various corporations have generally re-organized their activities so that ancillaries and distinguishable activities are established as 'profit-centres' and independent bodies, often registered as companies. The extent of cross-subsidy can thus be known, and if necessary controlled. When the Conservatives returned to power in 1970 they set out to promote a different policy: instead of encouraging frontier development, they curtailed it. In particular, they returned to private enterprise the travel agency of Thomas Cook Ltd, and the breweries and public houses in the State Management Districts of Carlisle, Gretna and Cromarty.

For this chapter, the main point is that the competitive environment of a public enterprise is a vital consideration in determining its commercial, social and political objectives. Since the mid-1950s there has been a gradual shift of emphasis from the idea of 'administering industries' in the management of public enterprises, to the notion of the 'public firm' responding to economic criteria. With such a change of concept, the rules about frontier delimitation must surely be modified.

A REASSESSMENT

It is now possible to attempt a summary and an evaluation of the various arguments set out in this chapter. It is convenient to begin by reiterating the old case for a commercial or 'purely economic' approach.

Its main administrative appeal lies in its clarity. It provides in most cases an unmistakable criterion by which to test the success of a policy. Moreover, it is a criterion which can be used to compare dissimilar activities, and which can be understood (and enforced) throughout the administrative structure of large organizations. The strictly commercial approach also has claims to be grounded in economic logic. The plain facts of economic life must eventually be faced, and if only projects that pay are taken up, then the facts will be faced sooner rather than later. The demand of consumers through the market is, moreover, a plain fact, and hence it is a surer basis for policy than the views of politicians and man-

agers about social needs, the national interest or future developments.

Even if commercial standards cannot be applied without exception, it is claimed that the commercial principle does provide a
practicable distinction between the responsibilities of the corporations, which should be entirely commercial, and those of the
Government, which may be based on other considerations. This
was the view of the Herbert committee, and a similar attitude
has been repeatedly taken up by the Select Committee on Nationalized Industries.

Most of the difficulties and objections to the rigorous application
of commercial principles have already been rehearsed. It may be
that its clarity – arising from its simplicity – is a reason for suspecting its validity, as well as being an administrative merit. The
old laissez-faire doctrines also had the merit of simplicity, but this
was eventually a cause of their downfall: they did not meet the
complexity of human needs. As the White Paper of 1961 insists,
the nationalized industries are not social services. But does it
follow that there can only be two styles of organization – the
social service, totally financed by the Government, and the
commercial enterprise, with no support whatsoever? In fact,
charges are made for some social services. It may also be convenient to meet the objectives of social policy, once they are
decided, by subsidies, cross-subsidies or measures of protection;
and the nationalized industries have no claim to stand aside from
this process.

The most popular form of the 'commercial solution' is undoubtedly the modified doctrine whereby non-commercial
activity is allowed, even welcomed, so long as it takes place at the
behest of the Government. A great deal turns on the practicability
and effectiveness of this doctrine. The Government certainly has
general responsibility for all aspects of national welfare and should
be in a position to give proper weight to social and political
factors. There are some things which can be done *only* by the
Government, such as determining an industry's role in a national
plan, or providing a degree of protection. In any case, the British
constitutional system gives the Government of the day the power

to impose its will, and it would be difficult for a Government to avoid final responsibility for industrial affairs.

Yet it may be doubted if this doctrine provides a real answer to the problem. Social and political considerations are not occasional occurrences: they pervade the whole conduct of industry. Moreover, the points at which they arise are not always national in scope: they are often local or individual. National rulings about social standards need to be interpreted, therefore, by managers well down the industrial hierarchy. To declare a doctrine of 'commercial operation only' is to pre-empt the social decisions of these managers. Again, the decisions of the Government on social matters cannot fail to be influenced by the attitudes of the chairmen of the public corporations. Ministers are under pressure from the public and their parties, but they will not be helped to wise decisions if they are confronted by the industries' universal hostility to all social claims.

The claims should not be trivialized. Convenient examples, such as rural electrification or a branch railway to a fishing port, may be over-used. Major sector policies – the effort to maintain electricity supplies at maximum winter peak demand without power-cuts; or the level of coal production; or the future balance between rail and road transport, for example – are major national issues, in which wider and social factors must be taken into account. They may be for the Government to decide in the end; nevertheless, the industries must play a part in the decision-making process. It cannot be shrugged off, as nothing to do with them, for from them must come much of the advice on which the decision depends.

The situation therefore calls at least for understanding and discrimination about social matters by the management of the industries themselves. Industrial decisions which involve social and political values – such as freedom, equality and accountability – will be better taken if the managers of nationalized industries participate in them, and if they are able to take a constructive attitude which recognizes the plurality of values usually prevalent in British society. Their examination of such issues will be improved, moreover, if they have some understanding of the distinctions between the types of factor involved.

There can be little doubt that the long controversy has resulted in great clarification[26] – at least, of the issues. It may be argued, however, that over the years authorities have produced sharp distinctions that provided apparent solutions. Unfortunately, they have not worn well in practice.

One of the great bogey-words in this controversy since the 1950s has been 'commercial'. The distinction between commercial and non-commercial activities has become one of the perennials of debate. Yet it may be doubted whether it does throw all that much light on the subject. The proponents of the so-called commercial approach do not advocate a short-sighted outlook derived from the unreformed Ebenezer Scrooge. They are in favour of compassion, good personnel and public relations and foresight. The Edwards report on *British Air Transport in the Seventies* found ten possible objectives 'for Government and Parliament to decide'. But the corporations themselves 'should take a *long-term view* of their prospects and their responsibilities just as major businesses in other fields would do'.[27] This means in fact that all sorts of considerations must be taken into account including the social and political perceptions of the corporations. They must moreover consider the social and political impact of their own actions. What is at stake is, in practice, not the range of topics the corporations consider, but the way in which the outcome is judged.

It is here that the pressure for a simple criterion, or at least a predetermined criterion, has been strongest. The economic marching orders are to an extent supposed to provide this; but these are still overshadowed in the public eye by the annual accounts, despite the over-simplification of deficit or surplus. In view of the financial troubles of the early 1970s, it cannot be said that the policies of 1967 – however well conceived – have survived very well. They may have provided the possibility of rationality, efficiency and independence, but they could not guarantee them against the insistent needs of national economic policy. It is perhaps significant that the Wilberforce report on the great mineworkers' dispute of 1972 brushed aside the constraints of the prescribed financial framework as 'somewhat artificial'.[28] Moreover, in spite of its lack of realism, as discussed in Chapter 4, the crude financial out-turn (quite apart from the financial target) must play a leading part, so long as it is published, in shaping the reputation of the industries; and good reputation is an inescapable part of their aims.

If crude 'commercialization' is an elusive phantom, then can anything be firmly stated?

Economic activity is concerned with the production of real wealth – goods and services. From the community's point of view, a successful economic project is one that produces a large difference between the value of what goes in (raw materials, fuel, depreciation of capital) and the value of the output. This difference (the economist's 'value-added') provides the income of labour and that of capital.

Now, the motives of the controllers of free-enterprise firms are complex, and the principles guiding their decisions have achieved some sophistication. The whole force of their legal obligations, however, lies in satisfying their shareholders. In the past this has been regarded as a sufficient explanation of their behaviour. There are now views that stress the multiple purposes of all enterprises. For private enterprise, however, the absence of any substantial system of public accountability means that any modifications of objective, economic or otherwise, must arise from within.

A nationalized industry has no built-in motives of this sort. Its economic purposes can only be understood as part of a wider operation – the maximization of value-added for the community. It will need some guidance, from national planners or market forces, on the scale of its contribution. It may be prudent for it to make some profit, as part of its investment programme. But the general measure of its economic success must lie in the value it adds to the community's goods and services, and not merely in the part of that addition which appears as a surplus or is used for the remuneration of capital-providers. Indeed, since some of this value may be distributed, not to labour or capital, but to consumers in the form of lower prices, its size may not be calculable at all.[29]

When their contribution is assessed, the nature of the existing British nationalized industries should be borne in mind. They are all basic industries or services, part of the 'infra-structure' of the economy. Their status as public utilities was noted by the 1961 White Paper. Efficient low-cost production on their part can make a great contribution to the success of other economic activities. It should be emphasized, perhaps, that the return-on-capital standard (implying a limited rate of profit) announced in the White Paper is a pragmatic device set up for administrative convenience. At the present time it suits the industries; but it will obviously be possible to raise or lower (or remove) the rate of profit in the future – the industries are not enjoined to secure *maximum* profits. The question in this chapter is, what principles should politicians and civil servants have in mind in fixing such standards?

Economic aims, however widely defined, cannot provide all the answers all the time. Insistence on them, narrowly defined, breeds criticism of and hostility to industrial enterprises. It was in the attempt to establish a more acceptable conception that ideas of 'public interest' and 'public service' were developed. They embody the desire to serve rural consumers, poor consumers and otherwise inconvenient consumers; and to operate in a fair and undiscriminating way. It has become clear that they are too vague to serve as working criteria for economic decisions. They demonstrate, however, that deliberately non-economic, let alone non-commercial, policies might be rationally pursued.

The upshot of all this seems to be as follows. First, the simplest criterion of policy appears to be the strictly commercial test, but it is elusive in practice. Secondly, it is desirable, and is probably possible by cost-benefit analysis and similar techniques, to replace this in some cases by an economic criterion that embodies full social costs (and here the principle of maximum value-added is relevant). Thirdly, however, national-economy considerations have dominated everything else in the mid-1960s and the early 1970s. And if long-term factors and social values are to play any part at all in administration and policy-making, it is hard to see that any single formula can be established for all circumstances. There is now, in America and Britain, a movement against defining business objectives in simple terms. It would be paradoxical, if, at this juncture, crude commercial rules were prescribed for public enterprise. The best available objective, therefore, seems to be a general regard for economic ends, including all social costs, modified repeatedly by a variety of other considerations.

This may not seem a very remarkable conclusion. It is, however, a mistake to assume simplicity where there is in truth complexity; and since the nationalized industries are large organizations, affecting significantly many aspects of life, it is not surprising that their policies need to respect a variety of human ideals. Nevertheless, there is no need to let complexity degenerate into confusion. The nationalized industries should know where their advantage lies; the social costs of likely policies should be carefully estimated where possible; and decisions involving other factors should be consciously taken and openly declared.

Several of the questions discussed in this chapter involve judgments about the sorts of relationships in society we consider desirable. For instance, emphasis on success by commercial standards often reflects a high valuation of wealth, especially material wealth. Stress on public accountability and the pursuit of 'social' objectives, on the other hand, usually goes with a belief that fair and harmonious relationships among people are a main value. The problem of ultimate objectives is never a technical one – of *how* best to achieve something; it concerns, rather, how far one objective (such as increased wealth) should be pursued in comparison with other things. This is not to suggest that such things as increased wealth and social justice are always competitive: on the contrary, they are often connected. Moreover, other social values, such as liberty, may be at stake. These are formidable issues which obviously cannot be fully discussed here.

In any case, the determination of aims for any organization – public or private, industrial or social – does not take place in a vacuum. The thinking of people in control is influenced by their environment, by the pressures they have to contend with. In nationalized industries, therefore, the boards' responsibility to the Government and the nation is a most pervasive factor; and the issues discussed in this chapter should always be related to the machinery of control and accountability described in Chapter 6. It has been a frequent hope in the last twenty years that some reformulation of the rules, or more drastically, some recasting of the organizational structure, would produce a solution to the dilemma of 'politics or business?' – that somewhere a calm haven might be found where unhampered business progress could be made. It has already been urged that this is unlikely, because there is a strong prevailing public expectation that economic and industrial failings – in almost all sectors – can be remedied by political action. While this expectation persists, major industries must expect to live in a world of politics *and* business.

At the beginning of this chapter it was pointed out that questions about the aims to be pursued, in nationalization as elsewhere, readily become questions of social and political philosophy. This does not mean that they cannot be rationally discussed. There is in Britain sufficient consensus of opinion to make clarification and comparison of value judgments a worthwhile operation. Yet the common acceptance of a general liberalism as a social attitude does not mean that there are no underlying differences. Liberalism, after all, can be interpreted in various ways. Discussion of the aims of nationalization is part of that interpretation.

8 The Politics of Public Ownership

THE MAIN concern of this book has been to examine British nationalization as it exists. It should be remembered, however, that problems of policy and administration have been dealt with against a background of political disputation. It remains, therefore, to give an account of developments in these controversies.

The concern with these matters is not an eccentricity of the British political scene, the outcome of accidental prejudice. Nor is it an odd quirk of history. In the circumstances of the age, the values esteemed by radical and reformist temperaments led naturally to a preference for public ownership. A tendency to mistrust the rich and powerful brings a liking for a system in which such people are in some way accountable. A habit of seeing issues in moral terms is readily associated with systems based on co-operation 'for the good of all' rather than private rivalry. Moreover, given a democratic political system in which each person has one vote, the working classes have obvious advantages in political control over industrial decisions, compared with market control, where they are handicapped by relative poverty. It is not difficult, therefore, to explain general attitudes to the issues of public ownership without accepting Marxist assumptions about social developments. These attitudes are not universal – they are particularly weak in North America – but they are widespread in most parts of the world.

In Britain and in other West European countries the range of controversy has been narrowed in recent years. Socialist and anti-socialist parties alike accept the 'mixed economy', in the sense that all assume that some industries will be publicly owned while others remain in private hands. It has certainly been a less frequent issue at elections in Britain.[1] Yet considerable differences still remain over the extent of public enterprise and the way in which existing nationalization is to be run. There have been many hopes and predictions that the controversy would fade away entirely. It has not yet done so; and the narrowing of the gap between the views of the main British parties does not necessarily make the issue less divisive. Only when issues are replaced by other controversies, arousing stronger emotions, are they effectively superseded.

At the beginning of the book, R. H. Tawney's distinction between questions of ownership and those of administration was quoted (see p. 15). In the previous three chapters, questions of administration in one form or another have been considered. These concluding pages return to the question of ownership itself.

LABOUR PARTY ATTITUDES

It is convenient to begin the discussion with the Labour Party, although it has been in opposition for most of the time since the industries were nationalized. As the party favourably disposed towards public ownership, it has spent most time discussing it, and there are in fact considerable developments in attitude to record.

In Chapter 2 it was noted that the Party eventually adopted the public corporation as its method of nationalization, and gave priority to the basic industries in its programme of action. In its professions of socialist faith the Party had always stressed two things: that it was democratic and would govern by parliamentary means; and that it was gradualist and would socialize industry only in stages.

This doctrine of 'gradualism' served as a policy of moderation in the 1930s. It ensured that the programme of 1945 was practicable and capable of execution by ordinary legislation. The 'stage by stage' idea, however, implied that the first nationalization programme would be succeeded by others. It was necessary therefore for the Party to prepare new policies on nationalization for the election of 1950. There were in the preparation of these policies the first signs of disagreements in the Party about nationalization, which were to persist for the next ten years. Briefly, the more cautious Labour politicians stressed the need for consolidation and the effective development of existing nationalization – for instance, the integration of transport envisaged by the 1947 Act had scarcely begun. The left wing in the Party, however, was anxious that the momentum of 1945–50 should not be lost, and that further progress should be made, in the event of success at the polls in 1950.

The programme for the election of February 1950 was therefore something of a compromise, though it appears radical enough today. The election manifesto proposed that public ownership in one form or another should be extended to beet-sugar manufacture and sugar refining; to the cement industry; to 'appropriate sections' of the chemical industry; to meat wholesaling and cold storage; to water supply; and to 'all suitable minerals'. It also declared that 'monopoly concerns which cannot be dealt with in other ways will be socialized.'[2] One of its most interesting proposals, however, was that for industrial assurance, where it suggested mutual ownership by the policy-holders. Ownership of insurance companies transacting life-assurance business by the weekly-collection method was to be transferred from shareholders to the policy-holders themselves, not to the Government or a public corporation.[3]

The General Election of 1950 was won by the Labour Party very narrowly, and no legislation in this field was practicable, though the already enacted nationalization of steel was carried out. At the election of October 1951 the Party made no specific nationalization proposals, and the Conservatives were narrowly victorious. The legislative situation was therefore reversed, and debate in the House of Commons centred on the denationalization of steel and road haulage in 1953. The difficulties of the Labour Party at this time were accentuated by its divided counsels. The left wing of the Party, inspired by Aneurin Bevan, was pressing for radical policies in foreign and defence affairs as well as in industry. The nature of these internal conflicts may be judged from two documents appearing in the same year. In 1953 the Trades Union Congress published a report on public ownership.[4] This was a cautious document which, though it commended existing nationalization as a success, displayed no great enthusiasm for its extension. Explicitly it favoured nationalization of water supply and the extension of the frontier of the National Coal Board to include some manufacturers of mining machinery. The attitude of the T.U.C. in this document (accepted by the 1953 Congress in Douglas) was cooler than that of many constituent unions, and the Confederation of Shipbuilding and Engineering Unions in particular favoured further wide measures of public ownership, including aircraft construction, the machine-tool industry, shipping and shipbuilding. The Labour Party itself issued a policy document in June 1953 setting out another group of proposals.[5] Steel and many road-haulage units were to be renationalized, and the State was to have power to 'build and operate new enterprises, or acquire a controlling interest in existing enterprises, or both'. This referred in particular to sections of the engineering industry, to key machine-tool firms and to a substantial degree of the chemical industry. The beet-sugar monopoly and water supply were also to be taken over, and a controlling interest acquired in a few firms making mining machinery. Industrial assurance would become a publicly organized service, and the State might manufacture requirements for the National Health Service.

In the General Election of 1955, which followed this programme, the Labour Party did badly and the Conservatives increased their majority. The proposals therefore came to nothing. A few months after the election, C. R. Attlee resigned as leader of the Labour Party, a position he had held since 1935, and Hugh Gaitskell was elected in his place.

A new approach?

A period of more fundamental discussion about public ownership now began. It was no longer a question of revising and adjusting a programme, but of examining the purpose of the whole line of policy. Unfortunately the Labour Party was only in moderate shape to do this. The leadership issue had been settled, but many of the disagreements and animosities were still little concealed. So far as public ownership was concerned, there was division between those who wished for considerable changes in attitude (eventually called the 'revisionists')[6] and those who believed in a reassertion of traditional principles, who became known as 'fundamentalists'.

It would be misleading to suggest that the disagreements were often clear-cut: indeed, it sometimes appeared that there were as many views as there were Labour politicians. The outlines of the revisionist case, however, became generally familiar. Socialism, it was argued, is not synonymous with public ownership. It consists of a set of values, of which social equality is probably the most distinctive. Public ownership, or nationalization, is a means to these ends. But, the revisionists said, it is not the only means, nor is it certain that mere transference to public ownership will by itself promote the ideals very much.

One of the grounds for supposing that nationalization promotes social equality is that it eliminates industries as sources of unearned income and capital gains for private individuals. In 1953 Mr John Strachey wrote:

> Socialists are determined to redistribute the national income not only more equally, but above all more justly ... The only final way of doing this is to do it *'at source'*: to transfer to the people, that is to say, the ownership of the *source* of the major unearned incomes which at present flow to the shareholding and property holding classes.[7]

In practice, argued the revisionists, the results of this brave doctrine were not so clear. Nationalization in Britain involves paying compensation to the former owners, who can reinvest it elsewhere and so maintain their advantages. Further capital for the industries is raised by borrowing, even if indirectly. There is some progress towards equality, indeed, because the interest paid by the industries is less than the distributed dividends would have been. But the effect is not large, and anyway progress towards social justice by this method is likely to be slow and cumbersome.

Another ethical argument for nationalization was that it substituted co-operation for conflict and competition. To this the revisionists replied that the elimination of competition did not by itself ensure a co-operative spirit in industry. In fact some rivalry and emulation were, on balance, desirable, and competition as such was valuable in many circumstances.

Other traditional arguments for nationalization were more practical and less idealistic in character. Some – such as the view that basic industries or monopolies ought to be controlled by the community – applied only to particular industries. Others, such as the need to improve efficiency, to co-operate in national planning, or to improve labour relations, might conceivably be achieved in other ways. All in all, it was argued, developments in mid-century had 'weakened but not destroyed' the case for general nationalization.[8] The situation, in the revisionist view, gave rise to a need to modify and re-present the habitual Labour Party approach to nationalization. The new outlook had two main aspects, one of which at least carried assent well beyond that of the more determined revisionists.

First, then, it was necessary to vary the methods of public ownership. 'Nationalization', in the sense of national ownership of whole industries, should apply only in one or two more cases than at present. Municipal ownership, co-operative ownership and ownership of competitive enterprises were to be stressed, and new forms were to be sought. In particular, the preparation of lists of industries scheduled for nationalization – known as 'shopping lists' – was to be stopped.

The second ambition of the revisionists brought sharper resistance in the Party from the fundamentalists. This was to reduce the promotion of public ownership from its central place in Labour policies to the status of 'one policy among others'. Stress was to be put on other measures – fiscal reform, educational changes, development of the social services – and public ownership advocated only in relation to other particular ends, not for its own sake. The mixed economy was to be recognized as permanent.

In the period after 1955 an attempt was made by the Labour Party to take stock of these views, and to resolve conflict in the Party by a process of full discussion, directed especially to framing new, agreed policies. Out of this process there emerged two policy statements about public ownership.

The first of these was a review of the existing nationalized industries called *Public Enterprise*. The Party had formed no dramatic new attitudes; no structural changes were proposed, but it was hoped that the machinery for consumer representation would be more effective.

The other statement, *Industry and Society*, was more adventurous and more controversial. It analysed the changes that had been taking place in industrial capitalism, and emphasized the distinctive nature of the large firm. A few hundred large companies dominated the economy, and were responsible for about half the investment and profits of the private sector. In these firms ownership had become separated from control, and, moreover, they obtained much of their investment funds from internal sources. National full-employment policies, ensuring high demand, meant that the prosperity of these firms was to a great extent underwritten by the Government.

The actual proposals of this statement stressed, as expected, the need for a variety of forms of public ownership. The Companies' Acts should be reviewed to develop more definite forms of public accountability, and a code of conduct should be set out to promote desirable social practices in industry. Besides the renationalization of steel and long-distance road haulage, public ownership might be extended in 'any industry or part of industry which, after thorough inquiry, is found to be seriously failing the nation'. Thus reports like those of the McGowan, Heyworth and Reid committees (discussed in Chapter 3) might again lead to nationalization. But the acquisition of firms, rather than industries, was a possible solution. The State should also participate in expansion and development by providing equity capital – that is, by making investments that receive a share of profits (instead of only providing fixed-interest loans) for new or existing enterprises. Furthermore, the pamphlet proposed the deliberate acquisition of shares in existing private-enterprise concerns, by accepting them in lieu of cash for death duties, or by investing social-security funds in industry.

These last proposals were the source of much dispute. The reason for including them was that they would promote equality, in spite of the doubts that had been expressed about the effectiveness of public ownership in this matter. In fact, it was the need to ensure a share in capital gains (rather than current profits) for the community at large that was stressed. Through share ownership a proportion of the increasing *wealth* of industry would become available for community purposes.

Though the statement had been agreed by a committee from all wings of the Party, it did not please most of the left when published. In its acceptance of the mixed economy and the absence of precise proposals for large-scale take-overs they detected a weakening of socialist purpose. Share-buying did not give active control either to the Government or to the workers, and it might commit the Government too closely to the outlook and interests of private business, rather than help to modify the behaviour of such concerns. At the Labour Party Conference in 1957 at Brighton there was an attempt to reject the statement as lacking the 'rich red blood of Socialist objective';[9] it was carried, however, and formed the basis of the Labour Party programme at the General Election of 1959.

Unlike the left wing of the Labour Party, the Conservative Party and private industry professed to see no moderation in the new policy. The discussion of the large firm and the share-buying programme were linked in allegations that all large firms were to be nationalized; and the criterion of 'failing the nation' was attacked for its vagueness. In the event, the Conservatives were victorious again in 1959, with an increased majority.

This third defeat brought on an unhappy period of recrimination and dispute in the Labour Party. It was felt by many leaders that what was wrong was not so much policies as the traditional Party 'image'. As a contribution to the presentation of a transformed view of the Party to the public, its leader, Hugh Gaitskell, proposed the repeal of Clause Four of the Party Constitution (see Chapter 2, p. 21), which stated the objects of the Party almost entirely in terms of common ownership. (By this time, 'distribution and exchange' had been added to 'the means of production'.) In fact, sufficient support for a change was not forthcoming, and the attempt was dropped in the summer of 1960. In this connection, however, a longer statement of Party objectives was formulated and approved by the Party Conference at Scarborough in 1960. This succeeded in placing public ownership as one aim among others. Two items in the declaration stated that the Labour Party

(i) ... stands for democracy in industry, and for the right of the workers both in the public and private sectors to full consultation in all the vital decisions of management, especially those affecting conditions of work.

(j) It is convinced that these social and economic objectives can be achieved only through an expansion of common ownership substantial enough to give the community power over the commanding heights of the economy. Common ownership takes varying forms, including state-owned industries and firms, producer and consumer co-operation, municipal ownership and public participation in private concerns. Recognizing that both public and private enterprise have a place in the economy it believes that further extension of common ownership should be decided from time to time in the light of these objectives and according to circumstances, with due regard for the views of the workers and consumers concerned.

The relationship of this declaration to Clause Four (still retained) is obscure. But the declaration was stated to refer to 'the second half of the twentieth century', so perhaps Clause Four is consigned to the remoter future. Election propaganda apart, it is clear that what are really important are the immediate programmes of the Party, and indeed whether it may be practicable in office for these to be carried out.

In the 1960s the Labour Party achieved a second major period of office, under the leadership of Harold Wilson, and the affairs of that period have further developed the Party's outlook on nationalization. Many of the actual events have been recorded in previous chapters. It is only necessary here to note what happened as an evolution of the Party's philosophy.

Paradoxically, though the period was one of great activity in many ways which affected public enterprise, there was only one example – the steel industry – of nationalization in the traditional manner, in which firms hitherto in private ownership become merged into a national public corporation by Act of Parliament. Whether this is the end of this sort of change remains to be seen. There is the question of the ports, and proposals about other industries are made from time to time. But it would be fair to assert that this style of transformation is no longer in the forefront of politics.

The Labour Government did nevertheless give attention to what can best be described as the pragmatic development of public enterprise. This included extension by way of openings on the frontiers – that is, of permitting or even encouraging existing nationalized industries to branch out into associated activities – by supporting enterprises through the Industrial Expansion Act, by involving public capital through the Industrial Reorganization Corporation. Moreover, the attempts to refashion the structures of existing nationalized concerns, especially transport; to put them on a sound financial and economic basis; and to carry out other developments and innovations, all served to raise not only the performance but also the public esteem of the industries. Thus what might seem technical developments are part of a preoccupation with the success of public enterprise that derives from the values of the Labour Party, and also helps to show that – properly understood and supervised – it can be a prime agent of national progress.

A pamphlet published by the Labour Party in 1969, *Labour's Economic Strategy*, made a number of tentative proposals for forwarding public enterprise. In particular it favoured '... a series of Investment Commissions ... or alternatively the creation of a new Ministry for the Public Sector' to investigate the distribution, priorities and plans for total public-sector investment funds; and the establishment of a State Holding Company to promote new public enterprises, perhaps in development areas and perhaps in co-operation with private enterprise. It was also concerned with the more effective deployment of the Government's holdings and directorships in companies with mixed ownership, and it recommended a fresh look at the possibilities of public ownership in the aircraft industry, the drug industry, North Sea gas and the building industry. When it came to the 1970 general election, the Labour manifesto[10] reverted to the theme of removing 'old restrictions on the activities of the nationalized industries' and 'opening up a new and more competitive concept of public enterprise'. It considered that the '... establishment of a Holding and Development Company ... may well be necessary' to exploit the possibilities of mixed enterprise.

The Labour Party was defeated in the election of 1970, and instead of putting this approach into effect, it found itself the critic of other developments. In 1972 it published a 'green paper' – a document designed for discussion rather than a definite programme.[11] This looked for 'new institutional arrangements to counteract the tendency to the automatic enlargement and enrichment of the rentier class'. Nationalization, a state holding company and diversification of existing public enterprises were ways of doing this. Other possibilities included investment of national superannuation funds in equity shares, and the creation of a national workers' capital fund, in which each worker gained a capital entitlement for each year worked. Companies would provide equity for this central fund by an annual levy.

CONSERVATIVE PARTY ATTITUDES

The Conservative Party has not grown any more sympathetic towards public ownership in the last twenty years.

In Chapter 2 it was noted that several of the pre-war public corporations were set up under Conservative auspices, and this at least implied that they might regard public ownership as appropriate in special circumstances. The Conservatives did not propose any nationalization at the 1945 election, but their opposition to some items in the Labour programme – the Bank of England, the coal mines, electricity – was not particularly vigorous. Transport, especially road haulage, and steel were different matters. The Conservative Party in Parliament used all the means available to resist and delay these measures, supported by the propaganda of the industries outside Parliament.

During these years the Conservatives had to formulate a long-term attitude to public ownership in the changed circumstances. There was a general movement of public opinion during the war which had to be taken into account, and the Labour Party in office had succeeded in establishing a number of new public corporations. It is the chief glory of British conservatism, as distinct from other right-wing doctrines, that it adapts itself to changing situations. The period of opposition from 1945 to 1951 was a time when adaptation was crucial for the future of the Party.

In the event, the Conservative rethinking – led and encouraged by Mr R. A. Butler – achieved a remarkably coherent (and electorally successful) set of principles. The social-service reforms of the Labour Government were on the whole accepted and even welcomed. Most of their nationalization measures were also accepted – but grudgingly, on the argument that 'eggs cannot be unscrambled'. Steel and road haulage were to be returned to private enterprise and the administration of the rest improved. Moreover, the Conservative Party accepted the doctrine of competition in industry more openly than it had ever done before. One consequence of this outlook has been that, though Conservative publicity now stresses the share of the Party in building the welfare state, in developing economic planning and even in trade union legislation, little attention is given to the creation of the public corporation.[12]

In July 1949 the Conservative Party published a pamphlet *The Right Road for Britain*, setting out policies for the forthcoming election. It declared firmly:

> The Conservative Party will undertake no further nationalization. It will restore free enterprise where that is practicable. But we refuse at this time of economic danger to aggravate industrial discord. We must ensure that those in control of industries are not persistently distracted from their task of management by watching the political weather. We have therefore no other course but to leave some industries nationalized but we shall radically overhaul their organization to make them more human, less centralized and more efficient.[13]

The iron and steel industry, road transport and the purchase of raw cotton were specifically marked for denationalization. The reorganization of the existing corporations would embody 'the greatest degree of decentralization', and parliamentary control would be strengthened.

Political formulae on these lines served the Conservative Party for many years: the existing nationalized industries were to be maintained, and run on business lines, but there was fierce hostility to any further extension. Denationalization in the 1950s did not proceed quite so far as envisaged, but, broadly speaking, the doctrine of 1949 did not receive much further adaptation. It remained the essence of the Conservative position at the elections of 1955, 1959, 1964 and 1966. In 1970 the Party election manifesto stated that:

> ... We are totally opposed to further nationalization of British industry. We will repeal the so-called Industrial Expansion Act which gives the Government power to use taxpayers' money to buy its way into private industry ...
> ... We will progressively reduce the involvement of the State in the nationalized industries, for example in the steel industry, so as to improve their competitiveness. An increasing use of private capital will help to ease the burden on the taxpayer, get better investment decisions, and ensure more effective use of total resources.[14]

Alongside these general pronouncements three persistent ideas may be discerned in Conservative attitudes to nationalized industries. First, they are readily suspected of being overcentralized. Conservatives have often argued that freedom is to be defended by diffusing power through the community; and, following this line somewhat vaguely, decentralization and local responsibility are desired in large nationalized organizations. An early check to the more dogmatic forms of this doctrine came with the publication of the Fleck report on the organization of the Coal Board in 1955, in which leading industrialists declared that decentralization in the industry was already excessive. There is still some political feeling towards decentralization among Conservatives, but moves in a contrary direction are possible, as with the creation of the British Gas Corporation, and the consolidation of the two airlines under the British Airways Board, in 1972.

A second Conservative idea is that the industries should as far as possible be subjected to competition, either between themselves or from private enterprise. This idea sprang from the enhanced prominence in Conservative thinking given to competition since the war. It was not possible to advocate uninhibited private enterprise without also emphasizing the virtues of competition, and to most members of the Conservative Party it seemed desirable to extend the competition as far as possible into the nationalized industries. The Government was able to carry this out in many cases, as described in Chapter 7, though there is some effective monopoly and protection left. The independent airlines, the fuel-oil industry and private road transport all made strong challenges in markets that were formerly the preserve of the nationalized industries. The establishment of independent television in 1956 and independent local radio in 1972 are further examples of the promotion of competitive and commercial arrangements. The converse of this approach, however, the encouragement of competitive forays into the private sector by nationalized concerns, is very far from acceptable to Conservative opinion.

The third preference commonly found among Conservatives is, of course, for a strictly commercial approach as propounded in the Herbert report and elsewhere. It has never really been adopted in full, and in the 1960s it was subsumed under the sophisticated economic criteria then devised. It continues to be reflected, however, in a reluctance to support subsidization on 'social' grounds and the hopeful search for ways of providing investment funds through the capital market.

When a party is in office its attitudes are not easily distinguishable from those of the Government. There was, in the early 1970s, a current of opinion among Conservatives, voiced by Mr Enoch Powell, which affirmed that large-scale measures of denationalization were possible. But the Government's policies were to restrict the ancillary and autonomous activities of the public corporations, to look for opportunities of 'hiving-off' such activities to private enterprise and to insist that the industrial corporations should play a leading part in price and pay restraint. These intentions probably reflected the general state of Party feeling on the subject. The pressure of events, however, led the Government to bring Rolls-Royce into public ownership in 1971 [15] and to put £35 million into support for shipbuilding concerns on the Upper Clyde in Glasgow in 1972. These were emergency expedients; but they served at that point to bring some disarray into Conservative attitudes to public enterprise, in view of the 'total opposition' of the 1970 manifesto.

LIBERAL PARTY ATTITUDES

The Liberal Party grew and prospered in the nineteenth century as the party of the industrial middle class, and its economic attitudes traditionally favoured freedom of enterprise and competition. It developed considerably, however, from being a laissez-faire party, and between the wars it played a part in fashioning the idea of the public corporation. It was also the party of Keynes and Beveridge, the formulators of the economic strategy for full employment.

In the 1940s it adopted a pragmatic attitude to nationalization, as distinct from what it regarded as Labour Party dogmatism. In Parliament it supported some Bills and opposed others, as described in Chapter 3. Steel nationalization was strongly opposed, and though in principle the Party retains a non-dogmatic attitude, it has not found it necessary to advocate any measures of public ownership since 1950. It is even more strongly attached than the Conservative Party to ideas of competition and free trade in industry, and stresses the need to remove any form of protection to public enterprise. In the late 1950s and 1960s it convinced itself that this coolness towards public ownership would enable it to become a great radical party of the left.

The Liberal Party's programme for the 1964 election made a brief reference to public ownership, declaring that the '... wrangle about nationalization and denationalization is irrelevant to most of the problems of modern industry'. In 1970 the manifesto scarcely offered any direct comment, though it suggested that a 'Commission for Manpower and Industry should devote particular attention to the nationalized industries.' It stressed, rather, another approach to industrial control, in which the individual worker

> ... is entitled to similar rights to those enjoyed by the shareholder. Industry must become a partnership between capital and labour, with management responsible to the partnership. Workers should participate in the election of directors. Works Councils should be established in every plant ...[16]

In general the Liberal Party has rarely been concerned with public enterprise as such, but has been more interested in adjusting it in some way to its philosophies of competition and co-ownership.

INDUSTRIAL OPPOSITION

An account of political attitudes to public ownership must include the opposition of private enterprise. Though not formally affiliated to the Conservative Party, industrial organizations usually find themselves in harmony with its major economic policies. Certainly they emphatically endorse its hostility to extensions of public ownership.

The steel industry has been most involved. The nationalization of steel was proposed by many socialist writers before 1939, and its inclusion in the Labour Party's 1945 programme set in train the events leading to the nationalization and denationalization described in Chapter 3. Between 1953 and 1965 the renationalization of steel remained firmly in the Party's programmes, even in the revisionist era. As a result there was a good deal of recrimination between the industry and the Party. By the early 1960s the need for drastic reorganization had become plain, and though there were critical Parliamentary debates the industry was eventually renationalized. The Conservative intention of denationalizing again had evaporated by 1970, and instead controversy turned on the size of the investment programme.

Until it was resolved, this controversy was the occasion for a good deal of anti-nationalization propaganda, especially before the General Elections of 1959 and 1964, when extensive advertising campaigns were conducted. The wisdom of this policy depended on its electoral effectiveness: if sufficient voters had been affected by it to keep the Labour Party out of office, it might well have been worth while. The Labour Party, however, regarded the campaigns as intimidation and 'political blackmail', and the emotions they aroused in Party loyalists were hardly such as to allow the leaders to change their intentions even if they had wanted. Whether the narrow result of October 1964 justified the industry's expenditure or not is a matter of conjecture.

Other industries and other organizations have also carried out anti-nationalization propaganda. Vigorous efforts were made in the late 1940s by the Road Haulage Association to restrain nationalization. Before the 1950 election, campaigns were organized with considerable skill by the sugar, cement and insurance companies, and these have been followed by extensive Press advertising, by industry, critical of nationalization, in every pre-election period before 1970. Many private businesses are also believed to contribute to the funds of the Conservative Party, either directly or through a body called British United Industrialists.

The Labour Party's response to this flow of hostile propaganda was to complain about the use of company funds (rather than personal wealth) for political purposes, and in particular about the secrecy with which this was done. Now, however, companies are required to disclose funds spent on political purposes. In any case, political advertising is scarcely a very secret activity. Nor is there any doubt about its legality, since it can obviously be claimed to be in the interests of the companies. Officially, the advertising campaigns are against nationalization and not against the Labour Party as such; the industrial subscriptions to the Conservative Party are presumably intended to have a more general impact.

The Federation of British Industries, the main top-level trade association of British industry before 1965, did not normally take part in partisan controversy. In 1958, however, it published a pamphlet setting out its views.[17] It did not recommend the de-nationalization of any industries already nationalized, 'but the country ought not to be content with their performance so far'. They had not met their financial obligations; they had maintained low prices irrespective of costs; and they had taken a more than proportionate share of national investment funds. The position of free enterprise, which worked in a 'dominant climate' of competition, was contrasted; there, the yardstick of profitability provided a clear measure of efficiency. The merit of the pamphlet lay in its point-by-point exposition of the whole range of anti-nationalization arguments; but a crucial weakness was its failure to acknowledge sufficiently the influence of Government policies on the results achieved by the industries.

There can be, of course, no counter-attack from the nationalized industries. Their constitutional position prevents them from indulging in very active political propaganda, though there is some prestige advertising. In defending themselves from nationalization, private-enterprise firms constantly criticize existing public enterprise, and so damage the general standing of the industries. It would scarcely be possible – even with a sympathetic Government – for public corporations to indulge in anti-capitalist advertising campaigns, but it might be possible to allow them to play a more direct part in protecting their own public reputations.

A further sphere of influence has opened to the nationalized industries in recent years. In 1965 the Federation of British Industries merged with some other employers' organizations to form the Confederation of British Industry. In January 1966 it was announced that the main nationalized industries were joining the C.B.I. as 'industrial associates' (though London Transport remained outside). They had obvious common interests as employers, and since then they have become full members. They now take an important part in the work of the Confederation, but dissociate themselves from any 'political' pronouncements it may make.

Harold Laski's thesis

In the 1930s the left wing of the Labour Party was inclined to doubt the practicability of socialist reforms, including large-scale public ownership, by conventional parliamentary means. These views were most forcibly expressed by Harold Laski in successive books and pamphlets.[18] The argument followed Marxist lines: if a group of people found its vital interests at stake, then it would take desperate measures, perhaps including violence, to protect them. The owners of industry naturally regarded public ownership as a threat to their fundamental position, and therefore they were unlikely to acquiesce merely because constitutionally elected socialists had legislated to this effect. Accordingly, a Labour Government should be prepared for non-cooperation, sabotage and possibly violent resistance. It should not be deterred from its course; it should be prepared to govern by emergency decree, and to meet force with force.

The experience of 1945–51 is generally regarded as disproving this thesis. Certainly it shows that under certain political conditions much nationalization can be carried out by orthodox legislation. It does not show, however, that any amount of public ownership can be achieved merely on the basis of a Government's constitutional prerogatives.

The non-cooperation of the steel industry in 1951 and the pre-election publicity campaigns might be held to give some support to a modified version of the theory. Certainly the controllers of private enterprise regard nationalization as a measure of an altogether different character from other industrial policies. It does not remove all of them from their posts, for high management posts must be held by people of the best quality available. Moreover, shareholders are fully compensated. But nationalization alters the basis of the controllers' authority, the conditions of their tenure and the extent of their accountability; in short, it strikes at their fundamental power. In these circumstances, a nationalizing party must expect determined opposition, which is not confined to other political parties.

The behaviour of any industries that may be faced in the future with nationalization is a matter for speculation. Though formidable in electoral terms, their opposition so far has been legal and constitutional, and seems likely to continue so. The situation can perhaps be assessed thus. The response of industrialists to the prospect of nationalization will be vigorous, but will remain peaceful and constitutional, provided that the transfers to public ownership are limited in scale, carry compensation and have a Government with moral as well as formal authority behind them. More extreme programmes might bring more extreme reactions. If Laski meant that *any* nationalization would be regarded as provocation to violence, then this is clearly untrue. The question of full-blooded opposition to a red-blooded programme has now become remote from practical politics.

In fact, the late 1960s and early 1970s showed the problem of democratic order to lie in a different direction. The risks of non-compliance with constitutional decisions or legislation on the part of business organizations were minimal, but a disposition grew up associated with the 'new left', to argue that failure to secure a certain type of social change merely showed the defects of the political arrangements. In this view, respect for constitutionality was a matter of tactics, and 'other methods' might be tried as convenient. The most conspicuous example of this attitude, perhaps, in national affairs was the attempt of trade unions to boycott the machinery of the Industrial Relations Act of 1971.

THE AGENDA

It will perhaps be helpful, by way of conclusion to this book, to set out what seem to be the main items of public discussion, in the early 1970s in Britain, on the subject of nationalization and industrial control. Many of these have been mentioned in earlier chapters, and are here recapitulated.

(*a*) Within the present structure of nationalized industries there are proposals for an independent efficiency audit. Rejected by the Select Committee and opposed by the industries, the practical possibilities do not look bright. There are also proposals for improving and strengthening the machinery of consumer representation.[19]

(b) Though the suggestion of a Ministry of Nationalized Industries seems to have failed, there is still some interest in the idea of a state holding company (or companies), in some way intermediate between the corporations as operating units, and the Government itself. This is associated by Professor David Coombes with a 'new style of state enterprise', where there are not nationalized industries as such but a number of state businesses, in which there are large public shareholdings, but which also have access to private capital.[20]

(c) A version of the state holding company idea in which the Labour Party has expressed sympathy is not so much concerned with the existing industries, as with the promotion of new enterprises, particularly in regions of the country needing new development. It would presumably be an agency for providing capital, though it would retain its equity holdings permanently.

(d) The Conservative Party has become antipathetic to all such ideas of piecemeal and fragmentary public ownership. When they came to office in 1970 the Conservatives announced a programme of 'hiving-off' detachable parts of the industrial corporations. How long this programme will be maintained remains to be seen.

(e) The attempt to provide stability and a degree of independence under the rules of the 1967 White Paper has met with such difficulties in the early 1970s that a new initiative in these matters has become a possibility. In particular, some recognized means of coping with the financial consequences for the corporations of acting as agents of Government economic policy was clearly needed.

It is difficult to pick out any linking factor from these various items. There is, however, an interest in more varied *forms* for public enterprise, though little confidence or clarity in explaining

H

what these might be. The structure of public enterprise in Italy is undoubtedly influential, and an inclination to look towards 'mixed enterprise', rather than the public corporation, as the way forward, is apparent.

There is relevance, therefore, in asking some questions about this type of institution.[21] In such undertakings the Government, or perhaps some intermediary public corporation, appears in the role of equity shareholder in firms registered as companies in the ordinary way. What degree or form of influence would the Government expect to exercise in this situation? Would the presumption be different in those enterprises where the Government (or its agency) held a majority or effective controlling interest from those where it did not? Would the efficiency controls – the investment and pricing rules, or project vetting – be applied to these concerns? One method of influence is to appoint 'Government directors'; these could be full-time businessmen; or civil servants attending board meetings among their other duties. To what extent would such directors be expected to act as active agents of current Government policies? In law, all directors are obliged to serve the interests of all shareholders, not to act especially for one of them. There is also the question of Parliamentary accountability. The tendency of the Select Committee on Nationalized Industries since 1967 has been to widen its scope, and presumably it would expect to be concerned.

This may appear a querulous approach to interesting new developments, and it may be better to suggest more positively claims that can be made for the existing structure. Richard Pryke has argued[22] that the efficiency of nationalized industries has been clearly improved by factors associated with public ownership. The unification of ownership and management makes possible rational structures which maximize economies of scale, and also enables collective bargaining to be improved. The financial constraints provide strong incentives to cost reductions, since there are few alternatives. The various forms of investigation and accountability – though often complained about – necessitate management reflection and rethinking, and are hence a stimulus to efficiency. Government supervision has similar effects:

But the most important way in which the Ministries promote and assist in the successful working of the nationalized industries is by asking questions and demanding explanations, and by ensuring that the industries plan ahead. In this way, Government ownership and departmental supervision discourage ill-conceived policies and promote rational behaviour.[23]

It is hardly necessary to say that not everyone would agree with these propositions. But they do constitute a challenge, in the sense of a claim that the industrial public corporations are not a second-rate set of arrangements, making the best of a bad job, but have positive advantages which other forms do not have. It certainly seems likely that experiments with other forms of public enterprise will take place; perhaps they can combine existing advantages with new ones.

Further possibilities

The origins of nationalization as a protest against capitalist control of industrial enterprises were noted in Chapter 2. There are other forms of public enterprise, as just described. There are also other possible ways of reforming industrial ownership, and in recent years there has been some interest in other methods of changing the structure of the firm. In a book about nationalization, it is not possible or appropriate to go into any detail, but it may serve to put the industrial public corporations in context by noting some other approaches.

First, there is 'wider shareholding'. A variety of schemes have been put forward which make easier the acquisition of shares in public companies. It is hoped by this means to end the feeling that capitalist ownership puts industry into the hands of a small, wealthy, group; instead, ownership will be diffused through the community, and its benefits (and outlook) will be widely shared. Unit trusts, which hold shares in a large number of individual companies, enable a person investing a small amount not only to spread the risks, but also to have this investment managed by experts. There are also methods of buying shares by small regular subscriptions.

A variant of this idea is 'employee-shareholding'. In these cases a company makes it possible for its employees to obtain its shares on specially favourable terms; they may be issued as a form of payment to established employees. A worker is thus enabled to acquire a 'stake' in his company and to share in its profits. If his shares carry voting rights, he also becomes a member of its ultimate controlling body.

These are the types of proposals most favoured by Conservative currents of opinion. It should be noted that such schemes do not disturb the principle of capitalist control at all. The benefits and rights of shareholders are made available to more people, but it is only by virtue of capital holdings that their position is improved. However, the more shareholders there are for any particular enterprise, the more difficult it is for shareholder control to be effective, and the stronger the position of the directors and managers. It has also been argued that the financial gains of employee-shareholders are no more than a variant of higher wage and salary payments.[24]

However, if employee-shareholding is carried out in an extensive and radical fashion, it can give workers a substantial part in the control of a company, and there are a few firms in which shareholding or partnership does make a real difference to the structure of the enterprise. A more fundamental charge, giving rights to employees as such, would require legislation. In West Germany a system of co-determination giving such rights has been established. In Britain the Liberal Party has declared its belief in *co-ownership*. This implied at first support for schemes of profit-sharing, employee-shareholding and co-partnership as they already existed. But in the 1960s the Party prepared schemes which took the matter further. The details varied, and the practicality was suspect, but they aimed at methods where directors and managers were responsible to both employees and capital-providers.

There are in existence, of course, a number of enterprises which have experimented in this direction. The best-known and most successful co-partnership is the John Lewis Partnership, which runs department stores and supermarkets. There are smaller and more radically disposed firms, such as Scott Bader Ltd of Wollaston, Landsman's of Huntingdon and Rowen Engineering Ltd of

Glasgow. An organization designed to promote this type of institution – the Industrial Common-Ownership Movement – has been set up; it defines a common-ownership enterprise as 'one that is wholly owned and controlled by those working in it'. It rejects, that is to say, the values of whole-community control embodied in the public corporation in favour of the primacy of the work-force.

The Labour Party remains mainly concerned with public ownership as such. The ideas of consumer co-operation and of full workers' control are, of course, associated with the Labour movement, and there have recently been some notable attempts to explore again the possibilities of this type of reform. A Fabian Society pamphlet, *The Company and the Community* by Paul Derrick, has proposed 'the socialization of the company'. This involves limiting 'the return to the shareholder so that he ceases to be an owner and becomes a creditor'. Another Fabian pamphlet, *The Democratic Firm* by Norman Ross, presented an analysis of the enterprise as 'a complex of group relationships in which conflicting objectives can and usually do exist'. The need was to create a system for the effective adjustment of these differing interests. The pamphlet proposed a supervisory representative council composed of shareholders' representatives and employee representatives in proportions which reflected their contribution to the income generated by the enterprise, as measured by net profits on the one hand and wages and salaries on the other. Though these Fabian schemes have some similarity to earlier proposals and to practice abroad, they effect a sharp reduction (on balance) in the power of the shareholders compared with that of employees or other groups.[25] The Institute of Workers' Control, with headquarters in Nottingham, seems mainly concerned with militant trade union action directed towards an ultimate goal of industrial control.

It must be noted that all these proposals would leave the structure of industry much as it is. They do not involve any change in Government control, nor do they contribute to improved economic planning. Few of them embody arrangements for public accountability. Indeed, they usually see the bureaucratic power of the State as an evil to be avoided at all costs. In so far as nationalization does deal with this sort of problem, therefore, the reform of the enterprise is not in the same field and does not undertake the same tasks. It is relevant, however, to the problem of industrial ownership conceived as a problem of social relationships. Thus there are currents of opinion in all parties that acknowledge the need for changes in industry not primarily designed to improve its efficiency.

In the current political context, public enterprise is usually judged by its contribution to economic ends, and the urgency of these problems is not to be denied. Nevertheless, it would be wrong to forget that public ownership sprang as much from criticisms of the injustice of capitalism as from its alleged in-efficiency. In the long run, the social and political aspects of the control of industry may not continue to be overshadowed by the economic.

Public ownership remains, in Britain, a party matter. There is great virtue in this. It brings the issues into the open. It means that few aspects are left obscure or unexamined by one controversialist or another. It is highly desirable that great industrial problems should receive the publicity and scrutiny that political debate ensures. Yet there is a danger of over-simplification. Many people will decide to oppose public ownership on principle. In doing so, they should be aware of the problems with which it attempts to deal; they should recognize that the question of how productive enterprises in society are to be controlled is one worthy of some attention, and that easy and dogmatic answers to it will certainly be unsatisfactory. In turn, those who support further public owner-ship should remember that, as a change from the existing situation, it needs to have a case made for it. It is presented as a remedy for alleged evils: economic, social and political. Its advocates have a duty to see that the forms it takes and the ways in which it operates ensure that it does in fact improve what it is meant to improve.

In short, nationalization has been treated too much as an *either/or* question. There are many ways of owning and directing industrial enterprises, and an economic system could do worse than adopt a great variety of them.

APPENDIX A

Major Reports of the Select Committee on Nationalized Industries

This list does not include procedural or other minor papers.

1. (No official title) Ministerial control; and the North of Scotland Hydro-Electric Board. House of Commons paper 304 of session 1956–7
2. (No official title) National Coal Board. H.C. 187-1 of 1957–8
3. *The Air Corporations.* H.C. 213 of 1958–9
4. (No official title) Special report on expert assistance. H.C. 276 of 1958–9
5. *British Railways.* H.C. 254-1 of 1959–60
6. *The Gas Industry.* H.C. 280 and H.C. 280-1 of 1960–61
7. *Reports of former committees* (i.e. nos. 1, 2 and 3 above). H.C. 116 of 1961–2
8. *Electricity Supply Industry.* H.C. 236-1, H.C. 236-II and H.C. 236-III of 1962–3
9. *British Overseas Airways Corporation.* H.C. 240 and H.C. 240-1 of 1963–4
10. *London Transport.* H.C. 313 and H.C. 313-1 of 1964–5
11. *Gas, electricity and coal industries* (evidence only) H.C. 77 of 1965–6
12. *The Post Office.* H.C. 340 and H.C. 340-1 of 1966–7
13. *British European Airways.* H.C. 673 of 1966–7
14. *Special report on the Committee's Order of Reference.* H.C. 298 of 1967–8
15. *Ministerial Control of the Nationalized Industries.* H.C. 371-1, H.C. 371-II and H.C. 371-III of 1967–8
16. *Exploitation of North Sea Gas.* H.C. 372 of 1967–8
17. *National Coal Board.* H.C. 471-i and H.C. 471-ii of 1968–9
18. *Bank of England.* H.C. 258 of 1969–70

19. *British Airports Authority.* H.C. 275 of 1970–71
20. *Relations with the Public.* H.C. 514 of 1970–71
21. *British Transport Docks Board.* H.C. 312 of 1971–2
22. *Independent Broadcasting Authority.* H.C. 465 of 1971–2

APPENDIX B

Reports of the National Board for Prices and Incomes concerned with the Nationalized Industries, 1965–1971

Report
number

79. *National Guidelines Covering Productivity Payments in the Electricity Supply Industry* (30.7.68) Cmnd. 3726
86. *Pay of Staff Workers in the Gas Industry* (24.10.68) Cmnd. 3795
88. *Pay of Pilots employed by the British Overseas Airways Corporation* (29.10.68) Cmnd. 3789
90. *Pay of Vehicle Maintenance Workers in British Road Services* (4.12.68) Cmnd. 3848
94. *Productivity Agreements in the Road Haulage Industry* (5.12.68) Cmnd. 3847
102. *Gas Prices* (Second Report) (13.2.69) Cmnd. 3924
107. *Top Salaries in the Private Sector and Nationalized Industries* (25.3.69) Cmnd. 3970
111. *Steel Prices* (21.5.69) Cmnd. 4033
112. *Proposals by the London Transport Board for Fares Increases* (15.5.69) Cmnd. 4036
121. *Post Office Charges: Inland Parcel Post and Remittance Services* (15.7.69) Cmnd. 4115
124. *Coal Prices* (21.8.69) Cmnd. 4149
128. *Pay of Ground Staff at Aerodromes* (28.10.69) Cmnd. 4182
129. *Pay of Pilots employed by B.O.A.C.* (4.11.69) Cmnd. 4197
137. *Proposals by the British Railways Board for fare increases in the London Commuter Area* (22.12.69) Cmnd. 4250
138. *Coal Prices* (First Report) (2.1.70) Cmnd. 4255
153. *Coal Prices* (Second Report) (13.8.70) Cmnd. 4455
     Coal Prices (Second Report) (Supplement) (27.4.71) Cmnd. 4455-1
     Coal Prices (Second Report) (Supplement) (27.4.71) Cmnd. 4455-2
155. *Costs and efficiency in the Gas Industry* (19.8.70) Cmnd. 4458
159. *London Transport Fares* (26.11.70) Cmnd. 4540
162. *Costs, charges and productivity of the National Freight Corporation* (13.1.71) Cmnd. 4569
170. *Fifth and Final General Report* (supplement) (29.4.71) Cmnd. 4649-1 (contains summaries of all reports)

FURTHER READING

There is a large body of literature on most aspects of nationalization. Many of the more specific books and articles have been indicated in the end-notes to the text. In a subject where there is constant change, however, books and new editions of books can rarely stay up-to-date for long, and readers should be prepared to look for official papers, including the reports of the Select Committee on Nationalized Industries and the Annual Reports and Accounts of the various corporations, for the latest information. These are all House of Commons papers, obtainable from Government bookshops.

A book deserving special mention is *Nationalized Industry and Public Ownership* by Professor W. A. Robson, 2nd edition (Allen & Unwin, 1962). This is a work of great scholarship that shows keen insight into many problems. It includes a complete bibliography of the subject up to the time of publication.

Two volumes of readings, prepared under the auspices of the Royal Institute of Public Administration, provide access to many important articles, pamphlets and selections from official documents. *Nationalization – a book of readings*, edited by Professor A. H. Hanson (Allen & Unwin, 1963), covers the development up to 1960. *The Nationalized Industries since 1960*, edited by Leonard Tivey (Allen & Unwin, 1972) contains material about the critical developments of the later period. A basic introduction to the subject is provided in W. Thornhill, *The Nationalized Industries: an introduction* (Nelson, 1968).

On the early development of ideas about nationalization, the student should consult E. Eldon Barry, *Nationalisation in British Politics* (Cape, 1965) and H. E. Weiner, *British Labour and Public Ownership* (Stevens, 1960). On the public corporation, see Herbert Morrison, *Socialisation and Transport* (Constable, 1933); W. A. Robson (ed.), *Public Enterprise* (Allen & Unwin, 1937); and G. N.

Ostergaard's article, 'Labour and the development of the public corporation', in the *Manchester School* (May 1954).

The evolution of accountability can be studied through A. H. Hanson, *Parliament and Public Ownership* (Cassell, 1961) and D. Coombes, *The M.P. and the Administration* (Allen & Unwin, 1966). Sir Toby Low's article, 'The Select Committee on Nationalized Industries', in *Public Administration* (Spring 1962) should also be consulted.

The classical official papers on the aims of nationalization are the report of the Herbert committee on *The Electricity Supply Industry* (Cmnd. 9672, 1956), the White Papers on *Financial and Economic Obligations of the Nationalized Industries* (Cmnd. 1337, April 1961) and *The Nationalized Industries – a review of economic and financial objectives* (Cmnd. 3437, November 1967). The serious student must give attention to the report of the Select Committee on Nationalized Industries, *Ministerial Control* (House of Commons paper 371-I of session 1967–8), which in fact reviews a great range of problems. There is also much important material in the volumes of evidence to the report (H.C. paper 371-II and -III of 1967–8), and in criticisms of it, some of which are reproduced in the R.I.P.A. volume of readings noted above. Christopher Foster's book *Politics, Finance and the Role of Economics* (Allen & Unwin, 1972) discusses related matters.

The representation of consumers is examined in a report of the Consumer Council, *Consumer Consultative Machinery in the Nationalized Industries* (H.M.S.O., 1968); and in the report of the Select Committee on Nationalized Industries, *Relations with the Public* (H.C. paper 514 of 1970–71).

The comparative study of nationalized corporations in other countries may be begun in *Government Enterprise*, edited by W. Friedmann and J. F. Garner (Stevens, 1970), and a shorter and livelier volume *State Enterprise – business or politics?* by David Coombes (Allen & Unwin, 1971).

The economic literature on nationalization in general or the various industries in particular is too extensive to list here. The Penguin book *Nationalized Industries* by G. L. Reid and K. Allen (1970) provides an excellent introduction, and there is a useful volume of readings, *Public Enterprise* edited by R. Turvey (Penguin, 1968). A major contribution to the economics of British nationalized industries in recent years, however, is Richard Pryke's *Public Enterprise in Practice* (MacGibbon & Kee, London, 1971). Michael Posner's essay, 'Policy towards Nationalized Industries', in W. Beckerman (ed.), *The Labour Government's Economic Record 1964-1970* (Duckworth, 1972), provides a useful survey of recent developments.

NOTES

CHAPTER 2: THE ORIGINS OF NATIONALIZATION

1. R. H. Tawney, *The Acquisitive Society* (Bell, 1921), p. 149.

2. See M. Beer, *History of British Socialism* (Allen & Unwin, 1919); G. D. H. Cole, *History of Socialist Thought* (Macmillan, 1953–60); and Henry Pelling, *The Challenge of Socialism* (Black, 1954).

3. See F. F. Ridley, *Revolutionary Syndicalism in France* (Cambridge Univ. Press, 1970); B. Pribicevic, *The Shop Steward's Movement and Workers' Control 1910–1922* (Blackwell, 1959); and S. T. Glass, *The Responsible Society* (Longmans, 1966).

4. See, for example, F. A. Hayek (ed.), *Collectivist Economic Planning* (Routledge, 1935).

5. *Manchester Guardian*, December 5th, 1918.

6. It is not entirely clear what 'responsibility' entails in this context: certainly it is not now the automatic practice for Ministers to resign after administrative errors.

7. See G. B. Shaw, *The Commonsense of Municipal Trading* (Allen & Unwin, 1904).

8. See F. M. G. Willson, 'Ministries and Boards', in *Public Administration* (Spring 1955).

9. Report of the Machinery of Government Committee (Cd. 9230, 1918), p. 11.

10. Report of the Broadcasting Committee (Cmd. 2599, 1926).

11. This was a network of high-voltage transmission lines linking major power stations and so providing a unified source of supply for the whole country.

12. J. M. Keynes, 'The End of *Laissez-faire*', reprinted in *Essays in Persuasion* (Macmillan, 1931).

13. 'The public corporation has no shares and no shareholders, either public or private.' W. Friedmann, 'The New Public Corporations and the Law', *Modern Law Review* (1947), p. 235.

14. See D. N. Chester, 'The Public Corporations and the Classification of Administrative Bodies', in *Political Studies* (February 1953).

CHAPTER 3 : THE MAJOR NATIONALIZED INDUSTRIES

1. Cmnd. 827 (1959).
2. E. Shinwell, *Conflict without Malice* (Odhams Press, 1955), p. 173.
3. Report of the Technical Advisory Committee on coal mining (Cmd. 6610, 1945).
4. See Lord Robens, *Ten Years' Stint* (Cassell, 1972).
5. *Hansard*, May 6th, 1946, col. 598.
6. Report of Committee of Inquiry into the aircraft industry (Cmnd. 2853, December 1965).
7. At first there was a single Road Transport Executive, but in 1949 haulage and passenger interests were separated.
8. *Hansard*, December 17th, 1946, col. 1890.
9. This Act embodied proposals set out in a White Paper, *Reorganization of the Nationalized Transport Undertakings* (Cmnd. 1248, 1960).
10. Report of Committee of Inquiry into the electricity supply industry (Cmd. 9672, 1956).
11. Report of Committee of Inquiry into the gas industry (Cmd. 6699, 1945).
12. A general account of controversies up to 1951 is given in G. W. Ross, *The Nationalization of Steel* (MacGibbon & Kee, 1965).
13. See Hugh Dalton, *High Tide and After* (Muller, 1962), ch. xxx.
14. See British Iron and Steel Federation, *The Steel Industry: the stage 1 report* (Benson report, 1966).
15. The Atomic Energy Authority is chiefly concerned with prototypes; other nuclear power stations are built by consortia of private-enterprise firms.
16. See White Paper, *Industrial Reorganization Corporation* (Cmnd. 2889, January 1966).

17. See White Paper, *Industrial Expansion* (Cmnd. 3509, January 1968).
18. See White Paper, *Public Purchasing and Industrial Efficiency* (Cmnd. 3291, 1967).

CHAPTER 4: THE PRACTICE OF NATIONALIZATION

1. See White Paper, *The Finances of the Coal Industry* (Cmnd. 2805, November 1965).
2. See the extracts on this subject in L. Tivey (ed.), *The Nationalized Industries since 1960* (Allen & Unwin, 1972); and also M. Howe, 'Financing State Steel: The Irrelevance of Public Dividend Capital', in *Public Administration* (Autumn 1971).
3. For example, *Public Expenditure to 1975–76* (Cmnd. 4829, November 1971), pp. 31–5.
4. For example, *Loans from the National Loans Fund 1972–73* (Cmnd. 4936, March 1972).
5. See Richard Pryke, *Public Enterprise in Practice* (MacGibbon & Kee, 1971), pp. 155–60; and the Edwards report, *British Air Transport in the Seventies* (Cmnd. 4018, 1969).
6. See *Report of a Court of Inquiry into a Dispute between the N.C.B. and the N.U.M.* (Wilberforce) (Cmnd. 4903, February 1972).
7. Richard Pryke, op. cit., p. 173.

CHAPTER 5: PROBLEMS OF ORGANIZATION

1. This group consisted of the chairman of the London County Council; a representative of the official advisory committee on London traffic; the chairman of the Committee of London Clearing Bankers; the president of the Law Society; the president of the Institute of Chartered Accountants; and the chairman of the L.P.T.B. itself.
2. Clive Jenkins, *Power at the Top* (MacGibbon & Kee, 1959), p. 43.
3. Lord Simon of Wythenshawe, *The Boards of Nationalised Industries* (Longmans, 1957).

4. The Fleck and Herbert committees (discussed later in this chapter) had different views of this question. The Fleck report recommends career appointments until retiring age; the Herbert report suggests that 'security should be achieved by results rather than formal contract'.

5. Richard Pryke, *Public Enterprise in Practice* (MacGibbon & Kee, 1971), p. 27.

6. Fleck report, p. 60, and Herbert report, p. 68.

7. See C. G. Lancaster, *The Organization of the Coal Board* (1948), and *Structure and Control of the Coal Industry* (Conservative Political Centre, 1951).

8. N.C.B. report, 1948, Appendix V.

9. Report of the Advisory Committee on organization (Fleck report) N.C.B., 1955.

10. See Alan E. Thompson, 'Organization in two nationalized industries', *Scottish Journal of Political Economy* (June 1957).

11. *Railways Reorganization Scheme* (Cmd. 9191, 1954).

12. British Railways Board, *Report on Organization* (H.C. 50 of session 1969–70), p. 10.

13. British Railways Board, *Second Report of the Board on Organization* (H.C. 223 of session 1971–2).

14. National Freight Corporation, *Report on Organization* (H.C. 72 of session 1969–70).

15. British Steel Corporation, *Report on Organization 1967* (Cmnd. 3363, August 1967); British Steel Corporation, *Second Report on Organization* (H.C. 163 of session 1968–9, March 1969) and British Steel Corporation, *Third Report on Organization* (H.C. 60 of session 1969–70, December 1969).

16. Herbert report, p. 9.

CHAPTER 6: CONTROL AND ACCOUNTABILITY

1. For example, in the Coal Industry Nationalization Act, 1946, section 3.

2. Select Committee on Nationalized Industries report (H.C. 120 of session 1955–6), para. 36.

3. Select Committee on Nationalized Industries report (H.C. 187-1 of 1957–8), pp. 50, 135.

4. *Hansard*, March 19th, 1956, col. 829 ff.

5. *Hansard*, November 21st, 1961, col. 1145.

6. *Lords' Hansard*, March 12th, 1953, col. 1504. This implies that the contact would be continuous and that the chairman would be a subordinate in an organization run by the Minister.

7. Cmnd. 1248 (1960), pp. 7, 14.

8. Select Committee on Nationalized Industries, report on *Ministerial Control* (H.C. 371 of session 1967–8), vol. II (Minutes of Evidence), p. 148.

9. See evidence of W. Thornhill to the S.C.N.I., report on *Ministerial Control*, vol. II, pp. 538–44.

10. S.C.N.I., *Ministerial Control*, vol. I, p. 28, para. 114.

11. ibid., ch. 4.

12. As a matter of principle. See White Paper, *The Reorganization of Central Government* (Cmnd. 4506, October 1970), pp. 4–5.

13. Quoted by the S.C.N.I., *Ministerial Control*, vol. I, p. 34.

14. Mr J. Diamond, M.P., quoted by S.C.N.I., *Ministerial Control*, vol. I, p. 24. The statement oversimplifies, but it shows that the activities of the different bodies arise from different duties.

15. The debate on the Address in reply to the Queen's Speech.

16. *Hansard*, May 12th, 1971, col. 352.

17. See the evidence of R. D. Barlas, an officer of the House of Commons, to the S.C.N.I. report on *Ministerial Control*, vol. II, pp. 472–94. An extract from this valuable evidence is reprinted in L. Tivey (ed.), *Nationalized Industries since 1960* (Allen & Unwin, 1972).

18. Lord Heyworth, evidence to the S.C.N.I. (H.C. 235 of session 1952–3, p. 84).

19. S.C.N.I. report (H.C. 235 of session 1952–3).

20. S.C.N.I. special report *The Committee's Order of Reference* (H.C. 298 of session 1967–8). An extract from this report is in L. Tivey (ed.), op. cit.

21. During this period the total membership of the S.C.N.I. was increased to about eighteen.

22. Sir Toby Low, 'The Select Committee on Nationalized Industries', in *Public Administration* (Spring 1962), p. 14.
23. The Comptroller and Auditor General is an independent officer of Parliament who audits Government accounts and calls the attention of the Public Accounts Committee to matters needing investigation.
24. Special report of the S.C.N.I. (H.C. 276 of 1958–9).
25. Sir Toby Low, op. cit., p. 9.
26. S.C.N.I., report on *Ministerial Control*, vol. II, pp. 526–44 and 560–65. Extract in L. Tivey (ed.), *Nationalized Industries since 1960.* See also E. L. Normanton, *The Accountability and Audit of Governments* (Manchester Univ. Press, 1966).
27. *Hansard*, July 14th, 1971, col. 113 (written answers).
28. See Consumer Council, *Consumer Consultative Machinery in the Nationalized Industries* (H.M.S.O., 1968), tables on p. 92.
29. See S.C.N.I. report on *Relations with the Public* (H.C. 514 of session 1970–71). Evidence prepared for the Public Enterprise Group by Richard Pryke and Leonard Tivey, pp. 507–49.
30. See G. L. McVey, 'The Public Accountability of Industry', in *Political Quarterly* (October 1960).
31. A. H. Hanson, *Parliament and Public Ownership* (Cassell, 1961), p. 175.
32. ibid., p. 221.

CHAPTER 7: THE AIMS OF NATIONALIZATION

1. Coal Industry Nationalization Act 1946, section 1(c).
2. See E. H. Phelps-Brown and J. Wiseman, *A Course in Applied Economics*, 2nd ed. (Pitman, 1964).
3. I. M. D. Little, *The Price of Fuel* (Oxford Univ. Press, 1953), p. 97.
4. Report on *National Policy for the Use of Fuel and Power Resources* (Cmd. 8647, 1952), para. 66.
5. Herbert report (Cmd. 9672), p. 97, para. 372. The report in fact generally refers to 'purely economic' rather than 'commercial'; but in the context of controversies at the time the two terms were generally interchangeable.

6. The Herbert Report's 'Summary of Main Conclusions and Recommendations' contains all the points mentioned.

7. ibid., p. 139, para. 507.

8. There might also be labour troubles. By the Coal Industry Act of 1965, renewed by later legislation, payments are made to the National Coal Board as part of the cost of redeployment, rehousing and redundancy payments in the industry, thus acknowledging a national responsibility for some of the matters mentioned in this paragraph.

9. See, for instance, M. S. Feldstein, 'Cost-Benefit Analysis and Investment in the Public Sector', in *Public Administration* (Winter 1964).

10. See report of the Commission on the Third London Airport (Roskill) (H.M.S.O., 1970); and Peter Self, 'Nonsense on Stilts: Cost-Benefit Analysis and the Roskill Commission', in *Political Quarterly* (July 1970).

11. Select Committee on Nationalized Industries report (H.C. 187-I of 1957–8), p. xxiii, para. 124.

12. Cmnd. 1337 (April 1961).

13. ibid., para. 32. This solution implies, of course, that non-commercial activities are to be financed by cross-subsidization.

14. ibid., para. 2.

15. ibid., para. 28.

16. John Hughes, *Nationalised Industries in the Mixed Economy* (Fabian Society, 1960), pp. 9–10.

17. Discounted cash flow is usually abbreviated to d.c.f. The cash flow from a project is estimated for a number of future years, and discounted at a prescribed annual rate, so that early returns become of greater value than later ones. Hence choice between different investments can be based on comparable data.

18. See Select Committee on Nationalized Industries report on Ministerial Control, vol. 1, ch. 5, pp. 49–57. See also the S.C.N.I. report on the *National Coal Board* (1969), pp. 64–7, for an even more vigorous statement of the same view.

19. Professor W. A. Robson, 'Ministerial Control of the Nationalized Industries', in *Political Quarterly* (January 1969), pp. 103–

12. Extract in L. Tivey (ed.), *The Nationalized Industries since 1960* (Allen & Unwin, 1972).

20. For example, the Coal Industry Nationalization Act 1946, section 1 (a), states that the duties of the National Coal Board are 'working and getting the coal in Great Britain, to the exclusion (save as in this Act provided) of any other person'.

21. There may be strong buying monopolies (monopsonies) – e.g. the Central Electricity Generating Board's position as a purchaser of heavy generating equipment.

22. See essay by John Hughes in M. Shanks (ed.,) *Lessons of Public Enterprise* (Cape, 1963), p. 143.

23. *Steel Nationalization* (Cmnd. 2651), paras 20, 28.

24. Report of the committee on *National Policy for the Use of Fuel and Power Resources* (Cmd. 8647, 1952).

25. *Co-operation between Electricity and Gas Boards* (Cmnd. 695, 1959).

26. Particularly relevant discussions may be found in the S.C.N.I. report, *Ministerial Control*, ch. 14, 'Social obligations'; and the Edwards report, *British Air Transport in the Seventies* (Cmnd. 4018), ch. 2.

27. *British Air Transport in the Seventies*, pp. 9–14.

28. *Report of a Court of Inquiry into a dispute between the N.C.B. and the N.U.M.* (Wilberforce) (Cmnd. 4903, February 1972), Appendix 2.

29. See M. Shanks (ed.), op. cit., p. 149, where this argument is set out at length by an anonymous young economist.

CHAPTER 8: THE POLITICS OF PUBLIC OWNERSHIP

1. At the General Election of 1950, election addresses showed 67 per cent of Conservatives mentioning nationalization (unfavourably, of course), while 56 per cent of Labour candidates gave it favourable mentions. At the 1970 Election the figures were 24 per cent and three per cent respectively. See D. Butler and M. Pinto-Duschinsky, *The British General Election of 1970* (Macmillan, 1971), pp. 441–2.

2. Labour Party, *Let us win through together* (1950).

3. Labour Party, *The Future of Industrial Assurance* (1950). Some companies, such as the Liverpool Victoria, were already mutually owned.

4. Trades Union Congress, *Public Ownership: an interim report* (1953).

5. Labour Party, *Challenge to Britain* (1953).

6. There was no connection, of course, with earlier groups of 'revisionist' socialists, who were engaged in revising Marxist doctrine.

7. John Strachey, M.P., 'The Object of Further Socialization', in *Political Quarterly* (January 1953).

8. Hugh Gaitskell, *Socialism and Nationalisation* (Fabian Society, 1956), p. 18.

9. Speech by Jim Campbell, General Secretary of the National Union of Railwaymen, Labour Party *Annual Conference Report* (1957), p. 132.

10. Labour Party, *Now Britain's strong let's make it great to live in* (June 1970).

11. Special number of *Labour Weekly* (July 1972).

12. The Conservative Party at least shared in the inception of the B.B.C., the Central Electricity Board, London Transport, B.O.A.C., the North of Scotland Hydro-Electric Board and the Atomic Energy Authority.

13. Conservative and Unionist Central Office, *The Right Road for Britain* (1949), p. 26.

14. Conservative Party, *A better to-morrow* (1970), p. 14.

15. See White Paper, *Rolls-Royce Ltd and the RB 211 Aero-Engine* (Cmnd. 4860, January 1972).

16. Liberal Party manifestos, *Think for yourself* (1964), p. 5, and *What a life!* (1970), p. 8.

17. Federation of British Industries, *Report on Nationalization* (1958).

18. H. J. Laski, *Democracy in Crisis* (Allen & Unwin, 1933), contains perhaps the clearest statement of the thesis.

19. See Chapter 6, and the sources of these proposals noted there.

20. D. Coombes, *State Enterprise – business or politics?* (Allen & Unwin, 1971), especially ch. 12. See also the evidence of Mr

Aubrey Jones to the Select Committee on Nationalized Industries, *Ministerial Control*, vol. II, pp. 682–7.

21. A useful discussion of legal aspects is in T. C. Daintith, 'The Mixed Enterprise in the United Kingdom', in W. Friedmann and J. F. Garner (eds), *Government Enterprise* (Stevens, 1970).

22. Richard Pryke, *Public Enterprise in Practice* (MacGibbon & Kee, 1971), ch. 20: 'Conclusions – the irrelevance of ownership?'

23. ibid., p. 456.

24. There is also a long history of 'profit-sharing' schemes, giving employees payments varying with profits (like dividends on shares), but no rights to a share in control.

25. Paul Derrick, *The Company and the Community*, and Norman Ross, *The Democratic Firm*, both Fabian Research pamphlets (1964). See also L. Tivey, 'The Reform of the Firm', in *Political Quarterly* (April 1963).

Index

JONATHAN CAPE PAPERBACKS